AUTHE

Umbria

C000197662

Touring Club Italiano
President and Chairman: *Roberto Ruozi*
General Manager: *Guido Venturini*

Touring Editore
Editorial Director: *Michele D'Innella*
Editorial coordination: *Cristiana Baietta*

International Department
Fabio Pittella
fabio.pittella@touringclub.it

Senior Editor: *Paola Pandiani*
Editor: *Monica Maraschi*
Writer and Researcher: *Pietro Ferrario*
with Banca Dati Turistica for Pratical info
Translation and page layout: *Studio Queens, Milan*
Maps: *Touring Club Italiano*
Design: *Studio Queens, Milan*
Cover photo: *The green below the Basilica S. Francesco, with Via S. Francesco
leading off to the right (Roberto Bucciarelli)*

Advertising Manager: *Claudio Bettinelli*
Local Advertising: *Progetto*
www.progettosrl.it - info@progettosrl.it

Printing and Binding in China

Distribution
USA/CAN – *Publishers Group West*
UK/Ireland – *Portfolio Books*

Touring Club Italiano, Corso Italia 10, 20122 Milano
www.touringclub.it
© 2007 Touring Editore, Milan

Code K8AAG
ISBN-13: 978 – 88365 – 4221 – 5

Printed in October 2007

AUTHENTIC
Umbria

TOURING CLUB
OF ITALY

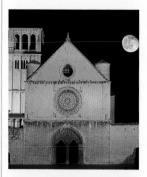

16   **HERITAGE**

Umbria, where you can still perceive the strong sense of peacefulness and spirituality. Its towns and villages are awash with medieval walls and austere monuments, and its gentle landscape comes straight out of a Renaissance painting.

Perugia
Day trips: Assisi, Bevagna, Cascia, Castiglione del lago, Città della Pieve, Città di Castello, Foligno, Gualdo Tadino, Gubbio, Lake Trasimeno, Montefalco, Nocera Umbra, Norcia, Panicale, San Manno Hypogeum, Spello, Spoleto, Todi, Trevi, Umbèrtide, Volumni Hypogeum.

Terni
Day trips: Abbey of San Pietro in Valle, Amelia, Carsulae, Ferentillo, Narni, Orvieto, The Màrmore falls.

94   **ITINERARIES**

In Umbria, birthplace of St Francis, even today, the protection of its natural heritage is an important priority. Visiting the places associated with St Francis is an enthralling experience. There are many options of itineraries which explore the unspoiled parts of the region, and special options for kids.

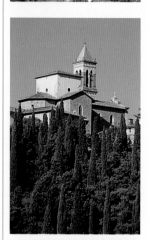

Parks	St Francis
Children	Medieval Umbria
Cinema	Biking routes

122   **FOOD**

Umbria has any number of typical foods because its landscape is so diverse: olive-oil, pork-meat products and exquisitely scented truffles. Quite rightly, the gastronomy of the region is one of its prime claims to fame. Simple, tasty cuisine based on excellent raw ingredients, with no fuss.

Traditional dishes	Oil
Pasta	Wine
Hams and salami	Cakes
Cheese	Food festivals

148 SHOPPING

Umbrian craftsmanship goes back centuries, but it is also receptive to new ideas and influences. Local markets are a paradise for people who love antiques and second-hand books, while factory outlets provide the chance to strike some real bargains.

Arts & crafts
Markets
Fashion

156 EVENTS

Umbria has an enormous number of traditional festivals in which tourists can participate actively, gaining insight into what makes Umbrians tick. Many high-level cultural events with a more modern focus are also staged in Umbria, attracting visitors from Italy and abroad.

Music
Folklore

166 WELLNESS

Umbria is justly proud of its many mineral springs, whose therapeutic value has been recognized since Roman times. Nowadays, people still come to its spas to drink the water, but it is also bottled and sold. Umbria has the perfect solution for people who need to re-charge their batteries and relax in a splendid natural setting.

Acquasparta	San Gemini
Città di Castello	Spello
Massa Martana	Spoleto
Melezzole	Tuoro sul Trasimeno

172 PRACTICAL INFO

The Practical Information is divided into sections on the hotels, restaurants, farm holidays and places of entertainment we recommend. The category of the hotels is indicated by the number of stars. In the case of restaurants we have awarded forks, taking into account the price of the meal, the level of comfort and service, and the ambience.

WHAT IS THE TOURING CLUB OF ITALY?

Long Tradition, Great Prestige

For over 110 years, the Touring Club of Italy (TCI) has offered travelers the most detailed and comprehensive source of travel information available on Italy. The Touring Club of Italy was founded in 1894 with the aim of developing the social and cultural values of tourism and promoting the conservation and enjoyment of the country's national heritage, landscape and environment.

Advantages of Membership

Today, TCI offers a wide rage of travel services to assist and support members with the highest level of convenience and quality. Now you can discover the unique charms of Italy with a distinct insider's advantage.

Enjoy exclusive money saving offers with a TCI membership. Use your membership card for discounts in thousands of restaurants, hotels, spas, campgrounds, museums, shops and markets.

These Hotel Chains offer preferred rates and discounts to TCI members!

How to Join

It's quick and easy to join.
Apply for your membership online at
www.touringclub.it
Your membership card will arrive within
three weeks and is valid for discounts
across Italy for the entire year.
Get your card before you go and start
saving as soon as you arrive.
Euro 25 annual membership fee
includes priority mail postage for
membership card and materials.
Just one use of the card will more than
cover the cost of membership.

Benefits

• Exclusive car rental rates with Hertz
• Discounts at select Esso gas stations
• 20% discount on TCI guidebooks
and maps purchased in TCI bookstores
or directly online at
www.touringclub.com
• Preferred rates and discounts available
at thousands of locations in Italy: Hotels -
B&B's - Villa Rentals - Campgrounds -TCI
Resorts - Spas - Restaurants - Wineries -
Museums - Cinemas - Theaters - Music
Festivals - Shops - Craft Markets - Ferries -
Cruises - Theme Parks - Botanical Gardens

ITALY: INSTRUCTIONS FOR USE

Italy is known throughout the world for the quantity and quality of its art treasures and for its natural beauty, but it is also famous for its inimitable lifestyle and fabulous cuisine and wines. Although it is a relatively small country, Italy boasts an extremely varied culture and multifarious traditions and customs. The information and suggestions in this brief section will help foreign tourists not only to understand certain aspects of Italian life, but also to solve the everyday difficulties and the problems of a practical nature that inevitably crop up during any trip.

This practical information is included in brief descriptions of various topics: public transport and how to purchase tickets; suggestions on how to drive in this country; the different types of rooms and accommodation in hotels; hints on how to use mobile phones and communication in general. This is followed by useful advice on how to meet your everyday needs and on shopping, as well as information concerning the cultural differences in the various regions. Lastly, there is a section describing the vast range of restaurants, bars, wine bars and pizza parlors.

TRANSPORTATION

From the airport to the city

Public transportation in major cities is easily accessible and simple to use. Both Milan and Rome airports have trains and buses linking them to the city centers. At Milano-Malpensa, you can take a bus to the main train station or a train to Cadorna train station and subway stop.

Subways, buses, and trams

Access to the subways, buses, and trams requires a ticket (tickets are not sold on board but can be purchased at most newsstands and tobacco shops). The ticket is good for one ride and sometimes has a time limit (in the case of buses and trams). When you board a bus or tram, you are required to stamp your previously-acquired ticket in the time-stamping machine. Occasionally, a conductor will board the bus or tram and check everyone's ticket. If you haven't got one, or if it has not been time-stamped, you will have to pay a steep fine.

Trains

The Ferrovie dello Stato (Italian Railways) is among the best and most modern railway systems in Europe. Timetables and routes can be consulted and reservations can be made online at **www.trenitalia.com**. Many travel agents can also dispense tickets and help you plan your journey. Hard-copy schedules can be purchased at all newsstands and most bookstores.

Automated ticket machines, which include easy-to-use instructions in English, are available in nearly all stations. They can be used to check schedules, makes reservations, and purchase tickets. There are different types of train, according to the requirements:

Eurostar Italia Trains **ES★** : Fast connections between Italy's most important cities. The ticket includes seat booking charge;

Intercity **/c** and **Espresso £** Trains: Local connections among Italy's towns and cities. Sometimes **/c** and **£** trains require seat booking. You can book your seat up to 3 hours before the train departure. The seat booking charge is of 3 Euro.

Interregionale Trains **iR** move beyond regional boundaries. Among the combined local-transport services, the **iR** Trains are the fastest ones with the fewest number of stops. No seat booking available.

Diretto D and **Regionale R** Trains can circulate both within the regions and their bordering regions. No seat booking available.

The Romanesque Duomo in Spoleto.

DO NOT FORGET: In Italy, you can only board a train if you have a valid ticket. Tickets without seat booking must be time-stamped prior to boarding (each station has numerous time-stamping machines).

If you don't have a ticket – or did not stamp before boarding – you will be liable to pay the full ticket price plus a 25 euro fine. If you produce a ticket that is not valid for the train or service you're using (i.e. one issued for a different train category at a different price, etc.) you will be asked to pay the difference with respect to the full ticket price, plus an 8 euro surcharge.

Taxis

Taxis are a convenient but expensive way to travel in Italian cities. There are taxi stands scattered throughout major cities. You cannot hail taxis on the street in Italy, but you can reserve taxis, in advance or immediately, by phone: consult the yellow pages for the number or ask your hotel reception desk or maitre d'hotel to call for you.

Taxi drivers have the right to charge you a supplementary fee for every piece of luggage they transport, as well as night and festivity surcharge.

Driving

Especially when staying in the countryside, driving is a safe and convenient way to travel through Italy and its major cities. It is important to be aware of street signs and speed limits, and many cities have zones where only limited traffic is allowed in order to accommodate pedestrians.

Street parking is organized using road signs and different colored street markings. No line or a white line is for free parking, blue is for paid parking and yellow is for reserved parking (disabled, residents etc). There may be time limits for both free and paid parking. In this case, use your parking disc to indicate your time of arrival.

Although an international driver's license is not required in Italy, it is advisable. ACI and similar associations provide this service to members. The fuel distribution network is reasonably distributed all over the territory. All service stations have unleaded gasoline ("benzina verde") and diesel fuel ("gasolio"). Opening time is 7 to 12:30 and 15 to 19:30; on motorways the service is 24 hours a day.

Type of roads in Italy: The *Autostrada* (for example A14) is the main highway system in Italy and is similar to the Interstate highway system in the US and the motorway system in the UK. Shown on our Touring Club Italiano 1:200,000 road maps as black. The Autostrada are toll highways; you pay to use them. The *Strada Statale* (for example SS54) is a fast moving road that may have one or more lanes in each direction. Shown on our Touring Club Italiano 1:200,000 road maps as red. *Strada Provinciale* (for example SP358) can be narrow, slow and winding roads. They are usually one lane in each direction. Shown on our Touring Club Italiano 1:200,000 road maps as yellow. *Strada Comunale* (for example SC652) is a local road connecting the main town with its sorrounding. Note: In our guide you will sometime find an address of a place in the countryside listed, for example, as

"SS54 Km 25". This means that the you have to drive along the Strada Statale 54 until you reach the 25-km road sign.
Speed limits: 130 kmph on the Autostrada, 110 kmph on main highways, 90 kmph outside of towns, 50 kmph in towns.
The town streets are patrolled by the Polizia Municipale while the roads outside cities and the Autostrada are patrolled by the Carabinieri or the Polizia Stradale.
Do not forget:
• Wear your seat belt at all times;
• Do not use the cellular phone while driving;
• Have your headlights on at all times when driving outside of cities;
• The drunk driving laws are strict – do not drink and drive;
• In case of an accident you are not allowed to get out of your car unless you are wearing a special, high-visibility, reflective jacket.

ACCOMMODATION

Hotels
In Italy it is common practice for the reception desk to register your passport, and only registered guests are allowed to use the rooms. This is mere routine, done for security reasons, and there is no need for concern.
All hotels use the official star classification system, from 5-star luxury hotel to 1 star accommodation.
Room rates are based on whether they are for single ("camera singola") or double ("camera doppia") occupancy. In every room you will find a list of the hotel rates (generally on the back of the door). While 4- and 5-star hotels have double beds, most hotels have only single beds. Should you want a double bed, you have to ask for a "letto matrimoniale". All hotels have rooms with bathrooms; only 1-star establishments usually have only shared bathrooms.
Most hotel rates include breakfast ("prima colazione"), but you can request to do without it, thus reducing the rate.
Breakfast is generally served in a communal room and comprises a buffet with pastries, bread with butter and jam, cold cereals, fruit, yoghurt, coffee, and fruit juice. Some hotels regularly frequented by foreign tourists will also serve other items such as eggs for their American and British guests.
The hotels for families and in tourist localities also offer "mezza pensione", or half board, in which breakfast and dinner are included in the price.
It's always a good idea to check when a hotel's annual closing period is, especially if you are planning a holiday by the sea.

Farm stays
Located only in the countryside, and generally on a farm, "agriturismo" – a network of farm holiday establishments – is part of a growing trend in Italy to honor local gastronomic and wine traditions, as well as countryside traditions. These farms offer meals prepared with ingredients cultivated exclusively on site: garden-grown vegetables, homemade cheese and local recipes. Many of these places also provide lodging, one of the best ways to experience the "genuine" Italian lifestyle.

Bed & Breakfast
This form of accommodation provides bed and breakfast in a private house, and in the last few years has become much more widespread in Italy. There are over 6,500 b&bs, classified in 3 categories, and situated both in historic town centers, as well as in the outskirts and the countryside. Rooms for guests are always well-furnished, but not all of them have en suite bathrooms.
It is well-recommended to check the closing of the open-all-year accommodation services and restaurants, because they could have a short break during the year (usually no longer than a fortnight).

COMMUNICATIONS

Nearly everyone in Italy owns a cellular phone. Although public phones are still available, they seem to be ever fewer and farther between. If you wish to use public phones, you will find them in subway stops, bars, along the street, and phone centers generally located in the city center. Phone cards and pre-paid phone cards can be purchased at most newsstands and tobacco shops, and can also be acquired at automated tellers.
For European travelers, activating personal cellular coverage is relatively simple, as it is in most cases for American and Australian travelers as well. Contact your mobile service provider for details.

Cellular phones can also be rented in Italy from TIM, the Italian national phone company. For information, visit its website at www.tim.it. When traveling by car through the countryside, a cellular phone can really come in handy.

Note that when dialing in Italy, you must always dial the prefix (e.g., 02 for Milan, 06 for Rome) even when making a local call. For cellular phones, however, the initial zero is always dropped.

Freephone numbers always start with "800". For calls abroad from Italy, it's a good idea to buy a special pre-paid international phone card, which is used with a PIN code.

Internet access

Cyber cafés have sprung up all over Italy and you can find one on nearly every city block.

EATING AND DRINKING

The bar

The Italian "bar" is a multi-faceted, all-purpose establishment for drinking, eating and socializing, where you can order an espresso, have breakfast, and enjoy a quick sandwich for lunch or even a hot meal. You can often buy various items here (sometimes even stamps, cigarettes, phone cards, etc.). Bear in mind that table service ("servizio a tavola") includes a surcharge. At most bars, if you choose to sit, a waiter will take your order. Every bar should have a list of prices posted behind or near the counter; if the bar offers table service, the price list should also include the extra fee for this.

Lunch at bars will include, but is not limited to, "panini," sandwiches with crusty bread, usually with cured meats such as "prosciutto" (salt-cured ham), "prosciutto cotto" (cooked ham), and cheeses such as mozzarella topped with tomato and basil. Then there are "tramezzini" (finger sandwiches) with tuna, cheese, or vegetables, etc. Often the "panini" and other savory sandwiches (like stuffed flatbread or "focaccia") are heated before being served. Naturally, the menu at bars varies according to the region: in Bologna you will find "piadine" (flatbread similar to pita) with Swiss chard; in Palermo there are "arancini" (fried rice balls stuffed with

ground meat); in Genoa you will find that even the most unassuming bar serves some of the best "focaccia" in all Italy. Some bars also include a "tavola calda". If you see this sign in a bar window, it means that hot dishes like pasta and even entrées are served.

A brief comment on coffee and cappuccino: Italians never serve coffee with savory dishes or sandwiches, and they seldom drink cappuccino outside of breakfast (although they are happy to serve it at any time).

While English- and Irish-type pubs are frequented by beer lovers and young people in Italy, there are also American bars where long drinks and American cocktails are served.

Breakfast at the bar

Breakfast in Italy generally consists of some type of pastry, most commonly a "brioche" – a croissant either filled with cream or jam, or plain – and a cappuccino or espresso. Although most bars do not offer American coffee, you can ask for a "caffè lungo" or "caffè americano", both of which resemble the American coffee preferred by the British and Americans. Most bars have a juicer to make a "spremuta", freshly squeezed orange or grapefruit juice.

Lunch and Dinner

As with all daily rituals in Italy, food is prepared and meals are served according to local customs (e.g., in the North they prefer rice and butter, in South and Central Italy they favor pasta and olive oil).

Wine is generally served at mealtime, and while finer restaurants have excellent wine lists (some including vintage wines), ordering the house table wine generally brings good results (a house Chianti to accompany your Florentine steak in Tuscany, a sparkling Prosecco paired with your creamed stockfish and polenta in Venice, a dry white wine with pasta dressed with sardines and wild fennel fronds in Sicily).

Mineral water is also commonly served at meals and can be "gassata" (sparkling) or "naturale" (still).

The most sublime culinary experience in Italy is achieved by matching the local foods with the appropriate local wines: wisdom dictates that a friendly waiter will be flattered by your request for his recommendation on what to eat and drink. Whether at an "osteria" (a tavern), a "trattoria" (a home-style restaurant), or a "ristorante" (a proper restaurant), the service of lunch and dinner generally consists of – but is not limited to – the following: "antipasti" or appetizers; "primo piatto" or first course, i.e., pasta, rice, or soup; "secondo piatto" or main course, i.e., meat or seafood; "contorno" or side-dish, served with the main course, i.e., vegetables or salad; "formaggi", "frutta", and "dolci", i.e., cheeses, fruit, and dessert; caffè or espresso coffee, perhaps spiked with a shot of grappa.

The pizzeria

The pizzeria is in general one of the most economical, democratic, and satisfying culinary experiences in Italy. Everyone eats at the pizzeria: young people, families, couples, locals and tourists alike. Generally, each person orders her/his own pizza, and while the styles of crust and toppings will vary from region to region (some of the best pizzas are served in Naples and Rome), the acid test of any pizzeria is the Margherita, topped simply with cheese and tomato sauce.

Beer, sparkling or still water, and Coca Cola are the beverages commonly served with pizza. Some restaurants include a pizza menu, but most establishments do not serve pizza at lunchtime.

The wine bar (enoteca)

More than one English-speaking tourist in Italy has wondered why the wine bar is called an enoteca in other countries and the English term is used in Italy: the answer lies somewhere in the mutual fondness that Italians and English speakers have for one another. Wine bars have become popular in recent years in the major cities (especially in Rome, where you can find some of the best). The wine bar is a great place to sample different local wines and eat a light, tapas-style dinner.

CULTURAL DIVERSITY

Whenever you travel, not only are you a guest of your host country, but you are also a representative of your home country. As a general rule, courtesy, consideration, and respect are always appreciated by guests and their hosts alike. Italians are famous for their hospitality and experience will verify this felicitous stereotype: perhaps nowhere else in Europe are tourists and visitors received more warmly. Italy is a relatively "new" country. Its borders, as we know them today, were established only in 1861 when it became a monarchy under the House of Savoy. After WWII, Italy became a Republic and now it is one of the member states of the European Union. One of the most fascinating aspects of Italian culture is that, even as a unified country, local tradition still prevails over a universally Italian national identity. Some jokingly say that the only time that Venetians, Milanese, Florentines, Neapolitans, and Sicilians feel like Italians is when the national football team plays in international competitions. From their highly localized dialects to the foods they eat, from their religious celebration to their politics, Italians proudly maintain their local heritage. This is one of the reasons why the Piedmontese continue to prefer their beloved Barolo wine and their white truffles, the Umbrians their rich Sagrantino wine and black truffles, the Milanese their risotto and panettone, the Venetians their stockfish and polenta, the Bolognese their lasagne and pumpkin ravioli, the Florentines their bread soups and steaks cooked rare, the Abruzzese their excellent fish broth and seafood, the Neapolitans their mozzarella, basil, pizza, and pasta. As a result of its rich cultural diversity, the country's population also varies greatly in its customs from region to region, city to city, town to town. As you visit different cities and regions throughout Italy, you will see how the local personality and character of the Italians change as rapidly as the landscape does. Having lived for millennia with their great diversity and rich, highly heterogeneous culture, the Italians have taught us many things, foremost among them the age-old expression, "When in Rome, do as the Romans do."

NATIONAL HOLIDAYS

New Year's Day (1st January), Epiphany (6th January), Easter Monday (day after Easter Sunday), Liberation Day (25th April), Labour Day (1st May), Italian Republic Day (2nd June), Assumption (15th August), All Saints' Day (1st November), Immaculate Conception (8th December), Christmas Day and Boxing Day (25th-26th December).

In addition to these holidays, each city also has a holiday to celebrate its patron saint's feast day, usually with lively, local celebrations. Shops and services in large cities close on national holidays and for the week of the 15th of August.

EVERYDAY NEEDS

State tobacco shops and pharmacies

Tobacco is available in Italy only at state licensed tobacco shops. These vendors ("tabaccheria"), often incorporated in a bar, also sell stamps.

Smoking is forbidden in all so-called public places – unless a separately ventilated space is constructed – meaning over 90% of the country's restaurants and bars.

Medicines can be purchased only in pharmacies ("farmacia") in Italy. Pharmacists are very knowledgeable about common ailments and can generally prescribe a treatment for you on the spot. Opening time is 8:30-12:30 and 15:30-19:30 but in any case there is always a pharmacy open 24 hours and during holidays.

Shopping

Every locality in Italy offers tourists characteristic shops, markets with good bargains, and even boutiques featuring leading Italian fashion designers. Opening hours vary from region to region and from season to season. In general, shops are open from 9 to 13 and from 15/16 to 19/20, but in large cities they usually have no lunchtime break.

Tax Free

Non-EU citizens can obtain a reimbursement for IVA (goods and services tax) paid on purchases over €155, for goods which are exported within 90 days, in shops which display the relevant sign. IVA is always automatically included in the price of any purchase, and ranges from 20% to 4% depending on the item. The shop issues a reimbursement voucher to present when you leave the country (at a frontier or airport). For purchases in shops affiliated to 'Tax Free Shopping', IVA may be reimbursed directly at international airports.

Banks and post offices

Italian banks are open Monday to Friday, from 8:30 to 13:30 and then from 15 to 16. However, the afternoon business hours may vary.

Post offices are open from Monday to Saturday, from 8:30 to 13:30 (12:30 on Saturday). In the larger towns there are also some offices open in the afternoon.

Currency

As in many other European Union countries, the Euros is the Italian currency. Coins are in denominations of 1, 2, 5, 10, 20 and 50 cents and 1 and 2 euros; banknotes are in denominations of 5, 10, 20, 50, 100, 200 and 500 euros, each with a different color.

Credit cards

All the main credit cards are generally accepted, but some smaller enterprises (arts and crafts shops, small hotels, bed & breakfasts, or farm stays) do not provide this service. Foreign tourists can obtain cash using credit cards at automatic teller machines.

Time

All Italy is in the same time zone, which is six hours ahead of Eastern Standard Time in the USA. Daylight saving time is used from March to October, when watches and clocks are set an hour ahead of standard time.

Passports and vaccinations

Citizens of EU countries can enter Italy without frontier checks. Citizens of Australia, Canada, New Zealand, and the United States can enter Italy with a valid passport and need not have a visa for a stay of less than 90 days.

No vaccinations are necessary.

Payment and tipping

When you sit down at a restaurant you are generally charged a "coperto" or cover charge ranging from 1.5 to 3 euros, for service and the bread. Tipping is not customary in Italy. Beware of unscrupulous restaurateurs who add a space on their clients' credit card receipt for a tip, while it has already been included in the cover charge.

USEFUL ADDRESSES

Foreign Embassies in Italy

Australia
Via A. Bosio, 5 - 00161 Rome
Tel. +39 06 852721
Fax +39 06 85272300
www.italy.embassy.gov.au.
info-rome@dfat.gov.au

Canada
Via Salaria, 243 - 00199 Rome
Tel. +39 06 854441
Fax +39 06 85444 3915
www.canada.it
rome@dfait-maeci.gc.ca

Great Britain
Via XX Settembre, 80 -
00187 Rome
Tel. +39 06 42200001
Fax +39 06 42202334
www.britian.it
consularenquiries@rome.
mail.fco.gov.uk

Ireland
Piazza di Campitelli, 3 -
00186 Rome
Tel. +39 06 6979121
Fax +39 06 6792354
irish.embassy@esteri.it

New Zealand
Via Zara, 28 - 00198 Rome
Tel. +39 06 4417171
Fax +39 06 4402984

South Africa
Via Tanaro, 14 -.00198 Rome
Tel. +39 06 852541
Fax +39 06 85254300
www.sudafrica.it

United States of America
Via Vittorio Veneto, 121 -
00187 Rome
Tel. +39 06 46741
Fax +39 06 4882672
www.usis.it

Foreign Consulates in Italy

Australia
Via Borgogna, 2
20122 Milan
Tel. +39 02 77704217
Fax +39 02 77704242

Canada
Via Vittor Pisani, 19
20124 Milan
Tel. +39 02 67581
Fax +39 02 67583900
milan@international.gc.ca

Great Britain
Via S. Paolo, 7
20121 Milan
Tel. +39 02 723001
Fax +39 02 86465081
ConsularMilan@fco.gov.uk

Lungarno Corsini, 2
50123 Florence
Tel. +39 055 284133
Consular.Florence@fco.gov.uk

Via dei Mille, 40
80121 Naples
Tel. +39 081 4238911
Fax +39 081 422434
Info.Naples@fco.gov.uk

Ireland
Piazza San Pietro in Gessate, 2 -
20122 Milan
Tel. +39 02 55187569/02 55187641
Fax +39 02 55187570

New Zealand
Via Guido d'Arezzo, 6
20145 Milan
Tel. +39 02 48012544
Fax +39 02 48012577

South Africa
Vicolo San Giovanni
sul Muro, 4
20121 Milan
Tel. +39 02 8858581
Fax +39 02 72011063
saconsulate@iol.it

United States of America
Via Principe Amedeo, 2/10
20121 Milan
Tel. +39 02 290351
Fax +39 02 29001165

Lungarno Vespucci, 38
50123 Florence
Tel. +39 055 266951
Fax +39 055 284088

Piazza della Repubblica
80122 Naples
Tel. +39 081 5838111
Fax +39 081 7611869

Italian Embassies and Consulates Around the World

Australia
12, Grey Street - Deakin, A.C.T.
2600 - Canberra
Tel. 02 62733333, 62733398,
62733198
Fax 02 62734223
www.ambcanberra.esteri.it
Consulates at: Brisbane, Glynde,
Melbourne, Perth , Sydney

Canada
275, Slater Street, 21st floor -
Ottawa (Ontario) K1P 5H9
Tel. (613) 232 2401/2/3
Fax (613) 233 1484 234 8424
www.ambottawa.esteri.it
ambital@italyincanada.com
Consulates at: Edmonton,
Montreal, Toronto, Vancouver,

Great Britain
14, Three Kings Yard, London
W1K 4EH
Tel. 020 73122200
Fax 020 73122230
www.amblondra.esteri.it
ambasciata.londra@esteri.it
Consulates at: London, Bedford,
Edinburgh, Manchester

Ireland
63/65, Northumberland Road -
Dublin 4
Tel. 01 6601744
Fax 01 6682759
www.ambdublino.esteri.it
info@italianembassy.ie

New Zealand
34-38 Grant Road, Thorndon,
(PO Box 463, Wellington)
Tel. 04 473 5339

Fax 04 472 7255
www.ambwellington.esteri.it

South Africa
796 George Avenue, 0083 Arcadia
Tel. 012 4305541/2/3
Fax 012 4305547
www.ambpretoria.esteri.it
Consulates at: Johannesburg,
Capetown, Durban

United States of America
3000 Whitehaven Street, NW
Washington DC 20008
Tel. (202) 612-4400
Fax (202) 518-2154
www.ambwashingtondc.esteri.it
Consulates at: Boston, MA -
Chicago, IL - Detroit, MI - Houston,
TX - Los Angeles, CA - Miami, FL -
Newark, NJ - New York, NY -
Philadelphia, PA - San Francisco, CA

ENIT (Italian State Tourism Board)

Australia
Level 4, 46 Market Street
NSW 2000 Sidney
PO Box Q802 - QVB NSW 1230
Tel. 00612 92 621666
Fax 00612 92 621677
italia@italiantourism.com.au

Canada
175 Bloor Street E. Suite 907 –
South Tower
M4W3R8 Toronto (Ontario)
Tel. (416) 925 4882
Fax (416) 925 4799
www.italiantourism.com
enit.canada@on.aibn.com

Great Britain
1, Princes Street
W1B 2AY London
Tel. 020 7408 1254
Tel. 800 00482542 FREE from
United Kingdom and Ireland
italy@italiantouristboard.co.uk

United States of America
500, North Michigan Avenue
Suite 2240
60611 Chicago 1, Illinois
Tel. (312) 644 0996 /644 0990
Fax (312) 644 3019
www.italiantourism.com
enitch@italiantourism.com

12400, Wilshire Blvd. – Suite 550
CA 90025 Los Angeles
Tel. (310) 820 1898 - 820 9807
Fax (310) 820 6357
www.italiantourism.com
enitla@italiantourism.com

630, Fifth Avenue – Suite 1565
NY – 10111 New York
Tel. (212) 245 4822 – 245 5618
Fax (212) 586 9249
www.italiantourism.com
enitny@italiantourism.com

The well-known slogan "Umbria: the green heart of Italy" conjures up a picture of peace and tranquility, of a gentle landscape dotted with medieval hill-top towns and fortifications. The dense network of small towns is linked by local roads and railways, in a landscape still very reminiscent of Renaissance paintings. In this region, home to St Francis and St Clare of Assisi and St Rita of Cascia, you can still capture the strong spiritual aura walking the streets of the towns with which they were associated. That is what this region of Italy has to offer, and much, much more. It was the land of the ancient Etruscans, and

Heritage

has always had spontaneous and frequent relations with nearby Tuscany, and thus the sea. Similarly, over the centuries, it has had close links with the region of Lazio. The Tiber River constitutes the border between them, flowing through 200km of the Umbrian countryside.

Highlights

- Perugia, with its extraordinary "underground city".
- The majestic Basilica of S. Francesco in Assisi, where the upper and lower churches date from different periods.
- Spello, the town with the largest number of Roman remains in Umbria.
- The facade of the Duomo in Orvieto, with its exquisite mosaics.

Bold, stars and italics are used in the text to emphasize the importance of places and art-works:

bold type ** → **not to be missed**
bold type * → **very important**
bold type → **important**
italic type → **interesting**

Inside

PERUGIA

Perugia, Umbria's largest city, dominates a maze of valleys and major communication routes between the Tiberina and Umbra valleys from its hill, 493m above sea-level. Here the visitor is afforded various sights, the best being the view when arriving from the direction of Cortona. The historic center appears like the cavea of a theater, from which areas of modern expansion have crept along and down the hill. To get a proper feel of the city, you should approach it by the ancient roads which wind up along the hill into the center of the town. Perugia is, first and foremost, a city of culture. Its state university and its university for foreigners attract large numbers of young people who enliven the historical center. This cultural vitality translates into high-level events, such as: Umbria Jazz (July) and the Sagra Musicale Umbra (September), dedicated both to sacred and contemporary music.

The city's monumental center, situated entirely in the higher part of town within the Etruscan walls, with the medieval Baglioni district, now completely underground, has a rich artistic heritage. To the north, outside the city walls, lie the town's charming medieval districts of Porta Sant' Angelo, Porta Sant' Antonio and Fonte Nuovo. Although they have now all been encompassed within later city walls, they have nevertheless maintained their "low-class" dimension in contrast with the higher noble part of the city. The elongated, narrow medieval district of Porta San Pietro, partly surrounded by fortifications (13C-14C), is the southern arm of the historic center, which is itself surrounded by the fortifications of later date (14C-15C) which enclose the caracteristic Borgo XX Giugno.

PERUGIA
IN OTHER COLORS...

ITINERARIES: pages 96, 100, 120
FOOD: pages 128, 134, 140
SHOPPING: pages 152, 154, 155
EVENTS: pages 158, 161
WELLNESS: page 168
PRACTICAL INFO: pages 182, 183, 184

Piazza IV Novembre ❶

This broad, lively square is the city's center of civic and religious power. It occupies the area of the Roman forum and, since its origins, has been the hub of the city's street network, to the extent of becoming, in medieval times, the starting point of the five *vie regali* (royal roads). These provided access to the main roads in the area, linking the city to Gubbio, Città di Castello, Cortona, Orvieto and Foligno. The square's charm derives from the harmonious relationship between the various monuments overlooking it: the Cathedral, the Fontana Maggiore and Palazzo dei Priori all playfully blend in alternating asymmetrical forms. The **Fontana Maggiore****, the visible hub of the square, is the symbol of the medieval commune and of the entire city.

The fountain, built in 1275-78, is a 13th-century masterpiece and has been

Perugia: Palazzo dei Priori

PLAN

1 Notaries' Chamber
2 Main doorway
3 Priors' arch
4 College of the Mercanzia
5 Old Priors' Chapel
6 Exchange college

described as "one of the most powerful medieval representations of human life". The monument consists of two polygonal marble basins surmounted by a bronze bowl, containing *three nymphs* (or *theological virtues*). The **marble reliefs** decorating the lower basin depict an agricultural calendar, the signs of the Zodiac and the seven Liberal Arts.

Cattedrale/Cathedral ❷

The long flight of steps leading to it is a favorite place for tourists to stop and enjoy a truly incomparable view of the square. The cathedral, dedicated to St Lawrence, was constructed in various phases. The initial structure, which became a cathedral in 969, was redesigned in the 14th century, restructured again in 1437, and consecrated in 1569. In the 17th century, the brick top was added. Its unfinished left side, in pink and white marble, has Gothic windows and additions from various periods, including the 15th-century *pulpit* from which St Bernardine of Siena is supposed to have preached. The bare facade, adorned with an elegant doorway (1729), is also unfinished. Its vast and luminous 15th-century interior has a high nave and aisles of equal height, separated by octagonal piers supporting Gothic vaulting. The structure is enhanced by 18th-century decoration and stucco-work. The decoration, consisting of paintings, frescoes and stained-glass windows of different periods (16 to 19C) make for a stylistically varied and harmonious whole. The carved wooden **choir*** (1491) in the apse is noteworthy.

The 15th-century frescoed *sacristy* (1573-76) can be reached via the chapel to the right of the presbytery. Connected with the sacristy are the inspiring **rectory cloisters**, with three superimposed arcades, where conclaves were held for some of the popes. The interesting **Museo Capitolare*** occupies part of the complex where the clergy lived and includes some artworks from the cathedral and from churches in the Diocese. Paintings of particular note include: a **Virgin Enthroned and Child, with Sts John the Baptist, Onofrius, Lawrence, and a Bishop** (probably the patron) **and a Musician Angel** (1484), a masterpiece by Luca Signorelli. Particularly noteworthy is a **Pietà** and the sculpture of a **deacon's head**, attributed to Arnolfo di Cambio. The Lapidarium contains architectural fragments dating from the Romanesque period, illuminated manuscripts (8C and 9C), a 12th-century breviary and a 13th-century missal. Near the cathedral, beneath the street level of *Piazza Cavallotti,* the **archaeological site** conserves the remains of a paved Roman road (you can still see the ruts made by ancient cart wheels) and part of a semi-circular fountain of the 2nd century AD.

Via Maestà delle Volte ❸

This street, spanned by archways and winding through one of the most charming parts of the city, once featured a *Maestà* painted beneath the supporting vault of Palazzo del Podestà, the remains of which are still visible at the end of the street. The **oratory of the Maestà delle Volte** was built to protect the fresco.

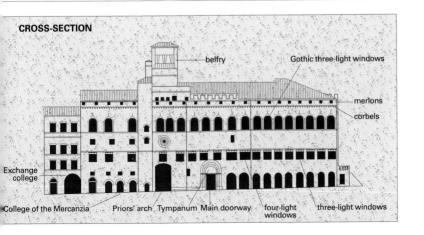

CROSS-SECTION

belfry — Gothic three-light windows — merlons — corbels — Exchange college — College of the Mercanzia — Priors' arch — Tympanum — Main doorway — four-light windows — three-light windows

Palazzo dei Priori/Priors' Palace ❹

Pride of the commune of Perugia, this magnificent building dominates the area between Piazza IV Novembre and Corso Vannucci. The city's ancient administrative seat currently houses the town hall and the Galleria Nazionale dell' Umbria. Its phase-by-phase construction (from 1293-97 to 1443), and its superimposition upon earlier structures explain the irregular layout and asymmetrical facade. The original part of the structure corresponds to the three windows overlooking the left side of the square and to the first ten overlooking Corso Vannucci, and was last broadened at the junction of Corso Vannucci and Via dei Priori. At the top of the steps which fan out onto the square is a large doorway surmounted by heavy consoles bearing the griffin (Perugia's coat-of-arms) and the Guelph lion (the originals are inside the palace). Inside is the austere **Notaries' Chamber*** (1582), with a transversal arched ceiling and frescoes dating from the last decade of the 13th century. Here, of particular interest are the wooden stalls along the entrance wall and the 16th-century seats along the other walls. On the side facing Corso Vannucci is the handsome **main doorway*** (1346), bearing an intricate allegorical *decoration* and, on the second floor, 19 very fine Gothic **three-light windows***. From the Gothic atrium, a boldly pilastered staircase leads to the upper floor, where, in the communal council hall, the Perugia **griffin*** and the Guelph **lion*** are displayed. They are the earliest example in Italy of medieval casting of large objects in one piece (ca. 1274), and possibly belonged to a fountain by Arnolfo di Cambio. Created from the original nucleus of the Accademia del Disegno (late 16C), the **Galleria Nazionale dell'Umbria** was expanded between the late 18th and early 19th centuries. In 1878, the art gallery was separated from the academy and transferred to the third floor of the Palazzo dei Priori. This important art collection, the most complete in the entire region, is arranged chronologically and divided by school, with works by artists active in this area from the 13th to the 19th centuries. The visit to the gallery begins with 13th-century sculptures, which also comprise **five works**** by Arnolfo di

Perugia 1 : 12 000 (1 cm = 120 m)

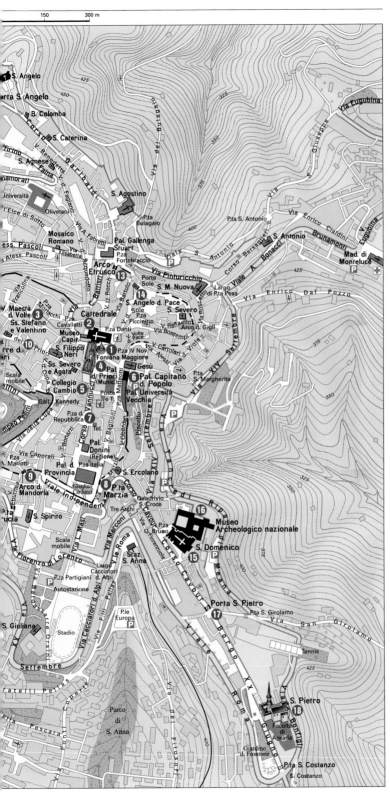

Cambio (1278-81). Pre-Giotto Umbrian painting has as its main representative the Maestro di San Francesco (**Crucifix****, 1272). Among the 14th-century works is a **Virgin and Child**** by Duccio di Buoninsegna, and the **Montelabate polyptych***, by Meo da Siena, ca. 1317. International Gothic reached Perugia in the early 15th century: examples include the **Virgin and Child with Angels**** by Gentile da Fabriano and the **Pietralunga polyptych*** (1404). The gallery's more significant Florentine Renaissance works include Beato Angelico's **S. Domenico polyptych**** and Piero della Francesca's **S. Antonio polyptych****.

One of Perugia's most important Renaissance works is the **Cappella dei Priori****, a chapel frescoed between 1454 and 1480. The works of Pietro Vannucci (known as 'Il Perugino') are given pride of place, including the **small panels*** (1473) in the so-called niche of St Bernardine, and the **S. Agostino polyptych****, a masterpiece of the artist's later years. One of Il Perugino's pupils, Pinturicchio, is also represented: the **S. Maria dei Fossi altarpiece**** (1495-96). These are followed by works dating from the 16th, 17th and 18th centuries. On the way round the exhibition, some areas are devoted to special exhibits or special collections: for example, the 19th-century *Rocchi collection* of 240 Perugian towels and **gold- and silver-ware** and **ivories** from the city's museums. In 1390, on the ground floor of the Palazzo dei Priori, the area to the left of the main doorway was assigned to the **Collegiata della Mercanzia***, one of the city's most impor-tant trade guilds. Inside, the rectangular **Audience Hall** has pine and walnut *wood paneling* (15C).

Collegio del Cambio/ Exchange college ❺

Next to the *Mercanzia* was the seat of the equally powerful money-changers' guild (the *cambiatori*), built between 1452 and 1457 alongside Palazzo dei Priori. Through a fine carved wooden doorway (1501) you enter the *Sala dei Legisti*, with its inlaid counters (1615-21). To the right, you enter the **Sala dell'Udienza del Cambio**, a vital testament to Italian Renaissance art. The beautifully inlaid wooden counters (1492-93) provide a perfect contrast to Il Perugino's **frescoes**** (1498-1500), which decorate the walls and the Gothic vaulting above. The fresco cycle follows a precise iconographical pattern: deities of the Ancient myths are depicted on the ceiling; on the walls, the *Four Virtues* and famous figures in Antiquity. On one of the pilasters separating the panels is a *self-portrait of Il Perugino*. Next-door is the *chapel of St John the Baptist (1506-1509)*, with an interior covered in frescoes.

Palazzo del Capitano del Popolo ❻

From the loggia supported by richly decorated consoles, heralds would read out official edicts and ordinances. Today, the building where those public

Frescoes by Il Perugino in the Exchange college.

Corso Vannucci, Perugia's main street.

the loggia are two stone bands engraved with Roman inscriptions. Porta Marzia provides access to the **"underground city"**, the unusual subterranean **Via Bagliona***, which penetrates the Rocca's extraordinary underground remains of the medieval quarter belonging to the Consorteria dei Baglioni (a political association of noble families). Here you can still see the structures of ancient houses and the street layout, warehouses, courtyards and small squares, still overlooked by a few windows, furnaces and shops. The many tower-houses include the 13th-century *house of Gentile Baglioni* with its tower still intact, and the *block of houses belonging to Ridolfo and Braccio Baglioni*, which has also survived.

Arco della Mandorla ❾

Also called Porta Eburnea, the archway was founded in Etruscan times, but remodeled during the Middle Ages, as can be seen by its ogival structure. Its upper stone blocks preserve traces of the original semicircular arch.

Via dei Priori ❿

This steep medieval street built on the line of the Etruscan street descends from Arco dei Priori below the tower of the town hall. The compact row of dwellings and religious complexes on this thoroughfare is intersected here and there by narrow, winding streets, which are a typical feature of the old city. Further on, the **church of S. Filippo Neri*** is the city's largest baroque building, with its facade preceded by a double flight of stairs. The interior, with side-chapels, is richly decorated with 17th- and 18th-century frescoes . Near Piazzetta degli Oddi notice the **Torre degli Sciri***, the only tower left (46m; built of finely cut stone) of the many which loomed over the city in the Middle Ages, symbolizing the power and wealth of the city's leading families. Via dei Priori bends right to reveal one of Perugia's most beautiful perspectives: **Piazzetta della Madonna della Luce***. Two 16th-century churches face one another on different levels. The church of *Madonna della Luce* (1513-19) has a Renaissance travertine facade and its interior is decorated with frescoes. To the right is the church of *S. Luca* (1586), designed for the Knights of Malta, whose *palace* (14C) was located close by.

proclamations were made, along with **Palazzo dell'Università Vecchio**, is a law court. This elegant Renaissance building erected in 1473-81 has a fine doorway surmounted by *two Perugian griffins* and, in the lunette, a statue of *Justice*.

Corso Vannucci ❼

The city's busiest, most elegant street, as well as a meeting-place and shopping venue. Opposite Palazzo dei Priori, on the corner of Via Calderini, stands **Palazzo del Collegio dei Notari** (1446). Next to it is *Palazzo della Sapienza Vecchia* (1363). Piazza della Repubblica is overlooked by the former church of S. Isidoro and by the Teatro del Pavone. The following stretch of the Corso has one of the best examples of an 18th-century private house, **Palazzo Donini**, built over a Roman cistern and an early-Christian hypogeum.

Porta Marzia ❽

This gateway set in the Etruscan perimeter walls (late 3C BC) was later encased within the eastern bastion of the **Rocca Paolina** to create a decorative entrance. Of the original gateway, only the semi-circular arch and crown remain. At the sides of the arch, two Corinthian pilasters support a capital, consisting of a loggia-like structure similarly resting on small Corinthian pilasters, amid which the busts of three male figures protrude and, at the end, two half-bust equine figures. Above and below

Piazza San Francesco ⑪

At sunset, the soft pinky hues of the buildings enhance the appeal of this broad and luminous square at the end of Via dei Priori, which is overlooked by the statues of Sts Francis and Bernardine. The Friars Minor installed themselves on the square around 1230, and built the aisled **church of S. Francesco al Prato**, now in ruins and roofless after the collapse of its vaults. The facade was restored in 1926, using local white and pink stone.

Oratorio di San Bernardino/ Oratory of S. Bernardino ⑫

This Renaissance masterpiece was built in 1452 in honor of St Bernardine to the left of the church of S. Francesco al Prato. Its facade (1457-61), is as striking as much for its decoration as for its delicate colors: azurite and malachite and the pink stone create special light effects. Inside, the structure is Gothic, and the high altar is a re-used *Christian sarcophagus* (mid-4C).

Arco Etrusco/Etruscan Arch ⑬

Also called the Arch of Augustus, the Etruscan arch was erected in the 3rd century BC, at the end of the Etruscan city's north-south axis (present-day Via Rocchi) as a main gateway through the walled perimeter. Practically intact, the arch has sturdy trapezoidal towers which protect the entranceway, and which are embedded in the colossal city walls. Above the double order of ashlars forming the arch is a frieze of round shields alternating with Ionic pilasters.

Sant'Angelo ⑭

This is one of Italy's earliest Christian churches (5-6C). Surrounded by cypress trees, it backs onto the city walls and sits on an outcrop facing the old city. Built on a circular plan, with an elevated central area covered with a retractile roof, it is internally supported by 16 columns, the shafts of which differ in height and materials, topped with Roman capitals. Near the church stands the *gateway* of the same name, composed of a combination of sandstone, limestone, and bricks, showing how many modifications this structure has undergone since 1326, when it was built by Lorenzo Maitani.

San Domenico ⑮

The Dominicans were well respected here in the 13th-century. In this small square, now dedicated to Giordano Bruno (the Dominican who was burned at the stake for heresy), a first church was built (1231-60), the remains of which are still visible in the cloister of the adjacent monastery (now the Museo Archeologico Nazionale). In 1304, work began on the imposing Gothic basilica we see today, completely restructured by Carlo Maderno (1632). Its striking plain facade is relieved by the doorway (1596). Inside, the plainness of the nave and aisles is offset by the large Gothic *stained-glass window* in the apse (1411, 23m) which is the largest of that period after the one in Milan Cathedral. In the right transept stands the **monument to Benedict XI***, who died in Perugia in 1304; in the apse is a carved and inlaid wooden **choir** of 1476. The ceiling of the church is particularly interesting. This extraordinary and unique architectural space was created—after the roof had collapsed and been rebuilt several times—between the roof and the extrados of the vaulting covering the interior of the church.

Oratory of S. Bernardino, a splendid example of Renaissance architecture.

Museo Archeologico Nazionale/ National Archaeological Museum ⑯

Relocated in 1948 to the Dominican monastery complex, and accessed to the left of the church, the archeological museum is divided into two sections: Etruscan and Roman artifacts and prehistoric finds. Much of the *Etrusco-Roman section* is arranged in the cells off the large 17th-century loggia. It contains finds of Villanovan material (9-8C BC) from Perugia and from the necropolises of Palazzone near Ponte S. Giovanni; there are also finds from other necropolises in the area: Monteluce, Frontone, Sperandio, S. Caterina and S. Giuliana. One of the highlights is the **Cippo di Perugia*** (3-2C BC), a stone with one of the longest Etruscan texts to have survived. One room contains the imaginative reconstruction of the Etruscan tomb of the Cai Cutu family (used from 3 to 1C BC), discovered in 1983. Notable Roman exhibits include the bronze **statue of the emperor Germanicus,** in a triumphal pose. The *prehistoric section* is organized according to where the finds were discovered, and chronological and cultural criteria. They include finds dating from the Paleolithic to the Eneolithic. Upstairs, in the *Room of the Bronzes*, is material from the Bronze

'Cippo di Perugia', Museo Archeologico Nazionale.

and Iron Ages from sites in Umbria, Marche, Abruzzi, and finds from excavations conducted at Cetona. The newly-exhibited collection of amulets, the finest of its kind, testifies to the survival of Archaic ritual beliefs in Italy until the 19th and 20th centuries.

Porta San Pietro ⑰

At the end of Corso Cavour, a gateway with two facades, also called *Porta Romana,* opens onto the medieval perimeter wall. On the Corso side, it appears as a plain 14th-century arch, surmounted by a sacred image painted in a niche (1765). On the outside, it has an elegant Renaissance facade. Built in 1475 by Agostino di Duccio and Polidoro di Stefano, it evokes Etruscan motifs in the lively figures on its two lateral structures, in the decorative patterns of the escutcheons, here alternating with rosettes, and in the plan to top the central arch with a large niche (never applied).

San Pietro ⑱

At first glance, the complex architectural history of this Benedictine abbey is not obvious. It was founded at the end of the 10th century on the site of an Etrusco-Roman necropolis and a pre-existing early-Christian church. The monastery (now the Faculty of Agriculture), which incorporates the basilica (of which the primitive structures still remain), is the result of various construction phases spanning the Middle Ages to the 18th century. The entrance courtyard (1614) is dominated by the imposing **campanile*,** which, respectively dodecagonal and then hexagonal in its lower parts, combines various styles. The belfry (1463-68) is Gothic-Renaissance. The entrance to the basilica is at the left rear corner, near the portico which conserves frescoes of the original façade. The 16th-century doorway, surmounted by a frescoed tympanum, opens onto the nave and aisles; the nave with its 16th-century coffered ceiling is supported by 18 ancient columns. Its simple medieval architecture is enhanced by rich decorations executed in the late 16th century and early 17th centuries. Highlights include: ten large *canvases* (Scenes from the Life of Christ, 1592-94) on the walls of the nave; five **little paintings*** by Il Perugino (1496) in the 15th-century sacristy; the wooden **choir*** in the apse, with its richly incised carvings and inlay (1526-35). Also featured are works by Guercino and Guido Reni. The former **monastery** develops around a Renaissance *main cloister* and a *smaller cloister* otherwise called *Chiostro delle Stelle* (1571). In the ancient *fishpond* of the friars is the **Orto Botanico Medievale** (medieval botanical garden), offering visitors the chance to learn about the religious symbolism of particular plants in the Middle Ages. In the **Giardino del Frontone,** monumental holm-oaks line the three parallel avenues leading to the small amphitheater and triumphal arch.

Mechanically-assisted walkways in Perugia

In the early 1980s, the municipal authorities in Perugia created a mechanically-assisted walkway to overcome the problem of the town's steep streets and make the historic center more accessible to anyone arriving on foot from the new town below.

This series of covered walkways, tunnels and escalators – from Piazza Partigiani to Piazza Italia, where it emerges underneath the portico of Palazzo della Provincia – flanks the historic Via del Circo before disappearing under the Rocca Paolina, the fortress built in the mid-16th century by Antonio da Sangallo the Younger for Pope Paul III Farnese. Here the route makes use of the hidden network of streets and squares of the old medieval quarter which Sangallo incorporated into the fortress, along with the Etruscan gateway known as Porta Marzia. From the Etruscan Porta Marzia, it is possible to enter the foundations of the fortress, which rested on vault structures placed over the houses and streets such as Via Baglioni. The stone houses, with their Gothic doorways, are still clearly distinguishable from the brick-wall foundations added by Sangallo.

This archaeological journey into the bowels of medieval Perugia has become

TOWN PLAN

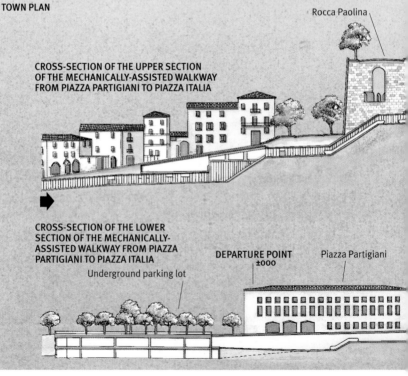

CROSS-SECTION OF THE UPPER SECTION OF THE MECHANICALLY-ASSISTED WALKWAY FROM PIAZZA PARTIGIANI TO PIAZZA ITALIA

Rocca Paolina

CROSS-SECTION OF THE LOWER SECTION OF THE MECHANICALLY-ASSISTED WALKWAY FROM PIAZZA PARTIGIANI TO PIAZZA ITALIA

Underground parking lot

DEPARTURE POINT
±000

Piazza Partigiani

a part of everyday life in the town. Each day some 20,00 people use the escalators and tunnels to climb up 50 meters in barely fifteen minutes, and well away from city traffic. Another similar system, the so-called "Cupa-Morlacchi" walkway, created in 1989 in the northern part of the town, has long stretches of open-air escalators protected by glazed canopies.
Two other routes are planned, one of which will connect the historic center with the expressway approach road and the Fontivegge shopping center.

Right, the arrival (and departure) point of the moving stairways inside the Rocca Paolina, the fortress built over the 13th-century Baglioni quarter. Via Baglioni was one of the main thoroughfares of the medieval town.

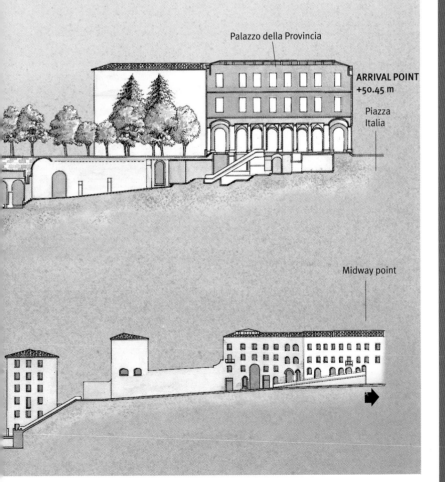

Palazzo della Provincia

ARRIVAL POINT
+50.45 m

Piazza
Italia

Midway point

ASSISI [24 km]

Before you arrive, Assisi appears spread out on terraces on the lower slopes of Mt Subasio. On entering the town you inevitably become aware of the atmosphere of St Francis, fed in part by literature, which, since the late 12th century, has always considered this small Umbrian town "the town of St Francis", and in part by the monuments which grace every corner of the town. In 1907, Herman Hesse wrote that Assisi was "[...] transfigured by the charm and enchantment that St Francis and ancient Umbrian art have transfused into this land". The city's former terrace structure is well exemplified by the **Piazza del Comune** ❶, with its broad rectangular shape. Between the mid-13th century and 1282, **Palazzo del Capitano del Popolo** was built along the entire upper section of the square, (note the standard measures in the wall for silk, flax and wool). In 1927, it was restored and crenellations were added, together with the extremely high *Torre del Popolo* (1305) nearby. Palazzo dei Priori (1475) was erected on the square's south side. The fountains with three lions dates from the 16th century, whereas Palazzo delle Poste (on the northwest side) is the result of restructuring in 1926, when a medieval fervor gripped the town as it celebrated the 700th anniversary of the death of its saint. The so-called **Tempio di Minerva/ Temple of Minerva★** ❷ built between the early 1st century BC and the Augustan period in the very heart of the town, may have been dedicated to the Dioscuri, Castor and Pollux. Used in the Middle Ages as a dwelling for monks, and later as a municipal prison, in 1539 it was turned into a church, with the name of *Santa Maria sopra Minerva*. Subsequently it was given a baroque facelift and dedicated to *St Philip Neri* (1634). The facade of the temple is perfectly preserved, with its original six grooved columns, Corinthian capitals, and plinths supporting the tympanum above the flight of steps which continues below street level. The construction of **Palazzo dei Priori** ❸ – the windows of which have been restored and which has fake crenellations – was very long and involved, since it

incorporates four pre-existing structures dating from before 1275. Beneath this complex, and to the right, is the so-called *Volta Pinta*, a barrel-vault passageway so termed because of its 16th-century decorations. By taking Via Arco dei Priori to the left of Palazzo dei Priori, you soon come to the **Chiesa Nuova**, built in 1615 upon the presumed remains of St Francis' birthplace. Completely decorated with wall paintings (1621), it contains some fine frescoes. Left of the presbytery there is access to what remains of the so-called *Casa del Santo*. The **Cattedrale di S. Rufino/Cathedral of S. Rufino★** ❹ with its tapering churchyard was probably founded in the 8th century – and first rebuilt in 1036. In 1140, reconstruction of the church began again, but it was only in 1253 that it was officially consecrated by Innocent IV. The **facade★**, an Umbrian

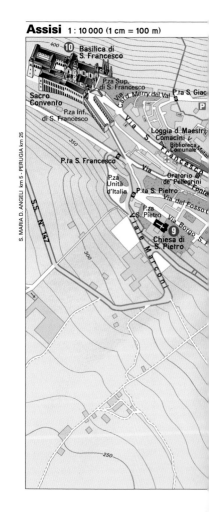

Assisi   1 : 10 000 (1 cm = 100 m)

Romanesque masterpiece, is horizontally divided into three registers, with geometric and ornamental decorations from various periods. It is flanked by a squat but imposing **bell tower**, also Romanesque, which rests upon a perfectly preserved 2nd-century BC Roman cistern. Its interior was completely renovated in 1571 and features, at the beginning of the right aisle, the *baptismal font* at which, tradition has it, St Francis, St Clare and perhaps Frederick II of Swabia, were baptized. The apse features a carved wooden **choir*** (1520). A small doorway to

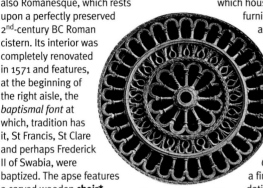

The rose window of the Cathedral of S. Rufino.

the left of the sacristy leads down to the underground *Oratory of St Francis*, where the saint is said to have prayed before preaching to the faithful. Adjacent to the right aisle is the **Museo della Cattedrale**, which houses paintings and sacred furnishings from the cathedral and other churches in the diocese. Of particular artistic significance: Puccio Capanna's **Deposition*** and a triptych by Alunno depicting the **Virgin and Child with Four Saints*** (1470). Adjoining the museum is the *Archivio Capitolare*, or archives, with a fine collection of documents dating from 963 and some illuminated codices (13-15C).

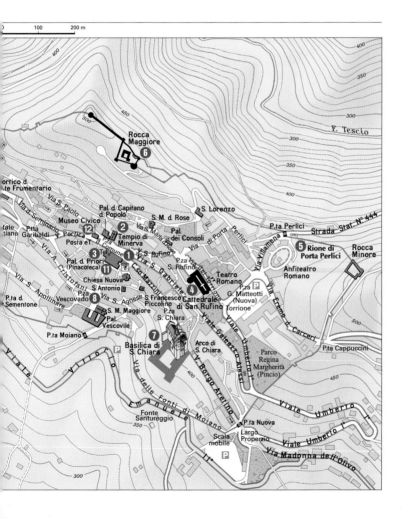

Basilica of S. Francesco, Assisi

The basilica, which was built in two stages in the 13th century, is in fact
two churches in one.
The *Chiesa Inferiore*, or lower church, built around 1230, consist of a single nave
with side chapels, a central barrel-vaulted transept and the crypt where
St Francis is buried. Above is the *Chiesa Superiore*, or upper church, which dates
back to the second half of the 13th century. This church, also with a single nave,
is an ensemble of strikingly Gothic elements that converge on the transept
and its polygonal apse.
The facade of the basilica takes its inspiration from the French Gothic style,
and features a large rose window surmounted by a smaller one, but the
monument's main attraction is without doubt its lavish fresco cycles that entirely
cover the interior walls, in keeping with the didactic aims of the Franciscan order.

Giotto's frescoes

Beneath the gallery of the central nave of the upper church is the cycle of the
Life of St Francis (1296-1300), attributed to Giotto but executed with the help of
assistants. The 28 frescoes that make up the cycle (in Roman numerals, I-XXVIII,
on the plan) depict the main scenes from the account of the saint's life
by St Bonaventure of Bagnoregio (the *Legenda Maior*). The most noteworthy are:
St Francis gives his Cloak to a Pauper (II), *St Francis drives the demons out of
Arezzo* (X), *St Francis celebrates the Feast of the Nativity at Greccio* (XIII),
St Francis creates a Spring to slake a Wayfarer's Thirst (XIV), *St Francis preaches
to the Birds* (XV), *St Francis receives the Stigmata* (XIX).

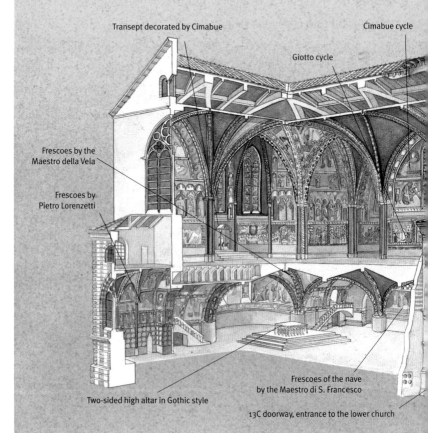

Transept decorated by Cimabue

Cimabue cycle

Giotto cycle

Frescoes by the
Maestro della Vela

Frescoes by
Pietro Lorenzetti

Frescoes of the nave
by the Maestro di S. Francesco

Two-sided high altar in Gothic style

13C doorway, entrance to the lower church

Basilica of S. Francesco, plan of the frescoes in the nave of the upper church

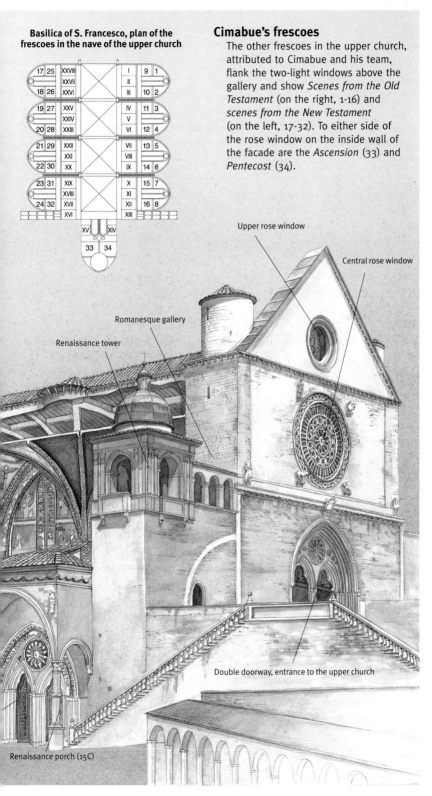

Cimabue's frescoes

The other frescoes in the upper church, attributed to Cimabue and his team, flank the two-light windows above the gallery and show *Scenes from the Old Testament* (on the right, 1-16) and *scenes from the New Testament* (on the left, 17-32). To either side of the rose window on the inside wall of the facade are the *Ascension* (33) and *Pentecost* (34).

Upper rose window

Central rose window

Romanesque gallery

Renaissance tower

Double doorway, entrance to the upper church

Renaissance porch (15C)

To the right of the facade there is access to the **crypt***, which contains painting fragments from the 11th century, a bishop's throne and a Roman Luni marble sarcophagus (3C AD), used as the coffin of St Rufinus. The **rione di Porta Perlici/ Porta Perlici district** ❺ northeast of the cathedral lies in an area whose Roman origins are belied by its regular road network. It was here that the densely populated medieval quarter, which has preserved its 14th-century layout, developed. On the northeast side of *Piazza Matteotti*, stands the *convent of Santa Caterina* (13C) which contains interesting paintings. The complex adjoins the area of the former Roman **amphitheater**, whose elliptical plan gave shape to the small houses later built in this area, a fine example of medieval re-use of an earlier building. Nearby, in Via del Torrione are the remains of the *Roman theater* (1C AD).

The **Rocca Maggiore*** ❻, poised on a hill overlooking the town and the valley, is an extraordinary landmark. Its striking visual effect is enhanced by the sinuous lines of the town walls which rise all the way to the corner towers, forming a trapezoidal perimeter which encloses a tall rectangular fortress. Frederick Barbarossa and a very young Frederick II are said to have stayed in the fort. Destroyed during a popular uprising in 1198, it was rebuilt in 1356 by Cardinal Albornoz according to the original plan. A path leads to the polygonal tower (1459-60), the top of which is linked to the

high chemin-de-ronde (not for the claustrophobic). Its 14th-century walls connect the **Rocca Minore**, otherwise known as the *Cassero di Sant'Antonio*, the smaller fortress which was built in 1360 to defend the castle's northern facade.

Since 1260, the **chiesa di S. Chiara/ church of S. Chiara**** ❼ has housed the remains of the saint to whom it is dedicated. Consecrated in 1265, it has similarities with the model of the upper basilica of San Francesco and almost seems to commune with it from the other side of the town. Its characteristic facade in pink and white Subasio limestone features a finely-wrought **rose window***, with a double wheel of small columns and arches, and an oculus in the tympanum. Its narrow front is marked by three colossal rampant arches (late 14C) which seem to balance the thrust of the vaults. The church's single nave, adorned with precious artworks, has four bays (corresponding to the external arches), and terminates in a polygonal apse with three one-light windows. The many fine works in the church's interior include an altarpiece of the **Crucifixion*** in the left transept; **St Clare and Eight Scenes from her Life**** in the right transept, attributed to the Maestro di S. Chiara (1283).

To appreciate the aura of the legend of St Francis, enter the **chapel of St George** (part of the original church), which is divided in two chambers by a stained-glass partition into the Chapel of the Sacrament and the Oratory of the Crucifix. It contains a fresco (**Virgin and Child**

The rooftops of Assisi with the churches of S. Rufino (left), and S. Chiara (right).

Assisi: Basilica di S. Chiara

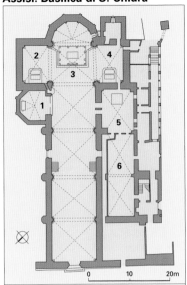

1 St. Agnes' Chapel
2 Madonna and Child by Maestro della Santa Chiara
3 Crucifix by Maestro della Santa Chiara
4 St. Clare and Eight Scenes From Her Life by Maestro della Santa Chiara
5 Chapel of the Sacrament
6 Oratory of the Crucifix

Enthroned with Saints*) and the wooden **Crucifix*** (late 12C) which, according to tradition, spoke to St Francis in the church of S. Damiano. Passing under the 13th-century *Arco di Santa Chiara* on Via Borgo Aretino, to the left of the basilica, make a short detour toward **Porta Moiano**, a gate built in the 14th-century perimeter, whose name derives from the ancient "Mons Iani", in reference to a temple dedicated to the god Janus which once stood on this spot. A spring, the waters of which are said to have curative properties, and the remains of Roman structures are located on the incline that slopes down beneath the road. **Piazza del Vescovado** ⑧, situated outside the first set of town walls, was the center of religious power, until the 11th century when **Santa Maria Maggiore** lost its cathedral status to S. Rufino. The Romanesque church has a plain facade, enhanced by a rose window bearing an inscription indicating that the church was restructured in 1163. It contains remains of frescoes dating from the 14th and 15th centuries. The **crypt** (closed) is all

that survives of the earlier church (9-10C), and leads to a subterranean chamber containing the remains of a *Roman house*, featuring fine mosaic pavements and wall-paintings. From the adjacent garden you can see the remains of the *Roman perimeter wall*, in Subasio limestone. After the cathedral was transferred, the only edifice symbolizing religious power in the square was the *Palazzo Vescovile* (Bishop's Palace), where St Francis made his vow of poverty and where, many years later, when he was seriously ill, he returned to be conveyed to the Porziuncola.

Proceeding along Via Sant'Apollinare and then *Via Borgo San Pietro*, the main thoroughfare of this densely populated 14th-century quarter, you come to the Benedictine **chiesa di S. Pietro/church of S. Pietro*** ⑨ built in the early 13th century and consecrated in 1253. Its beautiful rectangular facade is marked by three doorways, each with a rose window. Inside, the nave and side-aisles are decorated with 14th-century funerary monuments and frescoes from the 13th and 14th centuries.

St Francis died on October 3, 1226 and, two years later, work began on the grand **Basilica di San Francesco/Basilica of S. Francesco **** ⑩, which was destined to become both a spiritual reference-point for Assisi and for Christianity as a whole. The architectural peculiarity of the magnificent complex is largely due to the superimposition of two churches, each one representing a separate construction phase. This detail is enhanced by the double rows of very high arches of the Sacro Convento, the monastic complex that stretches out behind the church towards the valley, incorporating both that sense of strength and lightness which is perhaps one of the main prerogatives of the Franciscan order. Documentary sources relating to the construction phases after 1230, when the saint's body was moved to the lower basilica, up to its consecration by Innocent IV (1253), are less reliable. In 1367, the chapel of St Catherine was completed and, with it, the entire church, which was to undergo no change in the centuries that followed. The church was decorated by the leading painters of the time, who turned it into a "document" of exceptionally high quality, especially with

The facade of the Basilica of S. Francesco with its splendid Cosmatesque rose window.

regard to 13th- and 14th-century Italian fresco-painting. In sharp contrast to the interior, the basilica's **facade**, Gothic but re-adapted to local tastes, features plain lines broken by a twin doorway and a splendid double **rose window***. To the left stands the tall square Romanesque Umbrian-style **bell tower** (1239), despoiled of its crown in 1530. A double **doorway*** dating from the second half of the 13th century, and preceded by a Renaissance portico, leads into the nave of the **Chiesa Inferiore** (lower church), which is divided into five arched bays, the focal point of which is the saint's tomb. The walls along the nave, whose pavement inclines toward the main altar, are covered with **frescoes** by the Maestro di S. Francesco, were among the first to be painted (ca. 1253). To the right: **Scenes from the Life of Christ** and, on the left, **Scenes from the Life of St Francis**, stressing the link between Christ and the saint of Assisi. Half-way up the nave, two flights of stairs descend to the crypt where the plain stone urn above the altar in which the saint's body was found still contains the remains of the saint. It is surrounded at its four corners by the bodies of his closest companions (Leone, Rufino, Masseo and Angelo). The niche on the landing connecting the two rooms contains the remains of the Blessed Jacopa dei Settesoli, a Roman noblewoman and devout counselor of Francis, who called her "brother Jacopa".

Back in the nave, the 3rd side-chapel on the right is completely decorated with **frescoes*** by Giotto and his assistants. The famous **frescoes**** in the four sections of the cross-vault (1322) depict *Allegories of the Franciscan Virtues* (*Poverty, Chastity, Obedience*), and the *Glory of St Francis*. Recent critics attribute these works to various assistants working under Giotto's supervision. The vault of the right arm of the transept is entirely covered by two large tiers of *frescoes* painted by Giotto's assistants. The **Virgin and Child Enthroned with four Angels and St Francis**** is the only painting belonging to the previous decorative features, by Cimabue, to have survived; the *Crucifixion* is attributed to Giotto; on the end wall, *five saints*, the 4th of which is a beautiful image once believed to portray **St Clare*** (actually St Margaret). The semi-circular apse contains a fine carved and inlaid Gothic **choir***. The left transept is decorated with frescoes painted in 1315-20. Some of the finest, on the left, include a **Crucifixion*** and a **Virgin and Child between Sts Francis and John*** by the Sienese master, Cimabue. The **frescoes**** in the 1st chapel left of the nave, a masterpiece of mysticism and grace (1312-20), depicting stories in the life of St Martin, are the work of Simone Martini. Leaving the dimly lit lower church, we ascend to the **Chiesa Superiore**, or upper church, "suspended in air and light". In fact, the rose windows, the windows in the bays, and those of the apse all recall Nordic light-pervaded models, yet to some extent the result is a blend of Italy's architectural style and the pure forms of French Gothic.

Our visit begins with the transept, where the **Crucifixion**** is particularly striking, and is one of the Cimabue's most powerful and dramatic compositions. In the apse, there is wooden **choir***, (1491-1501), consisting of 102 stalls.

The upper walls of the nave are decorated with 34 frescoes depicting **Scenes from the Old Testament** (right) and **New Testament** (left). Instead, beneath the string-course, there is a stupendous 28-fresco cycle depicting the **Life of St Francis****, attributed to Giotto both as the principal artist and as supervisor of the various assistants who contributed to the project. The terrace behind the apse affords access to the **Museo-Tesoro*** which has paintings, gold craft, and textile artifacts linked to the history of the basilica. The museum's collection continues to be of great interest due to the 13th-century masterpieces of French gold-work and textile artifacts. The adjacent "red room" hosts the *Perkins Collection*, with paintings mostly by Florentine and Sienese masters of the 14th and 16th centuries.

The medieval **Via S. Francesco**, which runs from the basilica to Piazza Grande,

St Francis receives the Stigmata, a fresco traditionally attributed to Giotto, in the Basilica of S. Francesco.

shows evident signs of successive transformations over the centuries. Gothic-style dwellings were englobed by the large 17th-century noble palaces, including **Palazzo Barnabei** (17C), now the seat of Perugia University and the Italian Center for Advanced Studies in Tourism. After a row of medieval-looking houses, is the *Loggia dei Maestri Comacini* (13C), so called because of the coats-of-arms of families from Como on the architrave. On one side of the Loggia, the narrow *Vicolo Sant'Andrea* climbs up past old houses to the small square overlooked by the *church of S. Margherita* (13C), a quiet and peaceful corner of the town, with magnificent views over the basilica.

Back in Via San Francesco, you come to the long facade of **Palazzo Giacobetti**, with its monumental balcony and 17th-century railing, now the *Municipal Library*, together with the *Accademia Properziana del Subasio*.

The municipal art collections of the **Pinacoteca Comunale/Civic Art Gallery** ⑪ have recently been arranged in Palazzo Vallemani, in Via San Francesco. They include many *frescoes* (mostly by the Umbrian school from the 13 to 17C) which have been removed from churches, monasteries, oratories, and city gates, in the town and its environs.

In the following stretch of Via San Francesco is the **Oratorio dei Pellegrini*** (1457); the interior features 15th-century frescoes. Behind it is the fine **Portico del Monte Frumentario***, which was part of Assisi's earliest public hospital, founded in 1267 and converted into a bank in the 18th century. Next to it is the *Fonte Oliviera*, a fountain commissioned by Oliviero Lodovici in 1570. Beyond the 13th-century *Arco del Seminario*, boundary of the Roman walled town, Via San Francesco becomes **Via del Seminario**, where Palazzo Seminario has englobed the Sant'Angelo di Panzo Benedictine monastery (1270).

Located in the *crypt of S. Niccolò* (1097), a church demolished in 1926 to make room for the construction of the Palazzo delle Poste, the **Museo Civico/Civic Museum** ⑫ (entrance from no. 2 Via Portica) exhibits materials from pre-Roman times found in and around Assisi.

A long corridor leads to the archaeological site, commonly known as the **Roman Forum**, but actually an area below the so-called Temple of Minerva. You can still see the pavement with a water channel and a shrine containing the statues of Castor and Pollux donated to the city in the time of Tiberius by two wealthy *liberti* (freed slaves).

BEVAGNA [38 km]

Perched on a little ridge, and surrounded by waterways which have always provided a natural defensive system, lies Bevagna, still bearing signs of its Roman origins. Following the unchanged line of the Via Flaminia, we enter the city, which has been awarded the TCI's "Bandiera Arancione", through **Porta Foligno** (or Porta Flaminia). The structures above the Roman arch are medieval, whereas the top dates from the 18th century. Remains of the original Roman walls are visible at either side of the gate. From here we proceed down **Corso Matteotti**, which retraces the line of the Roman street. On the right, the facade of a former church boasts decorative pillars which were originally part of the former *church of S. Vincenzo* (12C), now in ruins. On the left are the remains of a Roman building, with a fine black-and-white mosaic pavement. The most important Roman landmark, however, is the *Roman theater* (1C), the remains of which constitute the foundations of the houses of Vico Anfiteatro (on the right) set around it in a semi-circle. Branching off to the right of the Corso is Via Crescimbeni, with the remains of a **Roman temple**, built perhaps in the 2nd century AD. In *Via di Porta Guelfa*, (no. 2), in the interior of a modern house, is a black and white **mosaic** dating from the first half of the 2nd century AD, depicting delightful dolphin scenes, and originally part of the Roman baths. After the Roman temple, the street leads to the long and narrow *Piazza Garibaldi*, where a stairway ascends to the **church of S. Francesco**, built after 1275 on the highest spot in the city. The stone facade, the doorway, and part of the square bell tower give us some idea of what the original building must have been like. In the interior, protected by an iron grating, is the stone upon which,

Francesco Torti Theater in Bevagna.

according to a legend, St Francis stood when preaching to the birds in Pian d'Arca. Return to Corso Matteotti. On the right of the Corso is the **church of the Consolazione** (1735). After that, you come to *Palazzo Lepri*, now the Town Hall (1800). The ground floor houses the **Civic Museum**, featuring archaeological finds, paintings, maps and documents illustrating the town's history from ancient times to the 18th century. The collection includes a **Virgin and Child** by Dono Doni. At the end of the Corso stands the 14th-century **church of Ss. Domenico e Giacomo**, together with the former Dominican monastery. The church's interior, modernized in 1737, houses interesting works, whereas, in the basement of the former convent you can still see the remains of a large barrel-vaulted Roman building. **Piazza Silvestri**** constitutes one of the region's most interesting medieval urban achievements: an area lacking symmetry and frontal alignments, and totally consisting of "corner-edge" perspectives which are further enlivened by the monumental presence of two churches, Palazzo dei Consoli, the *Colonna di San Rocco* (the shaft of a Roman column), and a pseudo-medieval fountain (1896). **Palazzo dei Consoli** (1270) stands out with its ground-floor loggia with ribbed vaulting. A broad staircase leads up to the small but harmoniously proportioned **Francesco Torti Theater**. A broad vault links the palace to the **basilica of S. Silvestro***, a jewel of Umbro-Romanesque architecture (1195), whose unfinished facade features an ornate marble triforium; the monumental interior is formed by a nave and two side-aisles. On the opposite side of the square stands the **collegiate church of S. Michele Arcangelo*** (late 12C or early 13C). The jambs framing its magnificent central **doorway*** are made from Roman moldings, whereas the solid pointed bell tower on the right dates from a later period. The next church, **S. Agostino**, was built in the 14th century, with Umbrian-school frescoes of that period and others of the 16th century.

CASCIA [103 km]

Several monuments replete with artworks are a reminder that Cascia, founded in the Middle Ages as a hill-top castle in a dominant position, overlooking the thoroughfares between the Norcia range and the Roman Campagna, served as the political and cultural pole for the surrounding area. At the entrance to the town is the **church of S. Francesco**, graced by a facade with a fine rose window (1424); the interior contains elaborate baroque stucco-work; of particular note are the 14th-century wooden **choir-stalls** of Gothic manufacture (apse). Emerging from the east doorway we come to the former **church of S. Antonio Abate** (14-15C), now the municipal *museum*, with altarpieces and furnishings from the 17th to 18th centuries, plus two important fresco cycles of the 15th century: sixteen panels depicting the *Stories from the Life of St Antony Abbot* (apse), and the *Scenes of the Passion* (1461, choir of the former monastery). Back within the old walls, near Porta S. Maria (or Porta Leolina), we come to the **collegiate church of S. Maria**, an ancient parish church erected in the 12th century, enlarged in the 15th, and then rebuilt in 1532. The church contains *frescoes* datable to between the 15th and 17th century. From Santa Maria, we continue towards the basilica of S. Rita, passing a succession of noble houses, each one restyled to some extent: **Palazzo Carli** (16C);

Palazzo Frenfanelli (16C), now the municipal council offices and **Palazzo Santi**, which recently became the *Museo Civico*, comprising an archaeological section and a picture gallery. The museum contains finds dating back to the 8th century BC; the gallery contains paintings by local artists (16-18C) and wood *sculptures* (13C). Now we come to the religious hub of the town, dominated by the impressive **Basilica of S. Rita** (1937-47) built on the site of an early Augustinian church annexed to the convent in which the saint died (1457).

The building, which seems excessively large compared to the surrounding fabric, is a blend of imitation Byzantine and Romanesque styles. The interior is adorned with marble and fresco

Interior of the Basilica of S. Rita.

decoration; on the high altar is the relic of *Corpus Christi*; in the chapel of St Rita, the mummified body of the saint is laid out in a crystal urn set in silver. The convent has several relics associated with the saint, such as the grape-vine she planted, the bee-hive, and the cell where she passed away. For centuries, episodes associated with the saint's life have struck a popular chord in terms of simplicity of sentiment. As a result, every May 22, huge numbers of pilgrims descend on Cascia for the procession held to commemorate the saint, which culminates in the blessing of the roses, St Rita's favorite flower.

CASTIGLIONE DEL LAGO [44 km]

In Etruscan and Roman times, the limestone promontory on which this town stands was an island of Lake Trasimeno. The town, enclosed by fortifications, is one the most interesting in the entire lake district. Entering the **historic center** through the 19th-century *Porta Senese*, on your left you immediately come to the *parish church of the Maddalena*, a Neoclassical structure, with an outside portico dating from 1867. Its interior features fine decorations. Proceeding along Via Vittorio Emanuele you come to a square, at the far end of which stands the *church of S. Domenico di Guzman* (1683). **Palazzo della Corgna***, situated at the center of the town, incorporating a former hunting lodge, was built by Ascanio della Corgna in 1563.

This L-shaped building resembles a noble residence and is a fine example of the lifestyle and decoration vogues of the time. The fresco decoration in the rooms, which celebrate the family to whom it belonged, is one of the finest examples of late Umbrian Mannerism. On the ground floor, used for leisure and gatherings of intellectuals, are the building's most refined paintings, among which the odd *Storie del mondo alla rovescia (Stories of the World Upside-down)*.

A long passageway, which was roofed over in the 17th century, connects Palazzo della Corgna to the **Castello del Leone**, ordered by Frederick II of Swabia in the 13th century as an army observation post, using a previous fortification which also included a parish church (remains visible). Its pentagonal plan, surmounted by a triangular crenellated tower, is today a charming backdrop for shows and other events.

CITTÀ DELLA PIEVE [43 km]

Set in a beautiful panoramic position, the town, which has been awarded the TCI's "Bandiera Arancione", is worth visiting for the quality of its buildings, monuments and artworks (the town is the birthplace on the great Pietro Vannucci, known as Il Perugino). Visitors are immediately struck by the warm color of its brick buildings, a reminder of the local brick-making industry for which the town was once famed.

The road leading into the town, beyond the defensive walls and the Porta del Vecciano, passes the **chiesa di S. Maria dei Servi/church of S. Maria dei Servi** ❶. Built in 1343 over the 13th century church of Madonna della Stella (now a chapel), it has a Gothic interior (not accessible) with 17th- and 18th-century reworking which largely cancelled out the votive frescoes commissioned from the illustrious Il Perugino; all that its left is a mutilated **Deposition from the Cross*** (1517), considered the most significant work painted by the aging master. Erected in the 13th century outside the defense walls, the **chiesa di S. Francesco/church of S. Francesco** ❷ was completely rebuilt in the second half of the 18th century, and was transformed into a *sanctuary* honoring the *Madonna di Fatima* after World War II. The six large stucco altars date from the 18th century. Next to the church stands the **Benedictine oratory of S. Bartolomeo**, earlier than the Franciscan church and subsequently used by the Friars Minor as a chapter house and a refectory. Built by inhabitants of Perugia in 1326 at the highest point of the town on land that was unencumbered with other buildings within the walls, the **Rocca/Fortress** ❸ has five square towers, and was commissioned by the dominating town of the time as a symbol of power. The building continues to be used for military purposes and is therefore closed to visitors. Opposite the fortress stands the *church of the Gesù*, erected in 1798. On **Via Vittorio Veneto,** the height of *Palazzo Orca* and the former *church of S. Anna*

The merloned walls of Castello del Leone.

Città della Pieve 1: 7 500 (1 cm = 75 m)

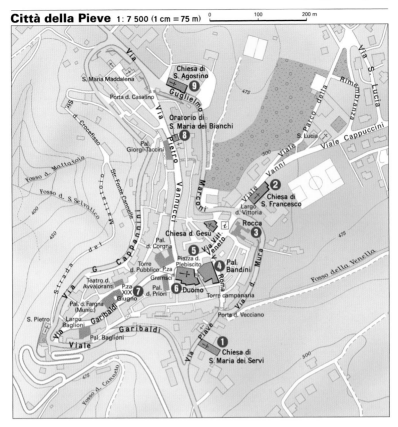

(1737-54) were raised in 1932 in order to accommodate the water tank of the town's aqueduct.

The brick facade of **Palazzo Bandini* ❹**, the result of merging several 14th-century structures, looks out over Via Roma. The palazzo has a fine Renaissance rusticated doorway. **Piazza del Plebiscito ❺** is right in the center of the town, bordered by the cathedral and by a series of buildings of varying architectural quality, such as the Neoclassical *Palazzo Cartoni* (1845). On the piazza itself, **Palazzo della Corgna**, with a decorated interior, encloses a lovely courtyard. It is now a university research center and the municipal library, as well as being used for temporary exhibitions. The **Duomo/Cathedral ❻** stands above an ancient parish church (8C), and it was reworked several times until the year 1600, when it became the cathedral. The single-nave interior on a Latin-cross plan contains fine *artworks*. The largest of the chapels (3rd right) has frescoes with *Scenes from the Old*

Testament (1714), on the back wall of the apse hangs a **panel** by Il Perugino, signed and dated 1514. The semi-dome of the apse was frescoed by Antonio Circignani, while the *Baptism of Christ* (1510) is another work by Il Perugino (1st chapel). From the right transept you can visit the *art collection* belonging to the Curia, comprising decorative material from the various phases of the church's construction, together with other works from the town and the surrounding area. Close to the facade of the cathedral rises the **Torre Civica** or **Torre del Pubblico**, the travertine base of which is Romanesque (12C) and the top in brick (14C). Opposite the cathedral stands **Palazzo dei Priori**, founded in the early 14th-century as a residence for the priors of the guilds and subsequently altered. **Piazza XIX Giugno ❼** was created halfway down Via Garibaldi, and is commanded by **Palazzo della Fargna** (now the town hall), erected in about the mid-18th century, with a *trompe l'oeil* background in the

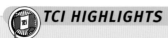

IL PERUGINO AND THE INVENTION OF THE MODERN LANDSCAPE

In the Adoration of the Magi (*see photo*) painted in Perugia in 1504 by Il Perugino, "Italy's greatest master", as his contemporaries described him, the procession of horses converging on the shed (the focal point of the composition) is set against one of the most elaborate landscapes ever created by the artist. The countryside slopes gently towards the center of the composition, perfectly framed by gently rolling hills, the horizon flattening out into a stretch of water, recalling the view from Città della Pieve towards Lake Trasimeno and Valdichiana, in one of Il Perugino's typical figurative

settings. Il Perugino's rendering of space and light creates landscapes that are a "perfect balance between the evocation of real life and the expression of an imaginary setting" (B. Toscano), in which contemplation of the Umbrian countryside represents the modern yearning for balance and order. This "almost modern manner", as Giorgio Vasari defined it in the 16th century, turned its back on the tormented Gothic visions of landscape, and marked a decisive change in taste. The countryside itself had only recently changed, especially because of developments in farming and especially improved land reclamation. From the middle of the 15th century onwards, this had altered the appearance of the Umbra valley and Valdichiana. The marshes ceased to be and were replaced by orderly arable land. Instead of being water-logged, this land was watered and farmed under human control. The rural scene thus took on new organic forms prompting a reappraisal of the ideal landscape, which was later captured so beautifully in Renaissance art.

courtyard and, inside, stucco decoration throughout. Also overlooking the piazza is the **Accademia degli Avvaloranti-Teatro Comunale,** with an auditorium of four tiers of seats. Almost at the end of **Via Garibaldi,** is **Palazzo Baglioni** and, further on, the **church of S. Pietro,** which was built in the 13th century below the defensive walls and frequently remodeled over the centuries. Inside is a fresco (transferred to canvas) attributed to Il Perugino but difficult to assess, owing to the multiple retouchings. Once again from Piazza del Plebiscito, passing rows of 18th and 19th-century town houses on Via Vannucci, we come to the *oratory* of **S. Maria dei Bianchi** ❽, where in 1504, Il Perugino painted his fresco of the

Adoration of the Magi*, one of his finest works. The Compagnia dei Disciplinati, to whom the oratory belonged, also sponsored the restoration of the neighboring *church,* completed in the late 18th century, which contains frescoes and canvases by Giovanni Miselli (1743-44), and contemporary stuccoes by Stefano Cremoni. The **chiesa di S. Agostino/ church of S. Agostino** ❾, erected outside the defensive walls in the 13th century, and remodeled in the late 18th century, is now a congress and entertainment center. The six altars inside the church were added in the 18th century and are decorated with 17th- and 18th-century paintings of the Umbrian and Tuscan school.

CITTÀ DI CASTELLO [54 km]

Green rolling hills and brightly sunlit farmland form the backdrop to the largest town in the Tiber valley. This town does not follow the usual medieval pattern but appears to the visitor in all the somber beauty of its broad, straight streets and 16th-century noble palaces. The creators of this small capital of the arts, embellished thanks to long sojourns by painters like Signorelli, Raphael, Vasari and Rosso Fiorentino, were the Vitelli, the sophisticated, cultured occupants of its castle between the 15th and 16th centuries, who renewed not only the town's urban layout but also the dwellings of this fortified medieval town. They left their mark in their large family palaces, one in each district and all splendidly decorated, involving whole areas of the town where streets and squares were broadened so as to give the town a new look, according to the Renaissance tenets of beauty. In the 11th century, the **Duomo/Cathedral** ❶

was erected in *Piazza Gabriotti,* a funnel-shaped square pivoting around the vertical hub of the civic tower. The complex was enlarged in 1356 and remodeled between the 15th and 16th centuries. Its 17th-century facade, however, is incomplete. Of the Romanesque church there remains a slender round bell tower, whereas the Gothic style can be seen in the left-hand doorway, adorned with twisted columns and reliefs. The interior, with its single nave and 18th-century coffered ceiling, is embellished with sumptuous 16th- and 17th-century altar pieces, in the form of paintings and frescoes. The large complex next-door houses the **Museo del Duomo*** and a splendid Gothic hall. Particularly interesting is the **Canoscio hoard***, a rare collection of embossed silverware consisting of objects used during the Communion service, dating from the 5th and 6th centuries; paintings include **Christ in Glory*** (1529-30), a masterpiece by Rosso Fiorentino; a *Virgin and Child*

HERITAGE

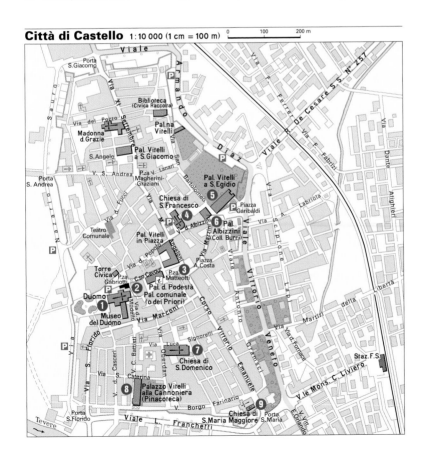

Città di Castello 1:10 000 (1 cm = 100 m)

41

and the Young St John the Baptist by Pinturicchio, and an *Angels* by Giulio Romano.

Palazzo Comunale* ❷ or Palazzo dei Priori, located in the same Piazza Gabriotti, is dated 1322-38. The palace has a rusticated facade adorned by an elegant doorway and fine two-light windows higher up. Opposite stands the **Civic Tower**, decorated with coats-of-arms, and affording an excellent view from its summit. Next to it is the former *Bishop's Palace*, dating from the 12th century (remodeled). The heart of the city's social life, **Piazza Matteotti**, ❸ was laid out in the 16th century as a noble square for **Palazzo Vitelli in Piazza**, which was completed around the mid-16th century. The 14th-century former *Palazzo del Podestà* (now the Prefettura) looks onto the square with its baroque 1686 facade, whereas the side overlooking Corso Cavour has maintained its austere Gothic forms. The **chiesa di S. Francesco/church of S. Francesco** ❹, erected in 1273, was almost completely remodeled during the 18th century. Parts belonging to the earlier building include the right side with its Gothic doorway and the three polygonal apses. Inside, near the entrance, there is an important Renaissance addition, the **Vitelli chapel**, designed by Giorgio Vasari and protected by a wrought-iron grille (1566). The chapel contains 26 inlaid stalls portraying *Scenes from the Lives of Mary and St Francis* and, above the altar, a *Coronation of the Virgin with Saints*, also by Vasari (1564). The power of the Vitelli family is fully symbolized by the size of the **Palazzo Vitelli a S. Egidio*** ❺, erected in the city's Sant'Egidio district in the second half of the 16th century. Its long facade is orchestrated by three series of windows and two rusticated doorways, whereas the interior is decorated by painters from Emilia and Bologna, especially Prospero Fontana. The coffered ceilings with their decorated panels are truly magnificent. At the rear of the garden is the *Palazzina*, a small palace with a beautiful decorated loggia.

Palazzo Albizzini ❻, a Renaissance building (late 15C), is the seat of the **Fondazione Palazzo Albizzini "Collezione Burri"**. The collection includes pieces executed between 1948 and 1989, arranged chronologically. The collection is completed by works on display in the **former tobacco-drying facilities***, on the southern edge of the town.

The Dominicans preferred to construct sumptuous buildings for themselves. The **chiesa di S. Domenico/church of S. Domenico** ❼, is no exception. However, its facade, begun in the 14th century and completed in 1424, was never finished. Its rectangular nave contains 15th-century frescoes.

Palazzo Vitelli alla Cannoniera* ❽ was begun in 1521 on the site of a former cannon foundry, after which it is named. It was enlarged in various stages and is a fine example of a 16th-century noble residence. The garden is overlooked by Vasari's *facade* (1532-35), decorated with graffiti; the decorations in the rooms inside are also very fine. The palace houses the interesting **Pinacoteca Comunale***. Highlights of the collection include a **Virgin Enthroned with Child** by the Maestro di Città di Castello; the **reliquary of St Andrew** (1420), an exquisite piece of craftsmanship; and the **standard of the Holy Trinity**** by Raphael. Between the late 15th and early 16th centuries, Luca Signorelli exercised a vital influence on local art. Here there is a fresco fragment by this painter of *St Paul* (1474) and a **Martyrdom of St Sebastian*** (1497-98). Not far away, in the medieval Farinario district (the so-called

Museo del Duomo, *Christ in Glory* by Rosso Fiorentino.

Mattonata), Niccolò Vitelli ordered the construction of the **chiesa di S. Maria Maggiore/church of S. Maria Maggiore** ❾, where, unusually, the Renaissance forms on the facade are complemented by the Gothic forms of the interior. On the walls are the remains of some 15th-century frescoes.

FOLIGNO [36 km]

Situated in the plain, Foligno differs from other towns in the region which tend to be built on hills. **Piazza della Repubblica** ❶ is the town's hub where the main civic and religious buildings are located. Around it is an intricate maze of secondary streets and squares forming the peripheral urban fabric, a sort of haphazard labyrinth providing a contrast to the linear forms of its most important buildings. The vast rectangular square was laid out in about the 13th century, when three of the public buildings were erected; Palazzo del Podestà, Palazzo dei

The facade of the Duomo overlooking Piazza della Repubblica.

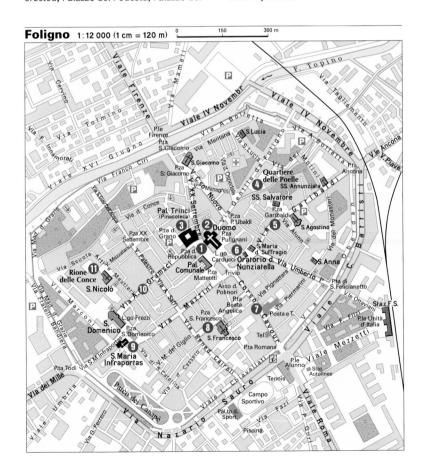

Foligno 1:12 000 (1 cm = 120 m)

Priori and Palazzo del Capitano del Popolo. In the following century, the ruling Trinci family built their prestigious family residence on the north side of the square. In the adjacent Piazza del Duomo, in the 9th and 10th centuries there was probably some kind of church, on the site of which the beautiful 12th-century **Duomo/Cathedral*** was built, dedicated to St Felicianus, one of the town's martyrs. Over the centuries, the church was progressively enlarged. Between 1772 and 1819, the church interior underwent a Neoclassical transformation. The facade of the cathedral facing Piazza della Repubblica is so richly decorated that the transept looks like a church in its own right, while the magnificent **doorway*** (1201) is richly adorned with decoration in the Classical style. To the left of the Duomo stands **Palazzo delle Canoniche** (11C), seat of the Diocesan art collection. Opposite, the 13th-century **Palazzo Comunale** was totally restructured between 1546 and 1642. The only medieval building to survive is the fine tower, the top of which was modified in the 16th century. In the rooms of **Palazzo Trinci*** ❸, which is also remarkable on account of its fine courtyard and monumental staircase, is the **Museo della Città** with an archaeological section and an art gallery. Note the **fresco cycle**, considered to be a veritable encyclopedia of cultural life in the early 15th century. The **interior***, which provides a striking setting for the municipal archaeological museum and art gallery, has a splendid **Gothic staircase**, with curious architectural features and late-Gothic decoration. The *piano nobile* upstairs has rooms with frescoes dating from the early 15th century: the **Hall of the Liberal Arts and the Planets*** and the **chapel***, completely adorned with wall paintings (1424). The **art gallery** has paintings of the Foligno and Umbrian schools from the 14th to the 16th centuries, whereas the **archaeological collection** illustrates the history of Foligno area and the town's Roman early settlement, situated on the Via Flaminia. Palazzo Trinci also houses the **Museo Multimediale dei Tornei, delle Giostre e dei Giochi**. The **Quartiere delle Poelle/Poelle district** ❹ developed in

TCI HIGHLIGHTS

THE PRINTING OF THE DIVINE COMEDY

Typography in Foligno dates back to 1470, which is a mere five years after movable type-printing was actually introduced to Italy. The protagonists of this undertaking were Johann Numeister and two other Germans, Craft (a type composer and punch setter), and Stephan Arndes from Hamburg, later active in Perugia and Lübeck. They were called to the city and funded by the Orfini brothers (Emiliano, Mariotto and Antonio), formerly papal engravers and minters, who also ran a typography business from their home on Piazza Grande. The Foligno printing presses turned out some extraordinary masterpieces, such as the first edition of Cicero's *De bello italico adversus Gothos*, and his *Epistulae ad familiares* and the first edition of Dante Alighieri's *Divine Comedy*, printed on 11 April 1472 (with a print run of between 200 and 300 copies), of which 14 originals are still in existence.

This first printing house, however, was short lived, perhaps because, in those early days, there was no well-organized distribution network to allow profits to be made from printing. The seed however had been sown, and many a qualified printer was later to contribute to Foligno's fame as a leading typographical center. Today, the building next to the Oratory of Nunziatella houses the Centro di Documentazione della Stampa, illustrating the development of the art of printing in Foligno. Also on display is an ancient printing press, supposedly the one used to print Dante's *Divine Comedy*. Although scholars do not all agree on this attribution, the press is the symbol of an artistic tradition which Foligno has preserved at the highest level.

the Middle Ages between the old bed of the Topino River and the new channel dug in the 13th-century. Its narrow streets are still arranged in a herring-bone pattern off the straight Via Mentana. The **church of S. Giacomo** is one of the three religious buildings around which the district developed. It has a characteristic white-and-red banded facade and an ogival doorway. The *church of S. Giovanni Battista* contains various attractive 15th-century frescoes, while the **monastery of S. Lucia** includes a church dating from the 14th-15th centuries, preceded by a graceful portico. Above the doorway, in the lunette, is a *fresco* (1471). At the end of the street you can see a long section of the medieval walls following the Topino River, with the picturesque *medieval* tower known as the *Torre dei Cinque Cantoni*.

Via Garibaldi ❺ is one of the axes of the "crossroads" around which the layout of the medieval city was based. By walking along this street, you pass some of the most important religious buildings erected during the period of architectural transformation that took place here during the 18th and 19th centuries. After the unfinished deconsecrated **church of the Annunziata**, you reach Piazza Garibaldi which is overlooked by the **church of the Santissimo Salvatore** (1138). Opposite stands the **church of S. Agostino**, which has a particularly striking 18th-century brick facade. Slightly further on is the 18th-century **church of S. Maria del Suffragio**, with a facade dating from 1826. The **Oratorio della Nunziatella/Oratory of the Nunziatella*** ❻, an oratory built in 1490-94, is a graceful rectangular Renaissance church, with a richly decorated *tabernacle* and two works by Il Perugino (**Baptism of Christ** and *God the Father*, 1507). The adjacent rooms house the civic *Centro di Documentazione della Stampa*, illustrating the early introduction of the art of printing to Foligno in 1470. From here, short detours take us to the late 17th century **church of S. Maria di Betlem** in Corso Cavour, and to the **convent of S. Anna*** in Via dei Monasteri, otherwise known as the *Monastero delle Contesse*,

originally only open to women. It was founded in 1388 and *decorated* in the 14th century.

At the junction we turn into **Corso Cavour** ❼ where, on the left, we come to the late-16th-century **Palazzo Iacobilli-Roncalli**. The palace has been altered since and only the Music Room has survived intact, with its masterful stucco decoration. Beyond it is the facade of the former **Teatro Apollo-Piermarini** (1827). Once again, two churches provide the structure of **Piazza S. Francesco** ❽: the **church of the Madonna del Gonfalone** (1724), with its plain unfinished facade, now used as a venue for exhibitions and other events, and the **church of S. Francesco**, a 19th-century re-make of a medieval church, featuring early 14th-century *frescoes* and a *Crucifixion* (late 13C). The **chiesa di S. Maria Infraportas/church of Santa Maria Infraportas*** ❾ was built in the 11th century, outside the city walls, with a white-and-pink stone facade and a small portico. To the right of the portico is a shrine (1480). Numerous votive frescoes grace its interior. The **chapel of the Assunta*** is well worth a visit to see its late 12th-century frescoes.

Via Gramsci ❿, the former Via dei Mercanti, continues to be one of the city's most elegant streets, because of the noble palaces which line its length. On the edge of the old town stands the deconsecrated **church of S. Domenico** (1285), now an auditorium. Stepping through its fine Gothic doorway you find yourself in a modern hall with a

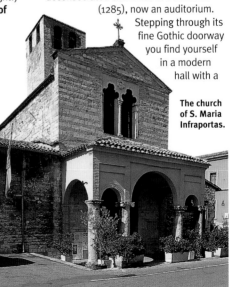

The church of S. Maria Infraportas.

BANDIERA ARANCIONE

THE QUALITY LABEL FOR TOURISM AND ENVIRONMENT IN ITALY'S INLAND AREAS

The BANDIERA ARANCIONE (ORANGE FLAG) is a label of quality for the development of tourism in Italy's inland areas. Municipalities with less than 15.000 inhabitants may be awarded it if selected criteria are achieved and maintained: cultural heritage, respect for the environment, hospitality, information and services, and quality local production. The ORANGE FLAG program is run by the Touring Club of Italy. The World Tourism Organisation has chosen the Orange Flag Program as a success in the sphere of environmental tourism.

For more information: www.touringclub.it/bandierearancioni

MONTONE

This attractive little oval town has retained all its medieval charm. A staircase with marvelous views climbs up to the *Gothic church of S. Francesco*, built in the 14th century. The church and the adjoining former Franciscan monastery have been restored and converted into a museum, the main feature of which is the decoration on the walls of the church itself. Note in particular the remains of the frescoes depicting **Stories in the Life of St Francis** and the standard with the **Madonna del Soccorso**. The spectacular *Rocca d'Aries* belongs to the municipal council.

VALLO DI NERA

The town stands on the top of a hill and is essentially still an early-13th century town, with concentric circles of streets surrounded by fortifications. Inside the town, arches spanning the narrow streets connect one house to another and the whole area is a pedestrian precinct. The *church of S. Maria* dates from the 13th century and contains votive frescoes; in the apse, an interesting fresco depicts *Stories in the Life of Christ and the Virgin Mary, the Saints and Prophets*. At the top of the hill is the church of S. Giovanni Battista (13 and 14C) with an apse entirely decorated with frescoes dating from 1536.

---

modern trussed roof, whose walls are covered with an extensive collection of votive frescoes by various artists. Among the street's civic buildings, of particular interest are: the 16th-century **Palazzo Brunetti-Candiotti**; *Palazzo Vitelleschi*; and *Palazzo Guiducci*.

The **rione delle Conce/Conce district** ⑪, traditionally the artisans' *rione* (district) consists of a dense medieval network of narrow streets. By walking along Via delle Scuole d'Arti e Mestieri, beyond the little deconsecrated *church of S. Tomaso dei Cipischi* (1190), you come to a square overlooked by the **church of S. Nicolò**. Having crossed the *Topinello Canal*, which flows along the old river bed, you reach the characteristic **Portico delle Conce**, with its ancient workshops facing the canal.

GUALDO TADINO [49 km]

The town lies at the foot of Mt Serra Santa. Our visit begins in Piazza XX Settembre, where the **church of S. Maria dei Raccomandati** and the 13th-century **church of S. Donato** are located. Not far away is **Piazza Martiri**

della Libertà, which still has a 13th-century *civic tower*, formerly part of Palazzo del Podestà. Opposite is *Palazzo Comunale*, erected in 1768-69 above the ruins of Palazzo delle Arti e dei Priori. The **church of S. Francesco*** stands on the west side of the square, facing it sideways on. The gabled facade facing Corso Italia has a Gothic doorway and a trilobate tympanum. (You may well wonder why it is the side of the church with its round buttresses that faces the present square rather than the elegant main facade. This is because the square was formerly the cloister of a monastery, which has since been demolished). The interior is decorated with 14th- and 15th-century *frescoes*. Suspended from the ceiling of the apse is a wooden **Crucifix*** dating from the 12th-14th century. The choir, high altar and the pulpit on the left date from the 14th century. The pilaster between the first and second chapel features a painting of the *Virgin and Child* by Matteo da Gualdo, the earliest-known work by this artist. The 13th-century facade of the **cathèdral of S. Benedetto** dominates the opposite side of the square. Parts of the original structure (1256, and remodeled during the 18th and 19th centuries) include the facade with its three doorways and a splendid rose window with a double wheel of small columns. To the right side is a 16th-century *fountain*, which was built at the same time as the sewage system (1573). The aisled interior of the cathedral was rebuilt in 1875, and between 1907 and 1924. The high altar (late 14C) was replaced in 1965. The decorated crypt contains an *urn* with the mortal remains of *Beato Angelo*, who died in 1324. The fortress of **Rocca Flea** dates from the early Middle Ages. It was rebuilt by Frederick II, restored in 1394 and, in the 16th century, was converted into a residence for cardinal legates, who enlarged the structure and decorated its interior. Its present-day structure is the result of the many uses to which it has been put. Walls with corner towers enclose the central courtyard with a large 14th-century keep. Today the complex houses the *civic museum* and *art gallery* with works from churches in the town and

the Gualdo area, including a **polyptych*** by Niccolò Alunno (1471); the *Antiquarium* has a display of finds from archaeological sites in the area, dating from prehistory to the Roman period.

GUBBIO [40 km]

A charming stone city which stands out at the foot of steep Mt Ingino, which almost seems to be carved out of gray limestone blocks, Gubbio provides the visitor with a spectacular and celebrated vision of a compact mass of monumental buildings. The urban development of the town, like the surrounding area, influenced by this city's "stony charm", has retained its medieval flavor.

Piazza Quaranta Martiri ❶, site of the medieval market situated on the edge of the city's most ancient core, has the best *view* of the upper city standing out against the mountain. Its northern side is delimited by the elongated 14th-century hospital, whereas in the 17th-century, the wool-weavers' guild added the *Loggiato dei Tiratori dell'Arte della Lana*, which surmounts the entire length of the latter

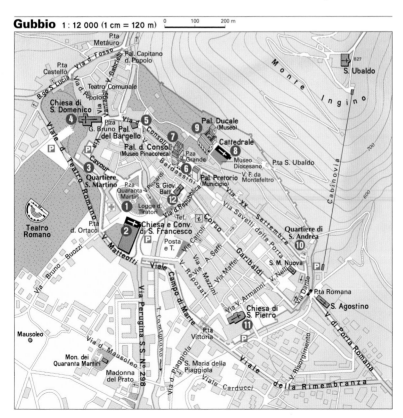

Gubbio 1 : 12 000 (1 cm = 120 m)

structure, using it as a pressing facility. The portico leading to the edifice was once adorned with mural paintings, of which there remains a *Virgin between Sts Peter and Paul* (1473). Adjoining the hospital is the **church of S. Maria dei Laici**, built in 1313, and later enlarged. The building, damaged during the latest earthquake (1997), is undergoing restoration and its movable art heritage is temporarily stored in the Palazzo Ducale. Near the Spadalonga warehouse, where tradition has it that St Francis, after leaving home, was welcomed and clothed, is the **Convento di S. Francesco/Monastery of S. Francesco* ❷** which today closes off the square's southern boundary (built in 1255). The church has Gothic forms and a simple facade, a Gothic doorway and a small rose window. A double doorway and small rose window (14C) adorn the church's left side, which is embellished with pilaster strips and tall one-light windows (some have been filled in). It has three polygonal apses which belonged to

The arches of the Roman theater in Gubbio.

the original church, upon which rests a polygonal bell tower (15C). Inside, the tall nave and spacious aisles lie below cross-vaults which, in 1720, replaced the open-beamed roof, still visible in the remodeled section towards the apse. In the right apse, the *chapel of St Francis* contains frescoes dating from the 13th-early 14th century, a small one-light window and

some decorated windows. The central apse is decorated with 13th-century frescoes and the left apse is decorated with **Scenes from the Life of Mary*** (c.1408 and 1413). The 14th-century sacristy leads to the cloister with its 14th-century frescoes. Elegant mullioned windows flank the doorway which leads into the *chapter house*, where there is a *fresco* (probably 14th-C), originally in the cloister.

The **Raccolta d'Arte di S. Francesco** includes archaeological finds, 14th- to 18th-century gold work, 16th-century vestments and vessels, and paintings. The seal known as the *Sigillo dell'antica custodia di Gubbio* (1350) is particularly noteworthy. At the end of the short street to the left of the church stands the Porta degli Ortacci. Turning down Via Buozzi you come to the **Mausoleum**, what remains of a Roman tomb, originally dressed with large square stone slabs and containing a barrel-vault burial chamber.

From the door of the tomb, by walking around the walls to the right, you come to the **Roman Theater**, dating from the 1st century AD, where we can admire some exceptionally finely-crafted and well-preserved mosaics. The lower vaulting and part of the upper vaulting can still be observed, together with the cavea which could seat almost 6,000 spectators, and the stage. In summer, classical plays are performed in this unique setting. The nearby Antiquarium has a display of finds from a Roman house and some polychrome Roman mosaics (1C). In **Quartiere S. Martino/ S. Martino district ❸**, *Palazzo Beni* is a typical example of a somber late 14th-century noble residence. The doorway dates from the 16th-17th century. Some of the original fresco decoration has been conserved in the smaller courtyard (coats-of-arms) and a room on the first floor (allegorical figures). From here you proceed to Piazza Giordano Bruno, dedicated to the Dominican friar, philosopher and man of letters, who was burned at the stake as a heretic in 1600. Here rises the Dominican complex, an area where a feudal settlement had developed in the 11th century, which was to give rise to the city's first medieval layout. Having relocated to the nearby monastery in the early 14th century, the

A view of Gubbio with the magnificent Palazzo dei Consoli on the left.

Dominicans enlarged the smaller church of S. Martino (which dated from 1180), pushing it beyond the city walls and changing the church's name to **S. Domenico** ❹. Mighty square towers support the apse. Inside are some 15th-century frescoes, wooden choir-stalls dating from 1563 and a beautiful **lectern**. We now proceed along Via Vantaggi and Via Gabrielli, where there was once a huge *palazzo* with a tall medieval defense tower. This brings us to the so-called **Palazzo del Capitano del Popolo** (late 13-C), currently used for exhibitions. The facade follows the curve of the street, and is decorated with three tiers of Gothic windows. Inside the palace there is a rather unusual stone basin. The street ends at **Porta Metauro**, the only gate of the city to have preserved its wooden door, with the remains of a mural painting in its tympanum. The main entrance to **Parco Ranghiasci**, which has preserved its original 19th-century layout, opens onto Via Gabrielli. Higher up, you can still see a tower and a part of the city walls. Situated outside the gate, is the **church of S. Croce della Foce**. Its interior has an impressive gilded coffered ceiling and stucco decoration from the 17th century. **Via dei Consoli*** ❺ is one of the city's most picturesque streets. Rising broad and curvilinear, it is flanked by ashlar-fronted buildings which, with their fine masonry and the broad street-level openings of the shops and warehouses, give an exact picture of a typical late-medieval street. The narrow ogival doorway (see house No. 49) on the ground floor, known as the Porta del Morto (Dead Man's Door), provided access to the upper stories via wooden (now stone) staircases. **Palazzo del Bargello** (1302) is a magnificent example of this type of house. Its well-preserved facade consists of three rusticated tiers decorated with stone window-frames with a scallop motif. Opposite is the small square of the *Fontana dei Matti* (the Madmen's Fountain), the heart of the *San Giuliano district*. A bold medieval architectural achievement, the "hanging" **Piazza Grande**** ❻ was conceived as a grandiose monumental churchyard connecting the two seats of the civic magistrates: Palazzo dei Consoli and Palazzo Pretorio. This monumental square (1321) looks out over the surrounding countryside, acting as a physical and ideal reference-point for the whole town. **Palazzo dei Consoli**** ❼, built between 1332 and 1349, is one of Italy's finest

Gubbio, Palazzo dei Consoli.

chronological order, the works in the **art gallery*** illustrate local artistry from the Middle Ages to the baroque. Standing opposite Palazzo dei Consoli, **Palazzo Pretorio** is an unfinished Gothic structure. To the left, inside the Neoclassical *Palazzo Ranghiasci-Brancaleoni* is a Roman mosaic. Nearby, it is worth looking briefly at **Via Baldassini**, which runs parallel, albeit at a lower level, to Piazza Grande. Lined by numerous antique shops, the street is dominated by the steep front of Palazzo dei Consoli and by a compact row of 13th-14th century houses, including the **Casa dei Baldassini** (which possibly belonged to the Accoromboni). To return to the square, take Via Gattapone, right opposite the house. A narrow passageway (on the northeast side of Piazza Grande) leads to the steps of *Via Galeotti*, a picturesque medieval street, leading to *Via Federico da Montefeltro* above. The street is overlooked by the 13th-century **Palazzo del Capitolo dei Canonici** (seat of the **Diocesan Museum**), with its elegant mullion-windowed facade. The museum is arranged on three levels. On the ground floor, in the cellar, is a huge 16th-century *barrel* (an extremely rare item of wine-making equipment). It also houses the art collections from the cathedral including Roman and medieval sculpture and *paintings* dating from the 12th to 17th centuries. Highlights include the magnificent gilt brocade *cope* attributed to Giusto di Gand and, in the frescoed room used for temporary exhibitions, a *fresco cycle* by Giacomo di Benedetto Bedi. The **Cattedrale/Cathedral*** ❽, dedicated to Sts James and Marianus, has a simple facade with an ogival doorway and a rose window surrounded by *symbols of the Evangelists* and the *Paschal Lamb*. The effect created by the church's broad nave, with its ten large pointed arches supporting the roof (a typical local model), is truly magnificent. Of particular interest are the *chapel of the Holy Sacrament* (17C), and in the *presbytery*, two organs with

examples of civic architecture. It is rectangular in layout and faces the square with a rusticated facade, offset at intervals by tiers of sturdy pilasters. The second tier is orchestrated by three pairs of windows and a cornice with a motif of small pointed arches and merlons above. A slender merloned tower rises from the left-hand corner of the building. Below the tower, a huge bell (2,500kg) is housed in the belfry. The bell is rung not with ropes but with kicks of the foot, which is very entertaining to watch. A fan-shaped stairway leads up to the Gothic doorway and thence to the *Arengo*, a magnificent barrel-vaulted hall where the popular assemblies of the commune were once held. The ground floor is occupied by the **Civic Museum** with finds, inscriptions, sarcophagi, architectural fragments, statues and marble work dating from the Roman and early-medieval periods. The palace's former sacristy contains a **coin collection** with specimens minted in Gubbio from the Umbrian period to the 18th century. In the former chapel of the palace are the famous **Eugubine Tablets****, seven bronze plaques of varying size inscribed partly with Umbrian characters of Etruscan derivation (2C BC), and partly in Latin (late 2C-early 1C BC) discussing such themes as worship, legal systems, augury and the religious ceremonies of the Gubbio community and the Atiedii brotherhood. On the upper floor, preceded by the *Sala della Loggetta*, there is a display of ceramics made in the Gubbio area between the 16th and 19th centuries. Arranged in

beautiful marquetry work (1550).
Also called *Corte Nuova*, the **Palazzo Ducale**** 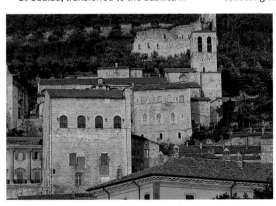 ❾, completed in 1480, consists of two central structures, one facing the valley and the other the mountain. The two blocks are connected by a splendid **courtyard***, with elegant Renaissance forms, accessed by a plain stone doorway. Today the palace houses a **museum**. Especially striking are two cabinets located in the first room (1493 and 1627); the **doors** of the main doorway, carved and emblazoned with symbols, attributed to Mariotto di Paolo Sensi – called Il Terzuolo – who was particularly famed for his marquetry techniques. Beneath the Renaissance complex lies an **archaeological site** (10-13C), featuring remains of streets, a tower, a *palatium*, a warehouse and two cisterns, also a some brick paving and an underpass which linked the cathedral churchyard to the road that leads up to Mt Ingino. However, still more interesting, especially from a historical point of view, is the fact that the stratification here dates from the early Middle Ages to the Renaissance. If you follow the steep, winding lane to the top of Mt Ingino past the pines and cypress trees, you eventually come to the **basilica of S. Ubaldo**. Alternatively, you can take the cableway which starts near the Roman gate; or the road from Porta Metauro, which goes up the Bottacione gorge past the *Parco del Coppo*. The church, with an elegant *cloister* with octagonal brick columns, has a nave and four aisles, decorated with 16th- and 18th-century paintings. At the high altar there is a Renaissance urn containing the body of St Ubaldo, transferred to the basilica in

1194. From Piazza Grande, by walking along *Via XX Settembre*, with its rows of characteristic 17th-18th-century houses, we reach the **quartiere di S. Andrea/ Sant'Andrea district** ❿. Here, in Via Savelli della Porta, is the 17th-century *church of the Muratori*, also called **S. Francesco della Pace**, where, during the night, as related in Saint Francis's Fioretti (XXI), the famous wolf tamed by the saint used to seek refuge. Inside is the stone upon which St Francis of Assisi is supposed to have preached to the people. On the same street stands **Palazzo della Porta**, with its elegant Renaissance doorway. At the end of the street is the **church of S. Maria Nuova**, built between 1270 and 1280. Its single nave is accessed via a plain ogival doorway, which is located asymmetrically with respect to the facade. Of the fine 14th and 15th-century frescoes which once adorned the interior, there remains only a **Madonna del Belvedere** (1413), encased in a sandstone tabernacle dating from 1510. The church also conserves furnishings from various local churches including a gilt plaster chest which once contained the remains of St Ubaldo. Beyond 14th-century *Palazzo Falcucci*, you come to Via Dante which, to the left, leads to the Umbrian *Porta Vehia* (4-3C BC), remodeled in the Middle Ages. Nearby stands the *monastery of S. Marziale*, with the *church of S. Andrea*, after which the district is named. By turning right, we come to medieval tower-shaped **Porta Romana**, a gate featuring in its interior interesting *collections of majolica* (16-19C) made in a reverberating furnace. Next to the tower are the offices once used for collecting taxes, which were in use in the 19th century. Just outside the gate is the **complex of S. Agostino** (1251), with its 18th-century facade and beamed ceiling supported by eight broad arches, a fairly common feature in Gubbio. The apse is entirely covered with 26 frescoes, portraying *Scenes from the Life of St Augustine*; the triumphal arch is decorated with an imposing scene of the *Last Judgment*. Continuing along the slope of Neri, you come to the

View of Gubbio on the steep slopes of Mt Ingino.

chiesa di S. Pietro/church of S. Pietro ⑪, one of Gubbio's most ancient monasteries. Here you can see traces of the successive phases of construction, such as a five-arched portico (late Roman period), the transformation of the church's layout from a nave and two aisles to a single arched nave (13C), and, lastly, the various Renaissance transformations to the interior (1519), when the central rose window was closed up and two lateral windows were made to make room for the *organ*. The *frescoes* in the chapel are by Raffaellino del Colle. After S. Pietro, beyond the medieval *Porta Vittoria*, we come to Borgo della Piaggiola, and the 15th-century **church of S. Maria della Piaggiola**, which boasts some baroque *decoration* and *stucco work* in its interior. *St Ubaldo's tabernacle* (1761) marks the beginning of the broad, straight **Corso Garibaldi**, the main thoroughfare of *S. Pietro district*, which developed in the early 13th century. At the beginning of the avenue stands the church of the Santissima Trinità, built in 1410 by Augustinian monks. At the end, to the right, Via della Repubblica leads to the **chiesa di S. Giovanni Battista/church of S. Giovanni Battista ⑬**, in the very heart of medieval Gubbio. The church, with its Gothic limestone facade and Romanesque bell tower, was built between the 13th and 14th centuries. The hexagonal Gothic chapel of the baptistery contains a Renaissance majolica *baptismal font*.

IPOGEO DEI VOLUMNI/ VOLUMNI HYPOGEUM [10 km]

From Perugia, first Viale Roma and then the scenic SS 75bis road to Assisi lead around the village of *Ponte San Giovanni* to this delightful 19th-century structure, which serves as a vestibule to the *hypogeum*, the most important of those so far explored in the vast Palazzone necropolis. The large chamber tomb, which belonged to the Velimna (Volumni in Latin) family, found by chance in 1840, is one of the finest examples of a Hellenistic-age noble Etruscan tomb. Dating from the second half of the 2nd-century BC, it reproduces the plan of an aristocratic home. The tomb is accessed via a steep flight of stairs which leads down to a rectangular area (*atrium*), with a sloping roof and three niches (*cubicula*)

on each of its longer sides. On the walls are carvings extolling the material virtues of the deceased. The rear side leads into the main room (*tablinium*), which contains **seven cinerary urns*** in marble and travertine. In line with the entrance is the urn of the head of the family, half lying on a drape-covered bed supported by winged funerary demons that keep watch above the painted doorway to the after-life. All around are smaller urns containing other members of the family.

IPOGEO DI SAN MANNO/ SAN MANNO HYPOGEUM [5 km]

Ferro di Cavallo is a complex which developed in the early 20th-century over a former nucleus resting on the *church of S. Manno*, which, despite its 14th-century appearance, is entirely decorated with fresco remains of the preceding century. Around the church, which was purchased by the Order of Malta, a rural fortified monastery was erected in the Middle Ages. Below this complex is one of the major monuments of Etruscan funerary architecture, the **S. Manno hypogeum** or *tomba dei Precu* (from the family's name), which was used as a crypt and cellar. Steps opposite the original entrance lead down to a rectangular dome-vaulted room made of large, perfectly squared blocks, opening onto two symmetrical cells. On the door to the left cell, which contained the cinerary urns, a lengthy three-line inscription can still be made out, which, although its meaning is obscure, has contributed to the tomb's fame.

LAGO TRASIMENO/ LAKE TRASIMENO [48 km]

If you have ever asked yourself how many shades of green there are in the wild, stop for a while at Lake Trasimeno, where you

Lake Trasimeno is home to many species of wildlife.

TCI HIGHLIGHTS

WATER CULTURE

The fishing-nets (*see photo*), the traditional fishermen's huts, the fishing-boats and sweep-nets, modern replicas of some of Trasimeno's most ancient fishing techniques: all these phenomena are outward manifestations of a trade which, in the past, provided the livelihood of the people who lived on and around the shores of Lake Trasimeno. The local practice of fishing is still alive in the traditions and the cuisine of this lake district, and is an important factor in local tourism. The Arte dei Pesciaioli, the medieval fishermen's guild that laid down strict rules about fishing and was responsible for the

territorial division of the lake, dates all the way back to the 13th century. Nowadays, modern craft like boats with outboard motors have long since replaced the old rowing-boats which were once used for fishing. In addition, the depletion of the numbers of fish in the lake has drastically undermined the fishing trade, to the advantage of more profitable agricultural activities.

Magione's Museo della Pesca del Lago Trasimeno in San Feliciano was set up in 1974 with the admirable aim of documenting local fishing, for centuries the primary economic activity of the locals. With its extensive display of objects and tools, the museum also demonstrates the techniques once used by the lake fishermen and aspects of their lifestyle, conserving a heritage which would otherwise have been lost. The presence of the lake and its products can be clearly perceived in the gastronomic specialties of the area, consisting primarily of pike, carp, tench (the *risotto* made with this fish is particularly worthy of mention), eel, and perch. On the shores of the lake, reeds grow in abundance. The reeds are turned into wicker by local craftsmen and used to make mats, baskets and chairs. San Feliciano is one of the best-known places for the working of lake reeds.

will be able to identify more than 100, as well as a whole spectrum of other colors: the soft yellow of primroses in spring, the bright yellow of the water lilies, the startling red of cornelian cherries and the orange *Lilium bulbiferum*. Lake Trasimeno is the largest inland lake in mainland Italy, and the country's fourth-largest (126km²) in terms of size. Surrounded by a plain and by rolling hills, where woods are sporadically interrupted by fields of corn or sunflowers, vineyards and olive-groves, the area attracts large numbers of birds. Nowhere is the lake more than 6m deep. With its very slow water reflux rate, it is one of Italy's most fragile and precious wetlands. A veritable paradise for botanists and bird-watchers, the three islands of the lake (Maggiore, Minore and Polvese) are home to various duck species, from mallards to garganey. You may well see groups of cormorant skimming low over the water, while the marsh harrier hovers above the reeds and you may even be lucky enough to see

penduline tits. With a little luck, you will also see an osprey diving into the water to collect its prey. The lake is home to many indigenous fish species such as pike, chubb, rudd and eel. In March 1995, the **Parco Naturale Regionale del Lago Trasimeno** was created, with the aim of protecting and making better use of the lake and the fragile natural environment around it.

MONTEFALCO [44 km]

From its hill, the town dominates the Topino and Clitumno plains, offering vistas of exceptional beauty. Because of its beautiful views, it is known as the 'Balcony of Umbria'. The symbiosis of this town, which has been awarded the TCI's "Bandiera Arancione", with its surrounding area is evident, because of its characteristic roads branching off from the town's circular square downward to the valley below. Entering the town through *Porta Sant'Agostino*, a gate which stands in a well-preserved stretch of the medieval walls, head up *Corso Mameli*, the main street of the **Castellare district** (early 13C). *Casa Angeli*, to the right, has an interesting facade set with remains of urns, chunks of Roman marble, and coats-of-arms. The entire district is dominated by the **church of S. Agostino** (1279-85), with its plain but elegant stone facade and handsome late 13th-century doorway, through which you enter the church's interior. The walls are covered with frescoes dating from the 14th, 15th and 16th centuries. The circular **Piazza del Comune**, situated at the top of the town, became the center of town life in the Middle Ages. This is where the five main streets that divide that town into segments converge. **Palazzo Comunale** (1270), the town hall, overlooks the square, along with the former **church** (now a theater) **of S. Filippo Neri** (1705), the *oratory of S. Maria di Piazza*, and the elegant 16th *Palazzo de Cuppis*. The **parish church of S. Bartolomeo**, founded in medieval times, was completely transformed after 1638. The unfinished interior, with its beamed roof, contains some fine 17th-century altars and paintings. A few steps down from the square is the deconsecrated **church of S. Francesco***, built at the same time as the adjoining monastery between 1336 and 1340. The chapels to the right, which form an extra aisle, were added in the 17th-century. Here we can admire the scenes from the life of St Francis by Benozzo Gozzoli, who was to influence Umbrian painting for the entire second half of the 15th century. The church houses the **Museo Civico*** which comprises not only the magnificent decoration of the former church but also the art gallery, housed in the former monastery. Starting with the church, we can admire frescoes by Benozzo Gozzoli in the **St Jerome chapel***, whereas the **Crucifix*** in the third bay is by the Maestro Espressionista di S. Chiara. It is the central apse, however, that captures the visitor's attention, with a fresco cycle depicting **Scenes from the Life of St Francis****, painted in 1452 by Benozzo Gozzoli. The first floor of the museum houses the **art gallery** with paintings by artists from Umbria and elsewhere dating from the 13th to 17th centuries. The semi-circular crypt contains the **lapidarium** with archaeological

The 13th-century Porta Sant'Agostino.

finds, marbles and inscriptions.
Borgo S. Leonardo is a 14th-century extension of the city on the road out of town in the direction of Spoleto. After a cylindrical tower in the perimeter wall, you come to the **church of S. Chiara** and the convent founded by the saint from Montefalco (Chiara di Damiano). At the far end of the *borgo* stands the **church of S. Illuminata***, a beautiful Renaissance building erected and frescoed in 1491. On Viale Marconi is the **church** dedicated to **S. Fortunato***. It is preceded by a 15th-century arcaded courtyard featuring four ancient columns and a frescoed *doorway*. Inside hangs a **St Fortunatus Enthroned*** by Benozzo Gozzoli, in addition to other fresco fragments by the same painter. In the wooded area nearby, the so-called *Grotte di San Fortunato* (underground caves) are worth a visit.

NOCERA UMBRA [55 km]

Through 16th-century *Porta Nuova*, or Porta Garibaldi, you access tree-lined Viale Matteotti, which in turn leads to *Porta Vecchia*, the main gate in the city's 13th-century perimeter wall. On either side of the gate is a fountain (1866) bearing an inscription extolling the virtues of Nocera's water. Proceed along the main street of the **Borgo** (now *Corso Vittorio Emanuele*), which leads to the upper part of the city, past houses which were renovated in the 16th-17th centuries. The houses in the side-streets are medieval. On the right, you descend toward the **Portico of S. Filippo**, a typical arcaded street built in the 17th century following the line of the medieval walls. In the small square at the end of the arcades is the neo-Gothic **church of S. Filippo** (1864-68), featuring pseudo-Renaissance decorative elements and, inside, the *Death of St Philip with the Apparition of the Virgin*. Across the square and to the left, return to the Corso and to the **church of S. Chiara** (13C), built above street level, which contains a *Birth of the Virgin*, an early work by Carlo Maratta, and a beautiful organ gallery decorated in the Venetian style. Further along is the *Palombara*, a Byzantine look-out tower, and Piazza Caprera, site of the **church of S. Francesco***, which was completely restructured in 1494-97. It has a fine stone facade with a late-Gothic doorway, and an even earlier side-door. The **Museo Civico** was set up in its interior, featuring a series of frescoes painted between the 15th and 16th centuries, paintings and sculptures from the cathedral and the surrounding area, and archaeological finds. The paintings include an altarpiece of the **Crucifixion*** by a late 13th-century Roman Umbrian painter and a **polyptych*** made especially for the cathedral by Niccolò di Liberatore (1483) with a magnificent carved, gilded Gothic-style frame. *Archaeological materials* include finds from the **Portone necropolis**, where 166 Lombard tombs (late 6C-mid 7C) were discovered containing rich grave-goods.

Located in Via Pontani, off Piazza Caprera, is the *church of S. Giovanni Battista*. Slightly further on is the picturesque and semi-circular **Piazza Torre Vecchia**. *Via San Rinaldo*, which climbs towards the higher part of the town, is overlooked on the left by the 18th-century *Palazzo Comunale* and the *Bishop's Palace* (19C) and, on the right, by the former *Bishop's Seminary* (1760). This building houses the *Biblioteca Piervisani*, with some 40,000 volumes, including rare editions and illuminated choir-books. Dedicated to the Assumption, the **Duomo** stands on the same high hill where the Rocca, the fortified castle of the local counts who commissioned the church, once stood. Originally Romanesque, the cathedral was completely rebuilt in 1448, and remodeled in the 18th and 19th centuries, whereas its stone-ornamented facade dates from 1925. The bell tower is 16th-century. The church has a large nave and a semi-circular apse, and is decorated with paintings of the Life of the Virgin dating from 1619.

NORCIA [97 km]

The town, which has been awarded the TCI's "Bandiera Arancione", grew up on the edge of the broad, fertile plain of S. Scolastica, bordered by a circle of mountains and irrigated by the Sordo and Torbidone rivers and the springs of S. Martino.
Its fame, apart from being the birthplace of St Benedict, rests on a centuries-long perfection of local crafts and farming. In the Middle Ages and the Renaissance, local wool and jewelry were in great

Piazza S. Benedetto, with Palazzo Comunale and the monument of St Benedict.

demand. Today, as in the past, the (pork) meats produced by the *norcini* (pork butchers) are very popular, along with the local black truffles.

The lunette over the doorway of church of S. Benedetto.

The visit begins in the town's main square, **Piazza San Benedetto***, which is overlooked by the most important civic buildings. At the center of the square stands the *monument of St Benedict* (1880). On the northeast side is **Palazzo Comunale**, with a medieval portico and a loggia above, reconstructed (1876) after the quake of 1859, and two lions at the foot of the steps. The *Council Chamber* contains the superb wooden seats of the Prior and the Consuls (16C), together with the pews for the councilors. On the walls the municipal coats-of-arms date from the 1400s. The neighboring *Priors' chapel* conserves the highly elaborate gilded silver *reliquary of St Benedict* (1450) in the Gothic-Renaissance style.

Tradition has it that the **church of S. Benedetto*** was erected in the early Middle Ages over the house of the saint's family home. Though remodeled several times, the church has kept its 14th-century facade. It was reconstructed after 1859, but only in the upper part, with a fine Gothic doorway complete with reliefs and wooden doors dating from 1578. Along the right side of the building stands the 16th-century **Portico delle Misure**. Under the portico is a stone slab containing a set of nine local measures for cereal crops. The church's interior contains frescoes of the *Madonna and Saints of Norcia*, and an imposing 16th-century carved wooden choir. Two flights of steps in the sides of the apse lead down to the small crypt, with its nave and two aisles, which, tradition suggests, was where Benedict and his twin sister Scolastica were born. The crypt contains a *St Benedict and Totila* (1621), and a *Raising of Lazarus* (1560). Set slightly back from the square, the **Cathedral** is dedicated to S. Maria Argentea, like the earlier medieval parish church

demolished in 1554 to create space for the fortress. The church is notable for its thick, sloping walls, an anti-quake device invented in the 18th century. The interior contains interesting artworks, a detached fresco from the Sparapane workshop (1528) and some fine marble sculptures.

The fort known as the **Castellina*** was commissioned by Pope Julius III as a fortified residence for the apostolic rulers to designs by Vignola (1554). Inside, you can still see some of the substructures of the parish church of S. Maria Argentea and the Palazzo del Podestà, also demolished to make room for the fortress. The building has preserved its square plan, reinforced at each corner by a tower with a sloping escarpment. The Castellina now hosts the **Museo Civico-Diocesano**, with a collection of paintings and sculptures from Norcia and the environs. The **church of S. Agostino**, built in the 1300s, was renovated in the 17th-century in the baroque style, in a way that did not clash with the earlier frescoes (14-16C), many of which have survived. Inside the church are votive frescoes and other works dating from the 15th and 16th centuries. **Via Anicia** leads to the northeast sector of the town, lined with small palaces which were the result of building programs in the 17th and 18th centuries. Worthy of note are *Palazzo Bucchi* (17C) and *Palazzo Colizzi* (17-18C). A little further on is the 16th-century *oratory of the Confraternita dei Cinturati di S. Agostino Minore* (known locally as **'S. Agostinuccio'**). The church has an elaborate gilded wooden ceiling; there are polychrome statues and stalls for the order's members (both ceiling and stalls date from the 1600s); over the baroque altar hangs a 15th-century *Crucifix*. The **Edicola***, also known as the *Tempietto*, was created in 1354, and is a small monument in limestone, built on a square plan as a votive stopping-place with therapeutic properties. A keen eye will pick out the curious mixture of classical architectural elements and the series of sculpted geometric, zoomorphic and anthropomorphic designs of the decoration. The **church of S. Giovanni** was built in the 14th century. The height of the roof was raised in the 18th century, when the fine wooden ceiling above the nave was built. To the right of the entrance is the *altar of the Madonna della Palla*, by Giovanni Dalmata (1468), to which stuccoes and paintings have been added.

PANICALE [34 km]

Founded upon one of Umbria's most beautiful natural terraces, Panicale looks over Lake Trasimeno on one side and the broad Nestore River valley on the other. This hill-town, which has been awarded the TCI's "Bandiera Arancione", has preserved its 13th-14th-century layout intact, centering on three main squares,

at three different levels, all of which are linked by the main street. **Outside the town walls**, the tree-lined thoroughfare leading to the walled town center passes the *church of the Madonna della Neve* (1625), also called *della Sbarra* (seat of vestments museum), in memory of the customs post which once stood here. Among the houses you can just make out the facade of the former *church of S. Agostino* (14C), in Piazza Regina Margherita, used today for art exhibitions. Inside, there are fragments of frescoes, some of which were painted by Il Perugino, and an interesting altar in *pietra serena* (1513). Skirting the walls you come to *Porta Perugina*, through which you pass into **Piazza Umberto I**. The octagonal limestone cistern (1473) at the bottom of the square was converted into a fountain in 1903. *Palazzo Pretorio*

TCI HIGHLIGHTS

LENTILS AND HANG-GLIDING: ATTRACTIONS OF THE CASTELLUCCIO PLATEAUX

Fry a little garlic with some *puntarelle* (a kind of vegetable) and when they turn brown, add the tomato, the sausage and the lentils to make the Norcia dish known as *lenticchie, puntarelle e salsiccia*, a dish invented by the inhabitants of the Castelluccio highlands to honor their famous local lentils.

In the lovely setting of the Parco Nazionale dei Monti Sibillini, the sight of this vast karst system known as the Piano Grande is breathtaking, with its lovely views down

to the Norcia valley. These three plateaux (Piano Perduto, Piano dei Pantani and Piano Piccolo) around Castelluccio form the most extensive enclosed karst landscape in Italy. The lentil fields here lie at about 1,400m above sea-level. This particular variety is small, green and very tasty, and is very popular because it doesn't take long to cook. What's more, the compact form of its seed means that it can withstand the cold winters of this high,broad mountain plateau. Lentil fields line the approach to the town of Castelluccio (1.400m above sea-level), with its beautiful views over the Piano Grande and the Piano Perduto. During the first ten days of June, the area is covered with a thick carpet of flowers – red poppies, white narcissus, blue cornflowers and the yellow flowers of the lentil plants themselves, transforming the plateau into a riot of color. Many will tell you that the best way to admire this stretch of almost 1,300 hectares of land is from the air, in a hang-glider. Hang-gliding experts take advantage of the high peaks above Castelluccio, using them as a springboard for their activities. Assisted by thermals and galvanized by the breathtaking views, they leap into the void, soaring above the fields in flower and the swallow-holes of varying sizes which, after heavy rain or when the snow is melting, are transformed into lakes of a myriad colors.

has a stone coat-of-arms (14C).

The **Collegiata*** stands in Piazza San Michele, where it was founded between the 10th and 11th-century. Enlarged in 1546 and rebuilt in the 17th-century, it features two Renaissance doorways framed by an unfinished facade. Inside there is a *Nativity* (1519) and a 16th-century wooden *Crucifix* with moveable arms. The street opposite the collegiate church leads to the scenic **Piazza Masolino**, and the 14th-century *Palazzo del Podestà*, with its triangular-topped bell tower (1769).

Back in Piazza Umberto I, go through the Porta Perugina, to the *church of S. Sebastiano*, where there are two frescoes by Il Perugino: the famous **Martyrdom of St Sebastian**** (1505) and the *Blessed Virgin and Child with Sts Augustine and Mary Magdalene*.

At *Tavernelle*, 7km southeast of Panicale, the **sanctuary of Mongiovino**, built in about 1524, is worth a visit. The sanctuary, built in sandstone, is built on a Greek-cross plan and has an octagonal dome resting on four pillars. The square interior is surrounded by four chapels and the main chapel with a famous painting of the *Madonna and Child*. As well as other paintings, note the stone high altar and the terracotta statues in the niches near the organ.

SPELLO [31 km]

An ancient hill-town, Spello stands on a narrow spur of Mt Subasio overlooking Umbria valley. This town, which has been awarded the TCI's "Bandiera Arancione", has more traces of Roman civilization than any other Umbrian site, from its walls and its Imperial-age city gates (re-used in medieval times) to the remains of the amphitheater and the baths, blending in a unique interplay of styles and colors. The town's plan is simple and rational, developed along a sole central artery linking the two main gates (Porta Consolare and Porta dell'Arce), which winds up gradually to the top of the hill.

The visit begins in the **Borgo/historic center ❶**. *Porta Consolare* was the main entrance to the Roman town, with three arches and, above, statues from the amphitheater placed there in the 17th century. On the right is a square medieval tower crowned with an olive-tree which is at least 500 years old.

From here you enter the district situated around *Via Consolare*, which winds upwards separating the symmetrical area of the Roman town (on the left) from the medieval area (on the right). On the way you pass the **Tega chapel**, which has important, sadly damaged, frescoes by Alunno (1461). A chain hanging on an ancient house to the left indicates that you are about to enter the Mezota district. Before going under Porta Consolare, it is worth turning left down Via Roma to see a beautiful section of the **Augustan walls***, one of Italy's best-preserved fortified structures, in Subasio limestone. At the end of the street stands **Porta Urbica**, dating from the Imperial period, with its Tuscan-style arch and, on the other side, the 12th-century *church of S. Ventura*.

S. Maria Maggiore* ❷, together with the collegiate church of S. Lorenzo, which marks the end of the Mezota district. Founded in the 11th-12th century, its facade dates from 1644 and has a Romanesque bell tower with a sloping roof. By the base of the tower are two grooved Roman columns. The height of the second bell tower at the back was raised in the 16th century. Stucco decoration covers the interior but, in the **Baglioni chapel****, notice the ma-jolica pavement (1566), and the **frescoes*** by Pinturicchio (1501),

Porta Venere in Spello, with its two twelve-sides towers.

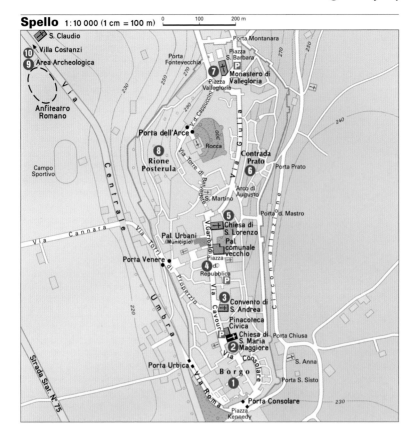

Spello 1:10 000 (1 cm = 100 m)

considered to be one of the artist's finest achievements. The **Virgin and Child**, situated above a small altar in the former chapel of the Canonici is by the same master from Perugia. The canopy above the high altar made of in *pietra caciolfa* (a type of local stone) is by Rocco da Vicenza (1515). In Palazzo dei Canonici (1552) is the **Pinacoteca Civica**. The collection displays in chronological order paintings, sculptures and local gold artifacts dating from the 13th to the 18th centuries. Continuing along the main thoroughfare of Via Cavour, you come to the **monastero di S. Andrea/monastery of S. Andrea** ❸ where Andrea Caccioli, a follower of St Francis, founded one of the first Friars Minor communities. Built in 1258, it underwent various renovations (17-18C), however, the facade and its simple, elegant Romanesque doorway are original. The interior is neo-Gothic (1913). It contains a *Virgin and Child and Saints* (1508) by Pinturicchio. To the rear of **Piazza della Repubblica** ❹, an area with

buildings dating from various periods, stands **Palazzo Comunale Vecchio**. Built in 1270, it was enlarged in the 16th century. The fountain bearing the coat-of-arms of Pope Julius III was added in the 16th century. On display in the atrium is a collection of Roman stone tablets and other finds, while the **Sala Emilio Greco** on the upper floor contains sculptures and drawings by the Sicilian artist. The history of the **chiesa di S. Lorenzo/church of S. Lorenzo** ❺ is entirely told by its facade. The small blind loggia above the right of the doorway dates from the 12th century (when the church was built), as does the band decorated with white and pink lozenges; the doorway, the three rose windows and the upper molding are from the 16th century; the decorations above the left door date from the 8th and 9th centuries. Of the works on display inside the church, in the chapel of the Sacrament designed by Piermarini, note the late 15th-century

One of Spello's Roman gates, the Arch of August, with a tower behind.

tabernacle for storing holy oil. The **Contrada Prato/Prato District** ➏ developed outside the Roman wall and was later enclosed by the 14th-century walls, around the central thoroughfare of Via Giulia. Besides the remains of the Roman gate, called the **Arco di Augusto**, situated opposite the shrine known as the *Maestà di Fonte del Mastro*, another building of interest is the **Teatro Comunale Subasio** (1787), a real gem of a theater. At the end of Via Giulia stands the **Monastero di Vallegloria/Monastery of Vallegloria** ➐. Built by the Poor Clares in about 1320, its 16th-century interior has picture cycle by Marcantonio Grecchi, Ascensidonio Spacca and Cesare Sermei. **Posterula** ➑ is the town's highest and most ancient point. Beyond *Porta dell'Arce*, the Roman arch built in the Republican age, is the tower and, on the left, the remains of a wall of the *Rocca* (14C). Our descent takes us down Via Torre Belvedere to the **Belvedere***, with wonderful views of the Topino plain and the hills stretching from Montefalco to Assisi.
Next to **Porta Venere**, so named in the 17th century because of a temple dedicated to Venus, which once probably stood nearby, are some Romanesque *twelve-sided towers*. In the **area archeologica/archaeological site** ➒ you can still see the remains of the *Roman*

amphitheater (1C BC). Here, the late 12th-century **church of S. Claudio*** was also built above a Roman edifice. Inside this church, which is often closed, the arches over the nave and side-aisles become progressively lower, making the church seem longer than it actually is. **Villa Costanzi,** formerly **Villa Fidelia** ➓ is a spectacular villa, built on the site of a terraced Roman sanctuary. The park of the villa, with its ancient trees and layout of descending terraces, is well worth a visit. A small 18th-century building here houses the **Straka Coppa Collection**. The gallery has a section dedicated to modern and contemporary painters and a classical section.

SPOLETO [66 km]

Spoleto's charm derives not only from its many remarkable monuments, but also its rather unusual setting. The hill of Monteluco not only functions as a scenic backdrop, but has also played a leading role in Spoleto's history. Special laws have protected its holm-oak forests from felling since Antiquity.
Our visit to the town follows two itineraries: the Traversa Interna and the higher part of the town. Afterwards we describe the churches lying beyond the river. The 'Traversa Interna', which runs from Piazza Garibaldi to the church of S. Paolo inter Vineas, cutting through the town from north to south, was really designed for cars, and has virtually no shops or restaurants. Having admired the broad, tree-lined *Piazza della Vittoria* and having inspected the remains of **Ponte Sanguinario**, with its three arches built of square blocks of travertine, much of which is now below ground, we enter **Piazza Garibaldi** ➊. *Porta Garibaldi*, through which we access the square, was first rebuilt in the 15th century, and again in 1825. Destroyed by the retreating Germans in 1944, it was subsequently rebuilt as a two-span bridge. Many Roman remains are to be found in the foundations of the square's public buildings. Often, Christian churches were built on earlier sites of cult worship, like the Romanesque **chiesa di S. Gregorio Maggiore/church of S. Gregorio Maggiore*** ➋, built in 1079 over an earlier church, near a cemetery. Opening onto the portico that was added in the 16th century is the 14th-century frescoed

Spoleto 1 : 12 500 (1 cm = 125 m)

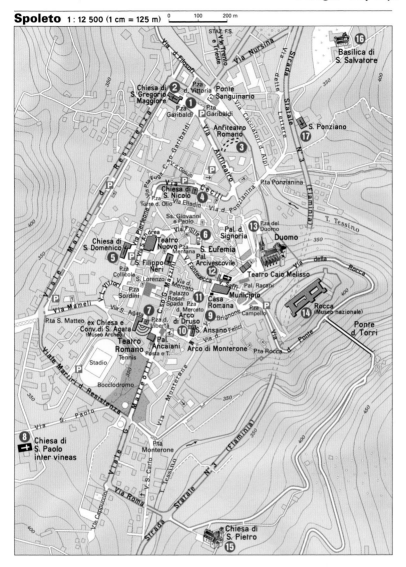

chapel of the Innocenti, whereas the mighty bell tower (12C) was erected in the late 15th century. Medieval frescoes adorn the interior walls. Built in the 2nd century outside the perimeter wall, the **Anfiteatro romano/Roman amphitheater** ❸ was probably built with two tiers of arches, as you can see from the remains of broad sections of the structure's outer covered passageway. In the Middle Ages, this area was occupied by the former *monasteries of the Madonna della Stella* and *San Gregorio Minore* or *del Palazzo*, which has two impressive cloisters: one late-medieval and the other late-16th century.

The Stella monastery church, dedicated to *Ss. Stefano e Tommaso*, dates from the late 18th century. At the beginning of tree-lined **Via Cecili** you can see the tall polygonal apse of the 14th century **chiesa di S. Nicolò/church of S. Nicolò** ❹, which you can access via the steep, cobbled Salita della Misericordia. Erected in 1304 at the same time as the Augustinian monastery, today, its interior houses a convention center and an exhibition hall. Having returned to Via Cecili and passed the *church of the Misericordia*, an oratory belonging to the Augustinian complex above, you can see

The outer portico of the Roman amphitheater.

an impressive section of the first **town walls**, and the tower built to defend a postern. If you look carefully, you will notice three layers of different wall-building techniques: large limestone blocks form the most ancient stratum (4C BC); above that is a squared buttressing section dating from 241 BC; and then elongated rectangular sections dating from restoration work carried out in the 1st century BC. The **Piazza Torre dell'Olio** is overlooked by a secondary facade of **Palazzo Vigili**, a combination of 13th- and 16th-century structures, including the tall, slender *Torre dell'Olio*. Continuing beyond the square through *Via Pierleone*, which has a characteristic medieval tower with megalithic stone walls, we reach a tree-lined square overlooked by the Dominican **chiesa di S. Domenico/church of S. Domenico** ⑤, which was built in the 13th and 14th century. In 1915, the Franciscans took over the church and restored its Gothic interior. This involved removing its 17th-century decoration and altars. The first altar features an important early 15th-century fresco (**Triumph of St Thomas Aquinas**); the frescoes in the St Mary Magdalene chapel date from the same period. Similarly noteworthy is a silver *reliquary* (1726), supposed to contain a nail from the Holy Cross, which, according to tradition, was brought here by the Blessed Gregorio. The underlying *crypt* is decorated with 14th- and 15th-century frescoes. As with other squares in the city, **Piazza Collicola** results from the nobility's desire to create areas suited to the prestige of their residents. The square is, in fact, dominated by the grand **Palazzo**

Collicola (1737), rich in artworks and now the seat of the **Galleria Civica d'Arte Moderna**. It has paintings and sculptures by artists of international renown. From the steps facing the palazzo it is a short walk to the former Romanesque **church of S. Lorenzo**, which conserves frescoes of the Umbrian School from the 15th and 16th centuries. Near **Via Filittèria** ⑥, paved in the 19th century, set back a little in Vicolo Corvino, stands the **church of Ss Giovanni e Paolo**, a plain 12th-century structure. The interior has one of the earliest representations of *St Francis* and a *Martyrdom of St Thomas Becket* (12C). After a bend with views, we come to **Palazzo Zacchei-Travaglini**. From here, proceed to *Via Walter Tobagi*, overlooked by **Palazzo Pianciani** (18C).

An impressive stairway links *Piazza Pianciani* to the Via di Fontesecca higher up, for which *Palazzo Leoncilli*, with its loggia and small balcony, provides a graceful backdrop. At the beginning of Corso Mazzini stands the **church of S. Filippo Neri**, with a grand travertine facade and a Roman-style dome. Its interior is enhanced by frescoes and an elegant 18th century sacristy. On **Corso Mazzini**, the first building we encounter is the former *monastery of the Filippini*. This area contains some of the town's earliest streets, such as Via del Mercato and the narrow *Via San Gregorio della Sinagoga*, where the Jewish community lived and worshipped. Especially interesting is the 20-meter long corridor of a Roman building, together with a mosaic-paved room, the purpose of which, however, remains a mystery. Almost at the end, on the right, Vicolo III leads down to *Palazzo Rosari-Spada* (17-18C), the first floor of which now houses the **Pinacoteca Comunale***. Highlights of the collection include a **Crucifix** on canvas fixed onto wood by an Umbrian painter of the late 12th century, and two painted **Crucifixes**, one dating from the 13th century, the other by the Maestro di Cesi (late 13-early 14C). There are two frescoes by Lo Spagna, especially the **Madonna and Child with Saints**, while 16th- and 17th-century works include a fine **Mary Magdalene**. There are also illuminated codices, gold- and silver-ware, and a selection of 19th-century paintings by local artists. Corso Mazzini ends at **Piazza della Libertà**, court of the noble Ancaiani family, once Umbria's most powerful landowners. In this square is **Palazzo Ancaiani** (late 17C), now the seat of the *Italian Center for Medieval Studies*. Not far away is the **chiesa di S. Agata/church of S. Agata** ❼, built as a Benedictine monastery at the end of the 14th century next to a *former church* of the same name (11C). The limited space afforded by the hillside inevitably meant that buildings had to be constructed on several levels. The monastery incorporated the medieval houses of the Corvi family, and now only the palazzo remains. Today the complex houses the **Museo Archeologico Nazionale**. Displayed in chronological order are rare Bronze Age finds from recent digs in the vicinity of the cave at Campello and the Rocca of Spoleto. The museum's Roman section (from the Republican to the Imperial period) features an interesting series of busts from the 1st to the 3rd centuries. Built within the town perimeter in the second quarter of the 1st century, the **Roman theater** was subsequently concealed and altered by the building of S. Agata, the houses of the Corvi family and the extension to the Benedictine

The Roman theater in Spoleto.

monastery (14-16C). The theater has been restored. Beyond the town walls, the **chiesa di S. Paolo inter Vineas/church of S. Paolo inter Vineas*** ❽ was rebuilt together with the convent in the 10th century and remodeled before 1234, when it was consecrated. Through its plain arched doorway you pass into the aisled interior, where the broad transept contains a cycle of 13th-century **frescoes** (depicting the *Prophets* and *Scenes from the Creation*).

This second itinerary explores the upper part of the town, where the most significant remains of the Roman town are situated, including the Arco di Druso (Arch of Drusus). The visit starts in **Via Brignone** ❾, a palimpsest of the town's history, dotted with the remains of dwellings and structures dating from Roman times, preserved in the basement of houses, and frequently reused since medieval times, and still being used even today. If you look inside one of the upper town's public buildings, you will see an unusual combination of architectural features. To the left, the street leads to *Piazza Fontana*, with its elegant 16th-century *fountain*. Nearby is the **Arco di Monterone** (3C BC), the massive limestone blocks of which span the street of the same name. Further on, *Arco delle Felici* is another structure built with huge blocks featuring fragments which possibly date from the 4th century. The **church of S. Ansano** was built in the 12th century above an earlier oratory dedicated to Sts Isaac and Martial (7C). The oratory was built above part of the Roman forum. The church was renovated in the late 18th century. In the side of the church, you can see sections of the earlier building. A stairway to the left of the main altar leads down to a Roman temple and the crypt of St Isaac. The **temple** was probably built by the second half of the 1st century along the south side of the *forum*, and, according to a traditional layout, comprised a *cella* preceded by a four-columned portico. The **crypt of St Isaac*** dates from the 12th century. Built on a rectangular plan, it has columns with roughly-hewn capitals and interesting fresco fragments on the walls. Yet another tangible remain of Roman Spoleto is the **Arco di Druso/Arch of Drusus*** ❿. It was the monumental entrance to the *forum*, built in the year 23 in honor of Drusus

Spoleto: the Duomo and above, the Rocca.

Minor and Germanicus (the son and nephew of Tiberius) and was covered over in the Middle Ages. The arch is simply decorated with pillars topped with Corinthian capitals. On the left-hand side of *Via dell'Arco di Druso*, which is a Roman street, is *Palazzo Leti* (17C). Beyond *Palazzo Parenzi*, another 17th-century palazzo set slightly back from the road, we are in the heart of the Roman town. The fact that, in the Middle Ages, **Piazza del Mercato ⓫** was still called Piazza del Foro, sheds light on the importance of this area over the centuries, even if, after the intensive building phase during the Middle Ages, very little remains of its broad Roman perimeter wall. The ornate **Fonte di Piazza**, in the Romanesque style, dates from 1746-48 (its coats-of-arms belonged to a previous structure of 1626). The charm of **Via del Palazzo dei Duchi** stems from the medieval-looking shops on either side. They actually date from the 16th century, when the arcades beneath the surviving bays of the church of S. Donato were converted into shops. Goods are still displayed on the original display counters. To the left stands the *Casa Spiga* (14C). Via del Palazzo dei Duchi intersects with **Via Fontesecca**, site of the *Casa dei Maestri Comacini*, with its characteristic pointed-arch doors and arched windows. Passing a number of aristocratic dwellings, renovated between

the 15th and the 16th century, we move towards the cathedral and the fortress. To the right, Via di Visiale affords access to a **Roman house** below the 20th-century Palazzo Comunale. This was a wealthy 1st-century residence looking onto the *forum*. The rooms are arranged in the usual way around a central *atrium* with an *impluvium*, with wings on either side and *cubicula* and a raised *triclinium* opposite the *tablinum*. The remains of the black and white floor mosaics with their geometric motifs show that it was a wealthy household. At the **Palazzo Arcivescovile/Bishop's Palace ⓬**, beyond the 16th-century portico, is the **Museo Diocesano**. Its collection includes many interesting exhibits of religious and historical interest, including a **bust of Pope Urban VIII** by Bernini (1640). Beyond the Sala del Passetto, where there is a display of 17th-century silverware and liturgical vestments, is the **Basilica of S. Eufemia***, which seems even more solemn and splendid when seen from the matroneums, or women's galleries, high above the nave. The church dates from the 10th century but was made wider in the 12th century. The interior is composed of a nave and side-aisles separated by columns and pillars using material from classical and early-medieval buildings. The marble altar is decorated with an **altar-piece** (13C) in the same material, with ornate Cosmatesque decoration and *reliefs*.

Piazza del Duomo* ⓭ has fine views of the cathedral. On the right-hand side is the 15th-century *Casa Fabricolosi* and a *sarcophagus* featuring a hunting scene (3C), which has been converted into a fountain. To the left, the red and white molded stone slabs of the *Casa dell'Opera del Duomo* (1419) and the small but elegant **Teatro Caio Melisso**. The following (former) **church of S. Maria della Manna d'Oro** was built on an octagonal plan in 1527, with Bramantesque influences, and was completed in 1681. Today, it is used for exhibitions. The Romanesque **Duomo****, erected in the late 12th century upon former S. Maria del Vescovato (8-9C), immediately catches the eye when you enter the square. You cannot fail to admire the large rose windows gracing the facade, surrounded by *symbols of the Evangelists*. Equally remarkable is the

Spoleto: Duomo

ELEVATION

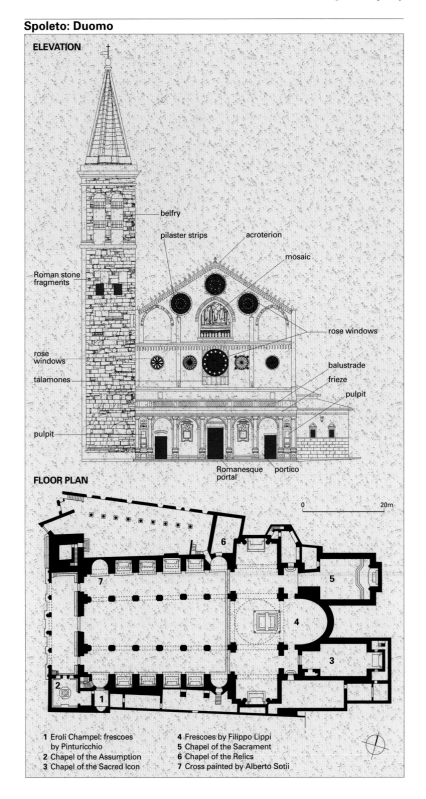

belfry

pilaster strips

acroterion

mosaic

Roman stone fragments

rose windows

rose windows

balustrade

talamones

frieze

pulpit

pulpit

Romanesque portal

portico

FLOOR PLAN

0   20m

6

7

5

4

3

2

1

1 Eroli Champel: frescoes by Pinturicchio
2 Chapel of the Assumption
3 Chapel of the Sacred Icon
4 Frescoes by Filippo Lippi
5 Chapel of the Sacrament
6 Chapel of the Relics
7 Cross painted by Alberto Sotii

majestic Byzantine-style mosaic (*Christ Giving the Blessing between the Virgin and St John*), dated 1207, located in the central blind arch of the upper tier. Completing the picture, to the left, stands the massive **bell tower**, built in the 12th century, with material recovered from Roman structures. The magnificent Romanesque **doorway***, with its impressive jambs and architrave decorated with a vine-leaf motif, and preceded by an elegant Renaissance portico, leads into the Latin-cross interior and to the semi-circular apse, which was extensively modified (17C).

The nave conserves most of the original 12th-century floor mosaic. On the right is the *Eroli chapel*, with frescoes by Pinturicchio (**God the Father with Angels**, the **Virgin and Child with Sts John the Baptist and Stephen***, and a *Pietà* on the front of the altar). The chapel is connected to the nearby frescoed *chapel of the Assumption*, by a vaulted chamber which was which was supposed to hold the tombs of the Eroli family. The **frescoes of the Life of the Virgin**** adorning the *apse* (1467-69) by Frà Filippo Lippi are truly magnificent. In the left aisle, the *chapel of Relics* (1540) houses a **Virgin and Child**, a finely crafted polychrome wooden sculpture (early 14C) and a rare autographed letter (to Brother Leone) from St Francis. At the beginning of the aisle is the **Crucifix***, a splendid painting on canvas fixed to a wooden panel dating from 1187. The *priest's house* contains the **Archive**, a collection of important documents and codices. From here, you can visit the **crypt of St Primianus**, a rare example of a semi-circular crypt containing fresco fragments from the same period.

To the left of the Caio Melisso theater, a brief detour from Via del Duomo takes you to Via dello Spagna, where recent restoration work has unearthed a **deambulatory** dating from the period of (1C), and consisting of a curved passageway approximately 30m long with a sharp bend and imposing arches overlooking the valley. The vast sloping **Piazza Campello** stretches from the walled city to the Rocca. The trees planted in the 20th century have altered the square's original perspective, concealing its complex access routes. On it stands the former **church of**

The huge Ponte delle Torri, near Spoleto.

Ss Simone e Giuda. Next to it is the *Fontana del Mascherone* (1763). **Palazzo Campello** (1597-1600) was erected on the site of medieval buildings belonging to the noble family after which it is named. At the top of Piazza Campello is the lane leading to the **Rocca/Fortress*** ⑭.

In 1359, Cardinal Albornoz decided to erect a castle here as a stronghold of papal power. The architect entrusted with this task was Matteo di Giovannello, known as 'Gattapone'. He designed a massive rectangular structure with six towers. It was divided into two quadrangles by an imposing wing, with the parade ground to the north and the courtyard of honor to the south. The fortress contains remarkable painted decoration dating from the late 14th to 18th centuries, including the **Camera Pinta**, inside the main tower, a room entirely frescoed with scenes of chivalry and courtly love. The rooms of the first and second floors looking onto the courtyard of honor will house the **Museo Nazionale di Spoleto**. The collection, which is displayed in chronological order and according to particular topics, includes inscriptions and archaeological finds from Late Antiquity to the late Middle Ages, previously on display in the Museo Civico. The display will also include fresco cycles detached from the church of S. Paolo inter Vineas (12-13C) and the former monastery of Palazze (late 13C), and a group of altar-pieces dating from the 12th to the 15th centuries, now on display in the Pinacoteca Comunale.

A splendid walk starts from Piazza Campello and proceeds down **Via del Ponte**, flanked by a stretch of polygonal Roman walls. First we pass an open area with marvelous *views* of forest-covered Monteluco, and then the breathtaking **Ponte delle Torri***, which joins the Rocca to the hill of Monteluco spanning a deep gorge. 76m tall and 230m wide, with its nine pillars connected by ten arches, this imposing limestone structure dominates the valley. The function of this bridge-cum-aqueduct (whose date of construction is set roughly between the 13C and 14C) was to convey water to the upper part of the town and to the Rocca, while at the same time providing access to Monteluco and to the small Mulini fortress. Its two tallest towers (hence the name) are hollow: one consists of two superimposed rooms with windows, and the other contains a room with an arched doorway, and was probably a former guard post. Leaving the city by Porta Monterone, along Via San Carlo, we cross the Tessino River and the main road. From here there is a magnificent view of the Rocca and the bridge-acqueduct. Steps lead up to a 5th-century panoramic terrace and the **chiesa di S. Pietro/church of S. Pietro* ⑮**, built by Bishop Achilleus to house a relic from the chains used to bind St Peter. The facade, which dates from the reconstruction of the 12th and 13th century, is a masterpiece of Umbrian Romanesque sculpture. Magnificent **reliefs**** adorn the three bands of the facade. Above the central doorway is a

horseshoe-shaped tympanum flanked by two eagles. The door-jambs and the architrave feature ornamentation of a more classical type, with two small side columns, and stylized animal and geometric motifs alternating with pairs of symbolic reliefs. The church's aisled interior, restructured in 1699, features a 15th-century votive fresco on the entrance wall portraying the patron kneeling in prayer. From Piazza della Vittoria take the road that leads to Norcia. Having crossed the Tessino River, you come to the so-called **Basilica di S. Salvatore* ⑯**. This is a most interesting early Christian structure (late 4C-early 5C), which has preserved its original (and very rare) architectural features – similar to those of the Tempietto del Clitunno, a blend of classical and oriental motifs. The lower level of its **facade*** has three marble doorways decorated with floral motifs, while the upper level is decorated with three broad windows. The central window is surmounted by an arch, while the ones on either side have tympanums. Its narrow nave and aisles, divided by Doric columns, produce a marked sense of verticality. The quadrilateral plan of the presbytery is quite separate from the nave, the ceiling of which has preserved its original beamed structure. At its four corners are pairs of tall grooved Corinthian columns. The central portion of the apse features a fresco of a monogrammed and jeweled cross, dating from the previous layer of decoration. The top of the apse is decorated with fresco fragments (13C) and there is a 16th-century *Crucifixion*. According to tradition, the **chiesa di S. Ponziano/church of S. Ponziano ⑰** stands on the site where St Ponzianus, the patron saint of Spoleto, was buried in 175 AD. The saint is depicted in the town's crest on horseback with a crossed shield (in a niche of the arch at the entrance to the monastery). The jambs on either side of the doorway are supported by two *lions* resting on Roman urns. The rose windows above the doorway (parts of which are missing) are encircled by *symbols of the Evangelists*. A room in its interior houses a *sarcophagus* from the early-Christian cemetery on the site. In the *crypt* are three other sarcopha-gi also from the ancient cemetery, and some 14th- and 15th-century votive *paintings*.

Reliefs on the doorway of S. Pietro, in Spoleto.

The famous ascent of **Monteluco**, which is particularly worth doing for its wonderful views, has the added attraction of visiting the Romanesque **church of S. Giuliano** (12C) and the **sanctuary of Monteluco**, which contains an oratory where St Francis used to pray. The woods below are dotted with magnificent viewpoints and small caves with a mystical atmosphere which evoke the ancient holy aura of this area.

Finally, the **fortified villages** dotted around the area between the fertile plain of the Maroggia Stream and the Martani mountains deserve a mention. This part of Umbria is worth exploring not only for its beautiful landscape but also for its splendid historic and artistic heritage. Villages like **Pontebari, S. Brizio, Castel S. Giovanni, Castel Ritaldi, Montemartano, S. Angelo in Mèrcole** and **S. Giovanni di Baiano**.

TODI [45 km]

The town of Todi is extraordinary because of the way it conforms to the shape of the hillside on which it is built, and its fortifications, erected above the line of the olive-groves in a defensive position. The oldest part of Todi lies between the two peaks of the hill and is enclosed by the first set of walls. In the 13th and 14th centuries, the city grew politically and economically, which determined its expansion towards the outlying countryside, essentially along pre-existing access routes. As a result, four districts developed. Three of those districts lie within the third perimeter wall (1244) and constitute the medieval part of the town.

In this context of steep hills, the utterly flat **Piazza del Popolo** ❶ comes as a surprise, built as it is, above a series of huge Roman cisterns (open to the public). This was once the heart of the Roman town, which was much larger than it is today. When, in the 13th and 14th centuries, the area was redesigned, it was decided that this was to be the site of the buildings representing religious and civic power. In fact, at opposite ends of the square we have the cathedral and the three palaces of the town magistrates. The **public buildings** appeared during the 13th century, with the construction on the square's eastern side of **Palazzo del Popolo**, or *Palazzo del Comune*. One of Italy's most ancient public buildings, the part facing Piazza Garibaldi was begun in the Lombard style. Its present

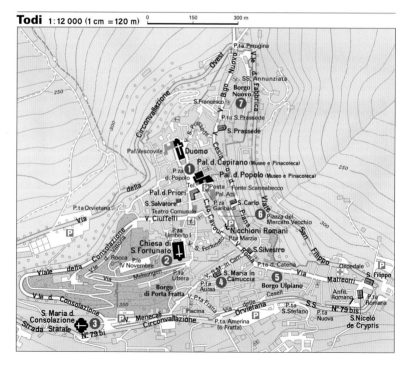

Todi 1:12 000 (1 cm = 120 m)

appearance is the fruit of restoration work carried out between the 19th and 20th centuries, when the structure was also topped with battlements. Set slightly further back, **Palazzo del Capitano***, also known as *Palazzo Nuovo*, was built in 1293. Its graceful Gothic facade is enhanced by a broad staircase connecting the two buildings, which currently

Medieval civic buildings in Todi.

house the Town Hall and the municipal museums. On the first floor of Palazzo del Capitano is the *Sala del Capitano del Popolo*, with fragments of 14th-century frescoes; opposite this lies the *Hall of the General Council* where a *Lapidarium* has been created, with displays of Roman inscriptions and architectural features. The top floor of the two palaces is taken up by the **Museo Pinacoteca**, where the municipal art collection is kept. Our visit begins with the *Museo della Città*, which illustrates the city's most significant historic events, from its legendary origins to the Risorgimento. Next is the *archaeological section*, the *numismatic collection*, the *fabric collection* and a section on *ceramics*, housed in the *Sala del Consiglio dei Priori*. Lastly, we come to a large hall housing the Pinacoteca, featuring an altar-piece by Lo Spagna (**Coronation of the Virgin, with Angels and Saints***, 1511). **Palazzo dei Priori*** stands on the shorter side of the square, opposite the cathedral. Originally built in the Gothic style, it was extended and completed in 1334-47 and altered again in 1513. The trapezoidal tower dates from 1369-85. Note the interesting fresco decoration in the *Sala delle Udienze*, built in about the 14th century. A grand travertine staircase leads up to the facade of the **Duomo****, begun in the 12th century and completed in the 14th century. It has a magnificent central **rose window***, begun in 1515 and completed a few years later. Note the huge carved wooden **door***. The

interior, with a nave and two aisles, has some fine *frescoes* and *panels*, and, hanging above the altar, a painted wooden **Crucifix*** of the Umbrian School (mid-13C). The **Cesi chapel** has frescoes on the ceiling dating from 1599. The *crypt*, also worth a visit, contains **three sculptures*** which originally adorned the facade. In a small courtyard behind the Duomo, the remains of an Imperial-age **Roman house** have been discovered, with a polychrome mosaic floor. On this side of the hill you can also see a stretch of the ancient city walls. Taking Via Rolli, which lies on the left of the cathedral, you come to the **Monastero delle Lucrezie**, which, from the cloister, affords one of the best views of the town.

In order to stress the importance of Todi's Franciscan settlement, the **chiesa di S. Fortunato/church of S. Fortunato*** ❷ was built in 1292 on the site of an existing church (1192).

Its facade, which remained unfinished (1415-58), has as its fulcrum the **main doorway***, with a pointed arch and sculptures decorating its outer frame. The interior, with a nave and two side aisles surmounted by cross-vaulting, contains a fresco fragment by Masolino da Panicale (**Virgin and Child with Angels***, 1432) and carved and inlaid wooden **choir-stalls*** (1590). The chapel of the Assumption (left aisle) is entirely decorated with **frescoes*** and paintings by Andrea Polinori. **S. Maria della Consolazione**** ❸ was erected by the outer (southwest) edge of the 13th-century walls, below the town. The church, with a central plan, was begun in 1508 and not completed until 1607. The Greek-cross plan of the church pivots around four apses, three of are which polygonal and the fourth semi-circular. Above is a terrace and, on the top, a very slender dome, for the size of the drum, flooding the interior with light. **S. Maria in Camuccia** ❹ is a church on two levels,

Todi: S. Maria della Consolazione

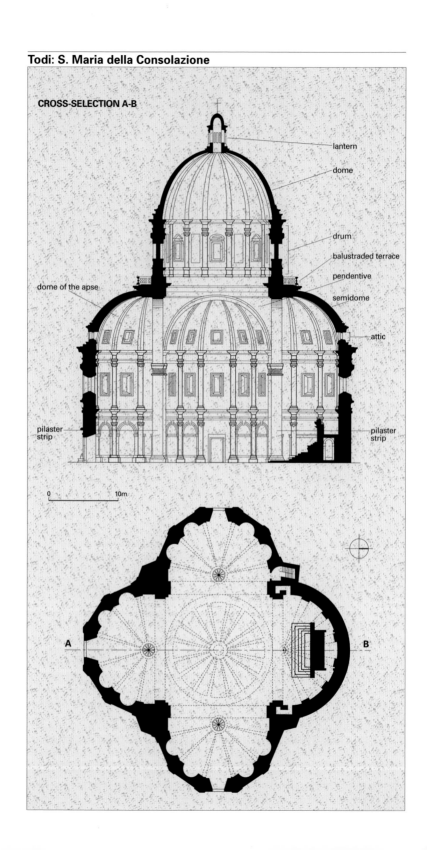

CROSS-SELECTION A-B

lantern

dome

drum

balustraded terrace

pendentive

dome of the apse

semidome

attic

pilaster
strip

pilaster
strip

0   10m

A   B

erected in the 7th-8th century and rebuilt in the 13th. It is the fulcrum of the *Camuccia district*, which stretches between the two Roman perimeter walls. The nave of the church contains a late-12th century wooden statue portraying the **Virgin and Child***. Branching off outside Porta Aurea, beyond the church, is the medieval **district of Porta Fratta**. Erected in the 13th-century between Porta Catena and Porta Romana, the **Ulpiano district** ❺ gravitates around the former **church of the Trinità**, which is now a museum. Another important building is the ancient **little church of S. Nicolò de Cryptis**, built in 1093 on the site of the Roman amphitheater. You can still see some of the remains of this imposing Roman building in the courtyard of the church. **Piazza del Mercato Vecchio** ❻ is dominated by the four so-called **Roman niches**. This monumental substructure was built in the late Republican and early Imperial periods. Beyond the *church of S. Carlo* (1112), you come to the **Fonte Scannabecco** (1241), comprising a portico supported by seven columns with capitals decorated in various styles. In the 13th century, the **Borgo Nuovo** ❼ district developed outside Porta S. Prassede, on a steep hill. The medieval buildings here were once occupied by craft workshops. At each end of the main road to Perugia, the street running through the district, is a religious complex. The *church of S. Francesco al Borgo* was annexed by the convent of the Poor Clares. Slightly further on is the **complex of the Santissima Annunziata**, with an *Annunciation* by Corrado Giaquinto. The street ends at *Porta Perugina*, the best preserved gateway in the town's third perimeter wall.

TREVI [50 km]

The road leading up to this town, perched on a hill overlooking the Spoleto plain has views over vast expanses of olive trees. From up here you only need to glance down to see the shape of the original town, where the 'lofty roofs' huddle in circles around the 'windy heights' described by the 19th-century Romantic poet Giacomo Leopardi. Below, the houses of the Piaggia district, built in the 13th and 14th centuries, fan out on the rocky terraced slopes surrounding the monastic buildings. On the beautiful

unspoiled mountain behind the town, olives are still produced in the traditional way, along with lime. Piazza Garibaldi is the edge of the medieval town, which has been awarded the TCI's "Bandiera Arancione". From the square, Via Roma quickly leads to centrally located Piazza Mazzini. From here, Via del Duomo climbs to the top of the hill, to the cathedral of S. Emiliano. This compact part of the town was the medieval nucleus, clustered around the cathedral. It was surrounded by a wall built at a 70-m radius from the Duomo. Cobble-stones and bricks pave the streets, forming very old traditional patterns. Leaving broad *Piazzale Garibaldi*, by following Via Roma you come to **Piazza Mazzini** ❶, by passing under an archway under the old town hall. This is the center of the town, dominated by **Palazzo Comunale**. An underpass leads to the *Torre del Comune*, a solid 13th-century construction. The hub of Trevi's most ancient settlement, the **chiesa di S. Emiliano/church of S. Emiliano** ❷ was built in the 12th and 13th century, and totally rebuilt in 1865, incorporating parts of the previous structures. The three small **apses*** of the Romanesque church are considered the most interesting structure of their kind in the region. The centerpiece of its aisled

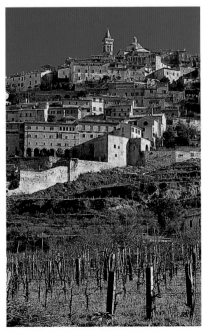

View of Trevi, with S. Emiliano at the top.

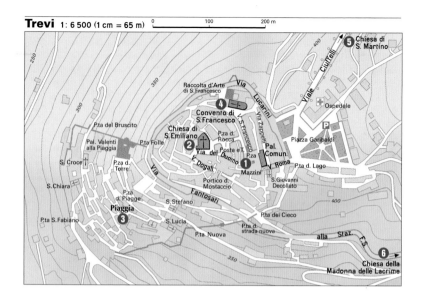

interior is the **altar of the Sacrament***, especially because of its extremely fine decorations (1522).

Facing S. Emiliano is the *Palazzo Lucarini* (15C). It houses the **Trevi Flash Art Museum**, used for contemporary art exhibitions. Periodically the museum's permanent collection is displayed, consisting of works by Italian and foreign artists, from the 1970s to the present. Narrow streets, winding downward below the city walls, descend to **Piaggia ❸**, an area which developed in the 13th century, enclosed by medieval walls and spreading out fan-fashion along the steep slope. As usual, churches constituted the area's first basic architectural reference points: the **church of S. Lucia**; on the western edge of the walls, the elliptical-plan **church of S. Chiara**; and, not far away, the Benedictine *church of S. Croce*. You come thus to *Piazza della Torre*. The main **palace** contains finds from Roman times and detached 14th-century frescoes. The former **convento di S. Francesco/ monastery of S. Francesco ❹**, documented in 1285, has undergone numerous modifications. Having been abandoned by the monks, the church was turned into a municipal grainstore. The entire complex has been restored and converted into a museum that hosts also the **Raccolta d'Arte S. Francesco** and the Pinacoteca Civica. Its collection comprises paintings by local artists (from the 15-18C), archaeological finds, sculptures

and documents pertinent to the city's history. Highlights include the **Coronation of the Virgin with Angels, St Francis and others saints*** by Lo Spagna. In the church there is a *Crucifix* (early 14C) and a fine Renaissance *organ* (1509). Along tree-lined pedestrian *Viale Ciuffelli*, which has wonderful *views* over the valley, a 10-minute walk from Piazza Garibaldi takes you to the site of the old parish church (Pieve) of Trevi, where the Friars Minor erected the **chiesa di S. Martino/church of S. Martino ❺** in the late 15th century. On the opposite side of the square is the **chapel of St Jerome** (1512), which contains one of Lo Spagna's best frescoes (1512) and the **Assumption of the Virgin** by Orbetto. From here, a road winds down through olive trees to the **chiesa della Madonna delle Lacrime/church of the Madonna delle Lacrime ❻, (off map)** (1487-1522) which was built to house a miraculous image of the Madonna, painted in 1483. Its vast and light-filled interior contains frescoes and an **Epiphany of Sts Peter and Paul*** by Il Perugino (1521), and a chapel decorated by Lo Spagna (1520). If you take the main road in the direction of Foligno, you come to the **church of S. Maria di Pietrarossa**: inside and out, this church is covered with votive frescoes, painted by Bartolomeo da Miranda (1449), Valerio de' Muti da Foligno (1477) and other contemporary painters from the Foligno area. Here the valley narrows.

After the octagonal *Chiesa Tonda* (16C), on your right is an elegant early-Christian structure dedicated to the Holy Savior, and better known as the **Tempietto del Clitunno***. There is clear evidence of the elements that were part of the typical pagan *sacella* (cult sites with altars to pagan deities). The frieze decorating the facade bears a dedicatory inscription to the God of angels.

With the *Castello di Passignano* on your left, you come to the **Fonti del Clitunno***: pools of crystal-clear, cold water form a small, placid lake dotted with verdant islets whose grassy shores are planted with weeping willows.

UMBÈRTIDE [34 km]

At the point where the Reggia flows into the Tiber River, set among hills scattered with remains of medieval fortifications, lies Umbèrtide. The town was named after Uberto, son of Ugo, an Italian king, who founded it in the 10th century.

Piazza Mazzini, the very core of the historic center, extends beyond the city walls, overlooked by the Rocca (fortress) and the *collegiate church of S. Maria della Reggia*, completed in the mid-17th century. What remains of the **Rocca** is a square tower, two round towers and a third bastion, in the part of the Rocca dating from 14th-century and 15th-century. This now place an important role in the cultural life of the town. Now the *Centro per l'Arte Contemporanea*, it often holds exhibitions. The central **Piazza Matteotti**, linked to Piazza Mazzini by short and narrow Via Stella, is the heart of this walled town. The 17th-century *Palazzo Comunale*, decorated inside with paintings and sculpture, dates from the late 17th century. The **borgo inferiore** (lower town) focuses on the oblong *Piazza San Francesco*, the most ancient and characteristic of the city's squares, with three churches on one side. The baroque *church of S. Croce* (16-17C) has been turned into the *Museo Civico*, and houses, among other works, Luca Signorelli's **Deposition** (1516), executed for this church and placed in a wooden frame in 1612, and a *Virgin and Child in Glory* by Pomarancio (1577). This painting comes from the adjoining 14th-century *church of S. Francesco*, which has a doorway with a three-lobed arch. A short detour into the northern part of the town leads to the **church of S. Maria della Pietà** (1486), which has a lunette above the doorway with a fresco attributed to Pinturicchio or Bartolomeo Caporali.

Il Perugino, *Epiphany*, 1521 (church of the Madonna delle Lacrime, near Trevi).

TERNI

The dual face of Terni, industrial center and historic town, began to develop in the last two decades of the 19th century, when the arrival of large manufacturing firms and hydroelectric power production of national importance earned it the nickname "the Manchester of Italy". The small town on the right bank of the Nera River was soon dwarfed by sprawling working-class districts on the left bank. A competition was launched for a new development plan. The deindustrialization process of recent years has halted the urban sprawl and focused attention on the historic quarters, on the older industrial areas, on the area's small towns and villages, and on environmental quality.

TERNI
IN OTHER COLORS...

■ **ITINERARIES:** pages 102, 104, 121
■ **FOOD:** pages 129, 136, 141
■ **SHOPPING:** pages 153, 154, 155
■ **EVENTS:** pages 160, 164
■ **WELLNESS:** pages 168, 170
■ **PRACTICAL INFO:** pages 185, 186

Cattedrale dell'Assunta/Cathedral dedicated to the Assumption ❶

The church, remodeled in the 15th century, enlarged in the 16th century, and extensively renovated before being reconsecrated in 1653, occupies the site of a former church dating from the 6th and 11th centuries, parts of which can be seen in the oratory-type crypt. The facade, with its balustrade and statues, has a fine late 12th-century doorway, with acanthus ornaments coiling

The elegant cathedral.

around animals. The interior with a nave and two side-aisles includes valuable art works and a superb 17th-century organ. The main chapel has a polychrome altar by Antonio Minelli (1762) with a grand tabernacle. The aisled and apsidal *crypt* is the burial place of St Anastasius, bishop of Terni; the *treasury* is also interesting.

Palazzo Rosci, a very interesting 16th-century palace opposite the cathedral, based on Roman models, has a rusticated doorway, a beautiful band of Angevin lilies, high windows on the *piano nobile* and a fine cornice. The decorations in the remarkable ground-floor hall, whose cloister vault is frescoed with grotesques, medallions and fine stucco cornices, depict *Allegories of the Arts and Sciences and Mythological Scenes*, partly repainted in the second half of the 16th century.
The fountain with travertine statues (representing the *Velino* and *Nera* rivers) by Corrado Vigni was added in 1935. Near the cathedral are the remains of the **Roman amphitheater**, built in 32 AD by Faustus Titius Liberal. It can be seen both in the curve of Via del Vescovado and in the remains of two-tone *opus reticulatum* wall facing, which survived the construction of the *Bishop's Palace* – enlarged in the 15th century – over the amphitheater.

Palazzo Gazzoli ❷

Located just off *Via XI Febbraio*, the former Via delle Carrozze and second main thoroughfare in Terni after the streets along the line of the original Via Flaminia, this palace was built for the future cardinal Luigi Gazzoli in 1795 to a design by Andrea Vici, who created a unified whole out of a number of existing buildings. Two rooms on the *piano nobile* have decorations with grotesques and *Scenes of Aurora* and

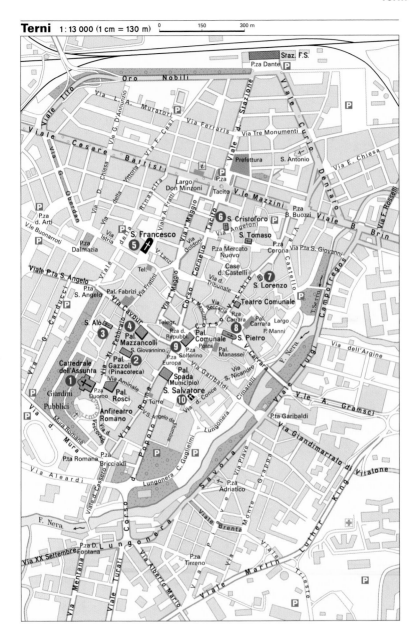

Terni 1 : 13 000 (1 cm = 130 m)

the Sun Chariot. An apsidal bathing pool found in the courtyard is believed to have been part of a Roman bath-house. A side-entrance to the theater was discovered in the stables.

The rooms of the palace now house the **Pinacoteca Comunale**, whose collection of artworks, mainly from abolished religious institutes, span the period from the late 14th to the

19th centuries. The finely decorated rooms display in chronological order such works as the **Crucifixion with Sts Francis and Bernardine of Siena*** by Alunno (1497) and a **Mystic Marriage of St Catherine*** by Benozzo Gozzoli (1466). One room has works by Orneore Metelli, a naïf painter from Terni, who worked between 1922 and 1938. The collection also includes works of contemporary art by Picasso, Severini, Chagall, Mirò and others. Palazzo Gazzoli also houses interesting *archaeological* finds from the excavations in the Terni area.

Sant'Alò* ❸

The name of this church, probably built in the 11th century, is a corruption of the name Aloysius, the patron saint of goldsmiths and blacksmiths. In the 18th century it passed into the hands of the Knights of Malta, who were based in the fine *house* built next to the Romanesque facade in the 14th century. Pillars and columns with interesting capitals divide the interior into a nave and two aisles; the aisles and the arch preceding the apse have unusual barrel vaulting.

The walls and apse were *frescoed* between the 12th century and the 15th and 16th centuries. At the end of Via XI Febbraio is a palazzo with a fine example of a 15th-century courtyard and loggia: *Palazzo Alberici.*

Palazzo Mazzancolli ❹

This very fine example of medieval architecture stands at the point where Via Cavour widens out into a small square. Built by Bishop Ludovico Mazzancolli in the 15th century over existing towers, it was restored in 1878 and again in 1927.

The nearby **church of Santa Croce** contains an altarpiece of the *Invention of the True Cross* attributed to the Giacinto Brandi circle and other valuable paintings.

Palazzo Fabrizi, whose 16th-century structures (including the elegant inner courtyard) were remodeled in the 18th century, stands on the corner of Via Cavour and Via Fratini.

The 18th-century doorway in the fine facade overlooking Via Fratini was altered by recent cement plaster work. The decorations on the *piano nobile* date back to the second half of the 18th century.

The Mystic Marriage of St Catherine, by B. Gozzoli.

San Francesco ❺

This church (1265) originally had a nave and transept in the Franciscan basilica style. Two aisles were added in 1437, together with the chapel of St Bernardine (destroyed during World War II air raids). Remodeling in the 17th century, repairs following the 1703 earthquake and far-reaching restoration in the 19th and 20th centuries, especially after wartime destruction, can be seen quite clearly on the facade, the central section of which has a Gothic doorway with an oculus above. The side walls, added in the 15th century, have doorways from that period and Gothic windows; the elegant campanile with two- and four-light Gothic windows is by Angelo da Orvieto. Inside there is a rare painting of the *Blessed Simone Camporeali* (early 14C), one of the original founders of the Franciscan community in Terni. The **Paradisi chapel*** has walls frescoed with scenes based on Dante's *Divine Comedy* (second quarter of 15C). The furnishings include a reliquary (late -15C and early -16C) made to contain a fragment of the Holy Cross. From Piazza San Francesco, Via del Leone leads to the **church of S. Marco**, whose frescoes include a *Crucifixion*, an *Our Lady of Mercy* and depictions of *saints*, dated between 1464 and 1468. The **Virgin and Child** fresco, near the high altar (in polychrome stucco), is regarded as one of Bartolomeo da Miranda's masterpieces; the frame dates from the 17th century.

From the church, crossing Via Lanzi at the corner with Via Goldoni, we reach the 16th-century **Palazzo Paglia** with an interesting Renaissance courtyard with loggias and 17th-century grotesques. The doors leading off from the entrance are late 15th-century; the portico is later and has three tiers on the entrance side of the small courtyard (the top level, made of wood, dates back to the 19C).

San Cristoforo ❻

This 13th-century church, built with spoil material and restored after being badly damaged in the last war, is divided into an ancient church and a modern one. Inside are Roman stone fragments from a nearby cemetery.

San Lorenzo ❼

Built over a probable Roman edifice in the 11th-12th centuries, and enlarged in the 17th century, this church has two three-light windows and a blind doorway dated 1492. Inside are two naves on different levels.
Almost opposite the church stand the **Case dei Castelli**, which can be accessed from the *Arco di S. Lorenzo*. Much of the medieval character of the area was lost during World War II. Only *Torre Dionisia,* some mutilated houses (remodeled in 1500), and the principal *palace* (late 16C) remain.
A little further along Corso Vecchio is the **Teatro Comunale Giuseppe Verdi**, on the site of the ancient Palazzo dei Priori with a neoclassical pronaos. In Via del Tribunale (right) stands **Palazzo Giocosi**, later Palazzo Mariani (16-17C), now the home of the Briccialdi music school, which contains a hall beautifully decorated.

Piazza Carrara ❽

The most noteworthy building in this square is **Palazzo Carrara** – which underwent extensive demolition and redevelopment work in the 20th century – an amalgamation of the medieval houses dating from 14th century and later, belonging to the Carrara family. The rooms on the *piano nobile*, most notably the *Room of Apollo and Daphne*, were decorated in the second half of the 17th century. Today the palace houses the **Biblioteca Civica (Civic library)**, whose collection includes some incunabula; the oldest are a text from 1472 and a *Breviarium Romanum* (1476-77), manuscripts and a collection of parchments. Close by, the **church of S. Pietro** has a Gothic doorway decorated with a 15th-century relief

(*Christ giving the Blessing*); the single broad nave contains fragments of frescoes dating from late 14th and early 15th century, which came to light during postwar restoration. There is also an interesting **Dormition of the Virgin with a Coronation of the Virgin** (14-15C). Nearby stands **Palazzo Manassei**, built in the 17th century in the street of the same name. The palace is in the typical style of noble buildings of Terni, based on the best-known Roman models, with a broad entrance for carriages, an inner courtyard and a fountain positioned so as to be visible from the main doorway. The rooms of the *piano nobile* are decorated with frescoes.

Main squares ❾

The center of Terni is a complex, disjointed system of squares and open spaces which together form a single and large urban area. Known as Piazza Maggiore in medieval times, today's **Piazza della Repubblica** remains the hub of town life. This square, which lost some of its unity with the creation of Corso Tacito, is closed on the north side by the elegant *Palazzo Manni*, while on the southeast side stands the old City Hall, or *Palazzo Comunale Vecchio*, rebuilt in the Renaissance style in 1878, by Benedetto Faustini. The ground floor still has remnants of the earlier 14th-century building. A 17th-century niche with an unusual fresco (*two cherubs*, one holding a lance, the other a sponge, beside a cross with the nails of Christ's martyrdom) has been opened to the left of the main entrance.

A view of the variously-colored countryside around Terni.

The work has been interpreted as a *signum pietatis*, or sign of piety, placed on the site where public executions took place.

Today the palace is a cultural center, housing, amongst other things, a multimedia library. On the left, before the adjacent Piazza Europa, on the south side of **Piazza Solferino**, stands the fine *Palazzo Montani*. It has rooms decorated by Girolamo Troppa with mythological, biblical, and literary scenes, and a loggia frescoed in 1624.

In the large, rectangular **Piazza Europa** stands **Palazzo Spada***, begun in the mid-16th century and completed in 1576 to a design by Sallustio Peruzzi.

The palace, now the town hall, was the first private monumental building in the town to have a courtyard. On the *piano nobile*, the so-called *Phaeton Room* is decorated with a cycle of frescoes (1575-76).

The decorations in the three adjacent rooms are attributed to Sebastiano Flori, a pupil of Vasari, and his assistants (1575-80). Remains of a mosaic floor belonging to a Roman *domus* have been found in the vicinity of the palace.

San Salvatore ⑩

Tradition has it (though the event is undocumented) that Lombard King Liutprand and Pope Zacharias met in this church, which now dominates the square overlooked by the eastern facade of Palazzo Spada. This interesting building has a circular body with rectangular apse and front section. Opening off from the 12th-century two-bay nave (a typical feature of the Umbrian Romanesque style) is the *Manassei chapel*, a 14th-century addition decorated with an interesting cycle of frescoes, probably from the middle of that century.

The present-day sacristy was formerly the 17th-century Filerna chapel, decorated with frescoes by Andrea Polinori and Ludovico Carosi.

An obelisk – 30 m high and in cast iron – stands on the crossroads between Viale C. Gugliemi and Corso del Popolo. It was created by Arnaldo Pomodoro to celebrate the centenary of the steelworks, and immediately became a symbol of industrial Terni.

ABBAZIA DI SAN PIETRO IN VALLE/ABBEY OF SAN PIETRO IN VALLE [22 km]

The hillock of Mt Solenne, on which the abbey stands, was chosen as the location of a hermits' retreat in 720, when Faroaldo II, Duke of Spoleto, retired to this place, and founded a nucleus of the Benedictine order. After the destruction wrought by the Saracens (end 9C), Otto III launched a restoration campaign (996), which was brought to its conclusion by his successor, Enrico III.

The present building is the result of renovations carried out in the 1930s, and comprises a very wide single hall with a trussed ceiling, rather reminiscent of models such as Cluny II and St Michael's church at Hildesheim. The imposing *bell tower*, dated to the second half of the 11th century (the same period as the sculptures of *Sts Peter and Paul* that grace the southern door) harks back to Roman models, with Lombard influences.

In 1995 work was completed on the restoration of the **cycle of frescoes*** that decorate the nave, considered one of the most magnificent testaments to Romanesque art in Italy (late 12-early 13C). The cycle is arranged on four registers: the first three with scenes from the Old and New Testaments; the last, badly damaged, probably depicted ornamental elements and votive imagery; each scene is set in a simulated frame with small, twisted columns, and commented by a *titulus*.

The central apse is occupied by a huge fresco on three registers, attributed to the Maestro di Eggi (ca. 1445).

The **high altar*** is a rare example of Lombard mastery by Ursus Magester. In the right transept lies the so-called **sarcophagus of Faroaldo II***, a Roman urn (mid-3C BC), in which the church's founder was supposedly buried. At the back of the transept, the other sarcophagi also date from the 3rd century BC.

The ex-monastery, now privately owned, has been converted into a hotel and conference center.

HERITAGE

AMELIA [24 km]

Attractively situated on a limestone knoll between the Tiber and Nera valleys, the town of Amelia has been inhabited since the times of the ancient Umbri.

The historic center, with its array of fine architecture from Romanesque times to the 18th century, is one of the most interesting in the whole of southern Umbria. The atmosphere of the town is enhanced by the splendid surrounding countryside, once celebrated for the medicinal properties of its apples, as well as for its pears and willow trees.

Porta Romana has always been the entrance to the walled town. To the sides, long stretches of the limestone *polygonal walls*★ (3C BC) can be seen. The **church of Ss. Filippo e Giacomo**, also known as the church of S. Francesco, dates back to 1287. In 1664, the nave was shortened and two side portions were added. Late-baroque modernization was completed in 1767. On the wall that was formerly the back of the facade are fragments of popular votive frescoes from the 15th century. The chapel of St Anthony contains *six tombs* of the Geraldini family. The adjacent former Collegio Boccarini houses the *Museo Archeologico Comunale,* whose collection consists mainly of stone sculptures and Roman remains. The museum collections also include an **art gallery** of works by Carlo Levi and Corrado Cagli.

Palazzo Farrattini is the finest noble palace in Amelia and was built by Antonio da Sangallo the Younger in the mid-16th century for the Farattini family. Sangallo's design was only partly realized, thus sparing the large cistern from the Roman baths (it was transformed into a *viridarium*). Inside the building are two 2nd-century Roman bath mosaics

(not accessible to visitors), still in their original position. **Piazza Marconi** stands on the top of the hill, once occupied by the ancient acropolis. It was accessed through the present-day *Arco di Piazza*, a medieval archway made from the arches of an ancient construction over which was built the *Loggia del Banditore*★, with a sail-vaulted bell tower and an 17th-century clock. On the right-hand side of the square stands *Palazzo Petrignani*. The frescoes decorating the rooms on the *piano nobile* are by local craftsmen working under Livio Agresti. Those in the antechamber and the first three rooms are traditionally attributed to the Zuccari school. At the end of square is the 15th-century *Palazzo Nacci*, which has a fine doorway and courtyard with an elegant *loggetta*. **Piazza Matteotti** was built over a huge Roman cistern from the 1st century BC, divided into ten vaulted, communicating chambers and serving as a substructure for the forum above. Here stands *Palazzo Comunale* (Town Hall), renovated in the 18th century and preceded by a courtyard. The simple exterior belies the rich ornamentation of the interior, which includes a notable painted frieze (17C) in the Council Chamber, inspired by works by Raphael, Giulio Romano, and Giulio Campagnola.

Erected at the top of the ancient acropolis in the 11th-12th century, the **cathedral** was destroyed by fire in 1629 and completely rebuilt in 1640-80. Of the original structure only the massive twelve-sided campanile (1050) remains. To the right of the entrance is a Romanesque pillar, to which St Firmina, the patron saint of Amelia, is said to have been tied and martyred. The Oratory of the Sacrament contains two canvases by Niccolò Circignani and a

A splendid view of Amelia.

Last Supper by Giovan Francesco d'Amelia (1538). In the presbytery are frescoes of saints by Luigi Fontana dedicated to the town's protectors, whose relics are kept below the 1648 altar.

On the first Saturday of each month, in May and on 15 August, a painting by Maestro dell'Assunta (*Assumption of the Blessed Virgin*) is displayed in the transept on the left.

CARSULAE [15 km]

Originally a Roman junction serving the Via Flaminia Antica, the first settlement developed in the 3rd century BC after the building of the consular road that crosses the town from north to south, but the first settlement planned as a town dates from the Augustan period, when Carsulae became a *municipium* of the 6th Region. Its open spaces and public buildings directly overlooked the Via Flaminia, with the sole exception of the theater (or games) quarter which is slightly off-center. The water supply depended on a series of cisterns, wells, and conduits. The Visitors' Center at the archaeological site has a display of the main finds.

A visit to the area begins at the little *church of S. Damiano,* built in the 11th century with material from Roman remains, which can partly be seen along the church's left side and facade. From here, by walking along Via Flaminia, you reach the remains of the aisled and apsidal **basilica**; to the left, around the area of the forum are public and religious buildings. To the south, on a man-made platform, the foundation remains of two identical **twin temples**. Next to the access stairway to the temple is a small *arco quadrifrons* or *four-sided arch*, of which only one side has been raised. A stairway behind the temples leads down to the Via Flaminia (note the remains of *tabernae*) to the so-called **Arco di S. Damiano**, a monumental arched gateway with three openings, of which the central one is preserved. Immediately outside begins the area of the **monumental tombs**, two of which have been partially restored: one, circular with a dome, resting upon a square base; the other with a more vertical structure.

Crossing the grass and following the modern road, we reach the **spectacle area**: the *amphitheater* was built in a

Area Archeologica di Carsulae

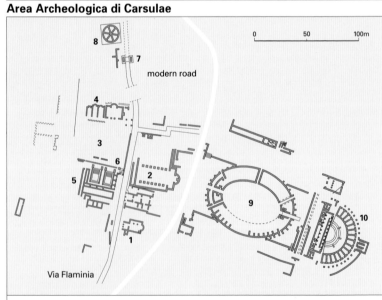

1 St Damian (11C, over Roman building)	**6** Four-sided arch
2 Basilica	**7** Arched gateway of St Damian
3 Forum	**8** Monumental sepulcher
4 Public Building	**9** Amphitheater
5 Twin temples	**10** Theater

The spectacular Màrmore Falls seen from the lower road.

natural depression of the terrain; in line with the latter lies the *theater*, of which the orchestra, the substructure of the cavea, and the stage foundations are still visible. Upon the summit, overlooking the Carsulae ruins from the east, rises the **Convento dell'Eremita**, founded on Roman remains by St Francis in 1213.

CASCATA DELLE MÀRMORE/ THE MÀRMORE FALLS [8 km]

This awe-inspiring "natural" spectacle was described even in Roman times and celebrated by travelers on the Grand Tour in the 18th and 19th centuries. The falls can be reached by either of two roads east of Terni (both sign-posted): the upper road (or "*Superiore*", 8 km), and the lower road (or "*Inferiore*", 7 km). An interesting road connects the lower road to the one higher up and passes a small loggia built in 1781 by the municipality of Terni. The **Osservatorio** enables visitors to have spectacular views of the falls without getting wet. The leap made by the Velino River here as it cascades down a precipice from the Màrmore plateau into the Nera River is, however, largely the work of man. In 271 BC, Roman consul Manius Curius Dentatus had a channel dug as a part of his land-reclamation scheme for the marshland around the Velino. The Cavus Curianus, as the channel was known, drained stagnant water from the river on the site of what is now the main waterfall. After endless bitter disputes between the populations of Rieti and Terni as to whether the channel should be closed or

merely diverted, the problem was partly solved by Antonio da Sangallo the Younger, who at the orders of Pope Paul III, dug the Pauline Channel. However, it was Domenico Fontana who made the Cavus Curianus deeper and who built a bridge that would limit the flow of the Velino River when it was in full spate. Finally, when the inhabitants of the Valnerina rebelled against the falls in the late 18C, at the orders of Pope Pius VI, Andrea Vici diagonally diverted part of the last leap. Today the foamy white mass of water makes three leaps, in a descent of some 165 meters.

FERENTILLO [18 km]

In a wooded gorge of great beauty at the mouth of the chasm known as Salto del Cieco (on the Nera River), stands Ferentillo, divided into two sections named Matterello and Precetto, of early medieval origin and closely bound to the abbey of S. Pietro in Valle. This ancient-looking town grew up in the valley bottom, but one can distinguish the two original settlements which built the fortifications on the mountainside. Close to Matterello stands the 13th-century parish **church of S. Maria**, rebuilt in the 16th century and altered in the 20th century, with interior decorations by Pierino Cesarei, Jacopo Siculo and Piermatteo Piergili.

The **church of S. Stefano** dominates from above Precetto, and is built on two levels: the lower one datable to the 13th-14th century, the upper to the

16th century (enlarged in the 18C). The crypt, which runs the full length of the building, after the construction of the upper story, was used as a burial ground. As the result of an extraordinary natural phenomenon, in the crypt of the church of S. Stefano, 30 m above the valley floor, the bodies of local people and foreigners who were buried here are preserved virtually intact. The floor of the crypt cemetery in which the bodies were buried is formed of a dry, porous sand, rich in nitrates, chlorides and calcareous salts which, combined with the continuous ventilation from the open windows facing southwest, contributed to the process of mummification. Around twenty cadavers lie in large cabinets around the walls and propped against the piers. Each mummy has a story behind it: one lost his life under the surgeon's knife; Sister Aurelia is still proudly dressed in her habit; and the two Chinese newlyweds who came here to drink the local water in the hope of a cure from the cholera contracted in Rome, where they had perhaps traveled for the Holy Year, and who died here in Ferentillo. The hill that rises behind Matterello is crowned by an impressive **Rocca** or fortress, with a bailey, cylindrical towers and a tall keep. Forming a counterbalance to the fort is another fort, situated on the crag overlooking Precetto.

NARNI [13 km]

The ancient town of Narni was built on a rocky spur overlooking the Nera gorge and the Terni valley for purposes of defense, and the town's development was largely dictated by the morphology of the site. This long, narrow town still has traces of the earliest Umbrian and Roman settlements in the north (the regular grid-pattern of streets), and the medieval layout (11-14C) of the Fraporta and Mezule districts. The fortress, a symbol of papal power built by Cardinal Albornoz, dominates the whole town. **Porta Ternana** ❶, part of the town's medieval fortifications, was rebuilt in the 15th century. Its rusticated arch is flanked by two sturdy towers. Beyond it, Via Roma leads up into the town with views over the Terni valley to **Piazza Garibaldi** ❷, dominated by the Duomo. This square was once called Piazza del Lago after the large medieval cistern, or *lacus*, built there on the site of a Roman cistern. Today it boasts a large *fountain*, rebuilt after 1527, with a 16th-century polygonal brick basin, and a 14th-century bronze pool decorated with animal-like figures. A narrow passage-way between the cathedral and the Bishop's Palace leads to the slightly higher *Piazza Cavour,* site of the cathedral and the edge of what was the Roman town. From Piazza Garibaldi the road leads up to the Mezule district, on the higher part of the rocky spur that ends at the castle. The panoramic route passes along Via del Monte and Via Cocceio Nerva, and takes in the **church of S. Margherita,** built in the early 17th century together with the Benedictine monastery, reserved for the nobility. The single-nave interior has stuccoes on the ceiling and frescoed walls. Via del Monte leads to the **Rocca*** or fortress, built in the second half of the 14th century by Cardinal Albornoz. Two elegant doorways lead into the delightful courtyard, which features an external staircase. Just below the castle is the *Fontana Feronia,* the site of a pre-Roman

Narni, the fortress.

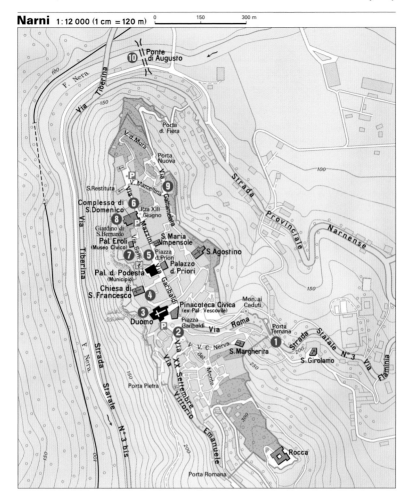

Narni 1:12 000 (1 cm = 120 m)

place of worship dedicated to the goddess Feronia, of which only an underground passageway to the natural spring survives. The **Duomo/ Cathedral*** ❸ stands on an early medieval necropolis – tombs dug out of the rock have been found under Piazza Cavour – from the time of the first bishop of the town, St Juvenal, to whom the cathedral is dedicated. Work on the building began in 1047 and continued for almost a century before the church was consecrated in 1145. In front of the simple, rectangular facade (transformed in the 14C) is an elegant portico with arches raised on columns. The main doorway dates from the 12th century. The large blocks of stone to the right of the portico are the remains of the Roman town walls. The basilica-style interior has

a nave divided from the two aisles by 16 columns with capitals in a variety of shapes and low arches. The left aisle was added between the 14th and 15th century to accommodate the **chapel of Sts Juvenal and Cassius***, more correctly referred to as the *tomb of the Bishops of Narni,* the front of which is divided into four orders of decorated pillars. Above the doorway is the *burial slab of Cassius and his wife Fausta* (558). The inner walls of the sanctuary, originally underground and thus hidden from view, are clad in slabs of marble, except for the wall on the left where several bishops are buried; on the back wall is a marble triptych from the above church (now destroyed), where St Juvenal was worshipped. The cave behind the altar contains the 8th-9th century *sarcophagus* which held the body of St Juvenal until 1642, when the new confessio was built below the altar. Above the entrance to the sacellum is a **Christ Giving the Blessing*** in a late 9th-century circular mandorla, flanked by frescoes of *saints*. In the south aisle are frescoes originally from the Romanesque church (12-13C) and a wooden **statue of St Anthony Abbot** (1474). The cathedral **bell tower*** can be seen from Via del Campanile, behind the church. This sturdy bell tower was built over Roman fortifications: the lower limestone part is Romanesque (12C); the upper part is Renaissance (15C) and built of brick, with decorative majolica inserts. The **chiesa di S. Francesco/church of S. Francesco** ❹ was built on the site where St Francis of Assisi is believed to have stayed in 1213, when he was summoned by Bishop Ugolino. The facade has an ornate Gothic doorway that was altered several times (most extensively in the 17C). In **Piazza dei Priori** ❺, forum of the Roman city and later the *Platea Maior* of medieval Narni, stand two of the most significant buildings of the town: Palazzo dei Priori and Palazzo del Podestà. Piazza dei Priori became a long, narrow square in the late 13th and early 14th centuries with the construction of the public buildings facing one another. **Palazzo dei Priori**, built in the mid-14th century, is dominated by the fine *Civic Tower* and embellished with a fine **loggia***; to the right of the simple doorway is the pulpit from which public proclamations were made. **Palazzo del Podestà*** (now the Town Hall) was built in the second half of the 13th century by joining together three tower-houses. The part to the right of the rusticated Renaissance doorway was originally the chapel, whose entry arch was later lowered with an unusual bas-relief composition (13C). The interior has a fresco from the first half of the 16th century. At the far end of the square, below the 16th-century *Palazzo Calderini,* stands the **fountain** with a bronze bowl decorated with six animal-like figures alternating with crests of the town. The dedicatory inscription reveals that it was built in 1303. **Via Mazzini** ❻ is lined with elegant old palaces, including the 17th-century *Palazzo Mosca* and *Palazzo Bocciarelli,* the latter standing opposite one of the oldest churches in Narni, **S. Maria Impensole*** (1175).

Bas-relief on the facade of Palazzo del Podestà.

The portico surrounds three sculptured *doorways* with sculpted acanthus scrolls in the classical style; the interior has a nave separated from the side aisles by Romanesque columns. Traces of late 14th-century frescoes can be seen on the wall; the high altar is clad in 15th-century marble. The subterranean area consists of three chambers: a niche-type tomb (6C) and two Roman cisterns. Further along the street is **Palazzo Scotti** (mid-16C): note the doorway, windows and inner loggia. The two lofty **Torri dei Marzi** on the right are a reminder of the illustrious Narni family of the 15th-century writer, astronomer and anatomist Galeotto Marzio. In the medieval Via Saffi is **Palazzo Eroli** ❼, a 17th- and 18th-century remodeling of 14th- and 15th-century buildings. The palace houses the Municipal Library, the Civic Museum and Art Gallery.

The **Art Gallery** houses the town's municipal art collections and the more valuable items of the cathedral treasury. The collections are displayed according to various themes illustrating the history of Narni and local art from the 15th to 19th centuries. Highlights include an **Annunciation*** by Benozzo Gozzoli (1451-52) and a large panel by Domenico Ghirlandaio and his workshop, painted in 1486 (**Coronation of the Virgin with Angels and Saints**). The Museo Civico contains a *collection* of archaeological finds from the Roman and medieval periods, including a sarcophagus with *hunting scenes*.

Tradition has it that the religious **complesso di S. Domenico/complex of S. Domenico** ❽ was built as the town's first cathedral in the 12th century, on the site of an ancient temple to Minerva (the central doorway comprises three monoliths, probably of Roman origin). Much transformed over the centuries, the church is now used for conferences. It contains fragments of frescoes (1409). The cross vault of the large chapel of the Rosary is frescoed with *Scenes from the Book of Genesis* by Flemish artists, dating from the second half of the 15th century. From San Domenico one can reach the *St Bernard's Garden*, once the herb garden of the convent (of which only the bell tower survives). Here is the entrance to the **underground chambers of S. Domenico**.

The walls of the *hypogean church* have been dug out of the living rock, plastered and frescoed (the oldest dates back to the 12C).

Via Gattamelata ❾ runs through a characteristically medieval district, which also features much Renaissance restoration work. Here stands the *Palazzo Capocaccia* (16C), which incorporates part of the *Oratory of S. Valentino,* traditionally held to have been founded by St Juvenal. The **church of S. Agostino**, which stands on a site above the walls, dates back to the 14th century. It was rebuilt in the 15th century and re-consecrated in 1728. The large interior, with its predominantly 18th-century decoration, contains a shrine painted in 1482 (behind the

Frescoes in the underground church of S. Domenico.

facade); in the Gothic apse, a fine stone altar (14C); the tribune in the apse is an important example of late 14th-century Umbrian painting, thanks to fragments still visible under the 18th-century frescoes. The *chapel of St Sebastian* is completely decorated.

The sacristy has a fine *Crucifixion* (1500). The modern bridge over the Nera to the north of the town near Narni Scalo is a good vantage point from which to observe the remains of the Roman bridge named **Ponte di Augusto/Bridge of Augusto*** ❿. Some 160m long and almost 30m above water level, it was once completely clad in travertine. Today only one of the original four (or three) arches survives. Near the bridge is the **sanctuary of the Madonna del Ponte**: the church incorporates a cave used as a chapel, which includes Roman structures.

Above is the Benedictine *Abbey of S. Cassiano* (12-13C) with a fine doorway with small columns and a later cusped bell tower; the complex is surrounded by a wall with Guelph-type merlons.

The **monastery of the Sacro Speco** stands at 13.5 km south-east of Narni in a beautiful wood of holm oaks and chestnut trees. It was founded by St Francis in 1213 and later enlarged by St Bernardine, and is named after the cave in which St Francis used to pray; the *oratory of St Sylvester* is decorated with a 14th-century fresco, while the wooden sculptures (*Crucifixion with Mourners*) in the convent church date from the 17th and 18th centuries.

ORVIETO [72 km]

The atmosphere of this ancient and mysterious place bolsters the myths surrounding Orvieto.

The town's main feature is the harmonious way it interrelates with the soaring tufa cliff, creating a continuum between the natural platform and the built-up fabric. Access to the town's historic center was helped by the creation of funiculars, elevators, and escalators. Besides improving the quality of life for its inhabitants, they enable visitors to enjoy the history of the town, documented in the monuments and museums, and through the tradition of wood craftsman-ship, wrought iron, lacework, and above all pottery. Orvieto's past resounds with the masters of the production of majolica, and, thanks to the colored *tesserae* of mosaics on the facade of the cathedral, their work continues to dazzle us even today.

The tour begins from the **Rocca dell'Albornoz/Albornoz fortress** ❶, raised at the orders of Cardinal Albornoz in 1364. This fortress has been turned into a public garden with the entrance near the top of the funicular. Destroyed in 1390, the fort was rebuilt in 1450-57 and a tower was added. In 1888, the moats were filled in for the work on the funicular. Thanks to the repair made to the chemin-de-ronde, visitors can proceed on foot to the late-13th-century

Porta Postierla (or della Rocca), built on an ogival plan with double archway, set into the 14th-century enclosure wall. Further up, in an alcove, stands the *statue of Boniface VIII*, dating from the end of the 13th century.

During the times of the Sack of Rome, Pope Clement VII decided to take refuge in Orvieto (1527-28). To guarantee the supply of water during a siege, he had the famous castle well built. The task was entrusted to Antonio da Sangallo the Younger, who dreamed up a unique system involving a double helix, thereby creating two separate, non-communicating routes up and down the well. The part of the well that emerges above ground is a low cylindrical construction with two doors on opposite sides. The well is 62m deep and 13m wide, and its stairways wind down to a central well in two spirals of 248 steps each, wide enough to accommodate pack animals sent down to bring up the water. Seventy-two windows give air and light to the stairways, while a small bridge crosses from one side to the other, just above the water level. The name **Pozzo di S. Patrizio/St Patrick's well* ❷** (according to the Servite friars) refers to the medieval legend that suggests – in compliance with the Irish saint's practices – spending a moment at the bottom of the well in order to purge one's sins, as if it were a kind of Purgatory, the third station of the afterlife. For others, the name comes from the vague resemblance to the chasm in Ireland where the saint used to retreat to for prayer. In a panoramic clearing near the well stand the ruins of the **Tempio del Belvedere/Belvedere temple ❸**; the deity to which it is dedicated remains unknown, and the place was discovered only in 1828 and excavated in 1920-23. The tetra-style temple is Etruscan, was possibly divided into three cells, and is datable to the early 5th century BC. Some of the statues at the entrance were found (now in the Faina museum), together with decorative furnishings for the votive cell. Accompanied by the medieval doorways and windows which enliven the facades of the ancient borough of San Martino,

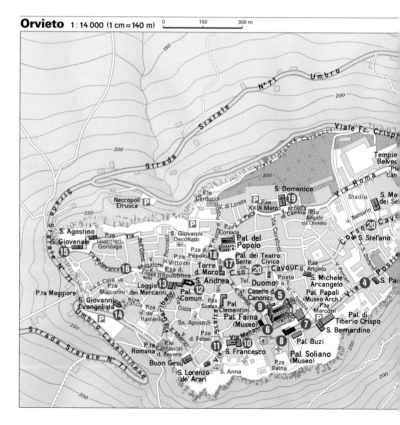

Orvieto 1 : 14 000 (1 cm = 140 m)

we continue up the ancient **Via Postierla** ❹, the link between the religious center of the town and Porta Postierla. The building work that took place in the 13th century in this corner of the town is documented by the **complex of S. Paolo**, a church and monastery founded in 1221 by the Benedictine order, when groups of monks began to transfer their facilities to the top of the cliff. Restructured in the 16th and 17th centuries, the ceiling and walls of the church are decorated (first half of the 17C).

Continuing up the same side we come to **Palazzo Tiberio Crispo**, named for a nephew of Pope Paul III Farnese. The building was raised around the mid-1500s on an earlier design by Antonio da Sangallo the Younger. Alongside stands the **church of S. Bernardino**, founded 1666. The neighboring **Palazzo Buzi** (ca. 1580) is pierced by handsome two-light windows. In Piazza del Duomo, seven steps of alternative white and red slabs lead

The double spiral staircase in St Patrick's Well.

up to one of the most impressive architectural creations of medieval Italy: the **Duomo/Cathedral**** ❺. The foundation stone was laid in 1290. Four centuries later the church was ready, and dedicated to Santa Maria della Stella, a name that was altered to *Santa Maria Assunta in Cielo* in 1800.

After 1309, the buttresses and six huge rampant arches were added, giving the building a new Gothic look, with extended transepts and a large four-sided tribune. The tri-part facade, a clear reference to Siena Cathedral, dates back to 1310; soon after the chapel of the Corporal (1350-55) and the St Brizio chapel (1408) were built and the transept was completed.

Between 1415 and 1456, the twelve Renaissance shrines were added to the facade, and Antonio da Sangallo the Younger redid the floor. In around 1890, conservative restoration was effected in a bid to restore the purity of the original design: the side altars and statues were removed (now on display at the Museo dell'Opera del Duomo, see below), and the stuccoes and frescoes realized between the 16th and 17th centuries were destroyed. From the piazza, the visitor is confronted with a huge, three-part design in which the relief elements are both structural and decorative, lending unifo-rmity, and the mosaic inserts accentuate with colors the overall geometry of the architecture. The **facade*** is an extraor-dinary synthesis of architec-ture and decorative detail. The skeleton of the building is composed of four composite pillars that rise out of solid piers and terminate in a crown of spires. Three richly ornate doorways punctuate the base. Each cusped tympanum meets with a delicate loggia of trilobed arches that

Orvieto: Duomo

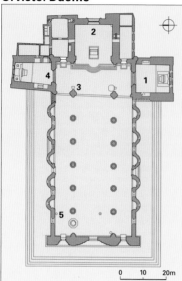

1 Chapel of S. Brizio
2 Wooden choir by Giovanni Ammannati, Crucifix by Niccolò Nuti, frescoes by Ugolino di Prete Ilario
3 Pietà by Ippolito Scalza
4 Chapel of the Corporal
5 Maestà by Gentile da Fabriano

the Old and New Testaments and Scenes from the Novissimi: six series of bas-reliefs depicting Scenes from the Creation to Jubal unfold among entwined ivy strands; acanthus leaves enclose two vertical series of frescoes depicting more Biblical scenes, particularly Messianic prophesies; also amid acanthus leaves arranged vertically are Stories of the Evangelists; and finally, once again in a crown of ivy, the Last Judgment. The bronze panels of the **central doorway** bear reliefs featuring the Works of Mercy (1964-70); the bronze and marble sculpture of the Virgin Mary and Child (1325), formerly in the lunette of the central doorway, is visible inside, in the left aisle. Above the piers are bronze statues representing the Symbols of the Evangelists. The splendid **rose window*** has a double circle of columns with interlaced arches and, at the center, the Head of the Redeemer. The figures of the Four Doctors of the Church decorate the corners of the panel around the window; along the border are 52 heads in relief dating from the 14th century. At either side, 14th-century marble statues of the Twelve Prophets are surmounted by travertine statues of the Apostles (1556). The entire facade is embellished with **mosaics** that pick out the architectural elements and outline the various depictions, while the larger spaces are devoted to depictions of the Life of the Virgin, this last almost entirely reworked over the centuries. Before entering the temple we recommend looking at the sides of the cathedral, in bands of black and white stone: the one on the right

divides the facade horizontally. The upper section is set with a splendid rose window and terminates in a repetition of the three-pointed scheme below.
In 1320-30, the **bas-reliefs*** that adorn the four pilasters between the doorways were added, giving the facade a singular wealth of decorative detail. Starting with the left pier, we can admire Stories from

View of Orvieto, with its tall Civic Tower, and Palazzo del Popolo to the left.

contains the **Porta di Postierla***, a stunning ogival doorway; the left wall is ornamented with a marble statue of the *Erythraean Sibyl*.

The **interior*** follows a basilica plan, with a nave and aisles resting on ten columns and two piers capped with elaborate **capitals**. One is struck immediately by the boldness of the original Romanesque forms. The effect created by the light filtering through alabaster panels, and the large four-light window in the apse, is further exalted by the soaring nave. The floor is in red

colonnade in the lower part and the windows higher up. From them, various illustrious figures look down on the scene, carrying books or scrolls, leaning on the banister in a illusionistic play of perspective which gives the viewer the feeling of being part of the painted scene. The center of the presbytery is overshadowed by a large wooden **Crucifix***; along the walls are carved and engraved **wooden choir-stalls*** in the Gothic style (1331-40 ca.). The tribune walls are decorated with *Scenes from the*

Resurrection of the Flesh, by Luca Signorelli (detail), from the St Brizio chapel in Orvieto.

Prodo limestone with a gradient from the facade to the apse, making the nave appear longer (88.33 m). After the *holy water stoup* (1485) in the nave and the five semi-circular chapels of the right-hand aisle, which have some interesting remains of frescoes (14-15C), we come to the right transept, which gives access to the **Nova chapel** (or **St Brizio chapel**), one of the finest examples of Italian painting. The **cycle of frescoes**** which adorns the chapel, realized in part by Beato Angelico (1447-49) and Luca Signorelli (1499-1504), together with the unusual concept of space, resulted in a totally unique expression of Italian art. In fact, Signorelli did not conceive it as a square chamber, but as a sphere in which all points have the same optical value from the focal point of the viewer. Between the two spandrels painted by Beato Angelico and the six spandrels by Signorelli there is a huge technical gap, due largely to the obsessional care and precision of the former, as if his painting would be viewed from only a few meters away, and the pictorial synthesis applied by Signorelli to create a sense of uniformity. The theme is the *Last Judgment* with a fake architectural framework, such as the

Life of Mary (1370-80). In the crossing, a **Pietà** in marble. In the left transept is the **chapel of the Corporal** (1350-55), a chapel that takes its name from the **reliquary of the Corporal***, which contained the sacred material of the miracle of Bolsena. A masterpiece of Italian craftsmanship, the reliquary is decorated with the translucent enamel technique, which involves incision with a burin of each scene on silver, and a further coat of enamel. Today the sacred cloth hangs in the marble **tabernacle of the Corporal** (1358). Of particular note is the **Madonna dei Raccomandati*** (1320) and, at the start of the left aisle is an important fresco by Gentile da Fabriano (1425), a **Maestà***.

Across the square from the cathedral stands **Palazzo Faina** ❻, built between 1846 and 1866. Today the palace houses the **Museo Claudio Faina**. The collection houses a prolific amount of bucchero ware, bronzes, coins, and masterpieces of antique gold-work and painted vases, mostly from the Orvieto area, covering a time-span ranging from the Archaic to the Hellenistic periods. The ground floor has exhibits from the **Museo Civico Archeologico**, with the so-called **Venus of**

Cannicella (530-520 BC), a striking nude figure; and an **Etruscan sarcophagus** (late 4C BC), with remains of polychrome decoration and bas-reliefs. On the first floor is the **"Gli ori dei Faina" exhibition,** with jewelry dating from the 6th century BC to the early Roman period. The **coin collection*** comprises some 3,000 pieces (origin unknown). The collection of painted vases includes certain examples of outstanding value, such as the black-and red-figure **Attic vases** attributed to Exechias (6-5C BC). The vases of Etruscan production include some dating from the 6th century BC and the **Vanth Group*** (320-300 BC). Completing the collection are prehistoric and protohistoric finds, datable from the Eneolithic to the Iron Age.

After some radical restoration, the **Palazzi Papali/Papal Palaces* ❼** have been united so that the three formerly separate buildings now form a single complex, a design that the ubiquitous use of tufa does not entirely conceal. Alongside the apse of the cathedral is **Palazzo Urbano IV** (1262-64), the first to be built, one facade of which is punctuated by a series of three-light windows which attenuate the

Museo Claudio Faina, a vase of the Vanth Group.

checkerboard pattern typical of the town. Next to this stands **Palazzo Gregorio X** (1272-73), a building with greater articulation than the previous one, but with similarities in the barrel-vaulted ceiling with timber trusses in the large hall on the first floor, and three-light windows in the facade. Standing on its own on the south side of the square is **Palazzo Martino IV** (1281-84), which has an open ground floor with a loggia and facades orchestrated with two-light windows, divided by frames without the checkerboard motif. On the ground floor stands the **Museo Archeologico Nazionale** which exhibits material from Etruscan and Italic necropolises of the Orvieto area. Worth noting are the detached **paintings** from the two tombs in Settecamini (late 4C-early 3C BC). An austere and forbidding mass of tufa stone whose construction began in 1297 at the behest of Pope Boniface VIII and left

unfinished upon his death, the ground floor houses the **Museo Emilio Greco**, with works donated to the town by the Sicilian artist. The collection comprises 32 sculptures and 60 lithographs, etchings and drawings. The **Museo dell'Opera del Duomo****, is soon to be set up in the Palazzi Papali and in **Palazzo Soliano ❽**; the collections are partially visible in the Museo Archeologico Nazionale on the ground floor. The collection in question (paintings, sculptures, and sacred furnishings from the cathedral and various private bequests) has been arranged chronologically into two main groups; the medieval and early Renaissance works will be installed in the Palazzi Papali; those from the Renaissance, Mannerism, and 18th-century in Palazzo Soliano; the buildings will be connected. Among the most important works to be put on display in the *Palazzo Papali* will be the **Virgin Enthroned with Child and Angels** (ca. 1270) and a **reliquary of the skull of St Savinus** (1340), in copper with gilded enamel; some **works** of Simone Martini, the *polyptychs of Saints Dominic and Francis* (14C). Other important works include the **Coronation of the Virgin** (ca. 1340) attributed to Andrea Pisano. *Palazzo Soliano* will accommodate large **statues of the Apostles and Saints** and various *drawings* by Ippolito Scalza, which reproduce the various designs for the transformation of the interior of the cathedral, dating from 1571-95. The southern border of the square opens out on the so-called Giardino delle Grotte, where one can visit the **hypogeum complex of S. Chiara**, one of the countless galleries dug out from the cliff over the centuries (around 1,200 have been discovered so far). The visit (only with guide) leads through various chambers, some of which have their own well; these were used until the 1800s as a *frantoio* or oil mill, and then as a quarry for pozzolana. In stark contrast with the imposing Palazzi Papali, on the north side of the square stand the **Casette dei Canonici ❾**, a set of unpretentious houses erected in the 15th century for the canons. The row of houses is closed (northwest corner) by the **Torre del Maurizio**, a tower on top of which is an automaton cast in 1348 with an alloy used for bell-making, which marked out the time for the cathedral building site by striking the bell. The name of the tower supposedly stems from a corruption of *ariologium de muriccio*, meaning "the site clock".

Taking **Via del Duomo**, a street traced out in the 1200s to link the new urban area with the religious center, we come to *Piazza Gualtiero*, with a *palace* of the same name, whose facade has been embellished with a doorway by Ippolito Scalza. Abutting the square is the 17th-century *church of S. Giuseppe,* while on the left, along Via de' Gualtieri, we come to *Palazzo Mangrossi*, an example of the restrained Mannerist style.

Begun in 1240, the **chiesa di S. Francesco/church of S. Francesco** ⑩ was consecrated in 1266. This is where Pope Boniface VIII proclaimed the canonization of Louis IX king of France (1297). The gabled frontage, with three pointed doorways, is part of the original design. The interior, with a single nave and intercommunicating chapels, was originally a single nave with five tall Gothic arches. In the first stretch of **Via Scalza** ⑪ we come to **Palazzo Clementini**, one of Scalza's finest bequests to his native Orvieto, the architect to whom the city owes much of its renovation in the 1500s. Also on the square stands **Palazzo Monaldeschi della Cervara**, the abode of one of Orvieto's most distinguished families, and allies of the papacy (1570-75). Worth seeing in the interior is the *Salone della Caminata* on the *piano nobile*, decorated with a cycle of frescoes; the coffered ceiling is divided into 15 parts, and the panels are painted with astrological and mythological scenes. Following the curve of Via Scalza, we come to the **church of S. Lorenzo de' Arari**, rebuilt in 1291 in the Romanesque style. Its walls are decorated with interesting paintings of the 14th-15th centuries. The main chapel houses the Etruscan altar from which church takes its name, and supports the slab of today's altar. Annexed to the adjoining Clarissan convent

(15-16C) is the **church of Buon Gesù,** built in 1618 and decorated throughout with baroque stuccoes and frescoes (1647). A line of old houses marks off the successive **Via degli Alberici**, overlooked by **Palazzo Saracinelli**, the work of Scalza again, with a plain late-Renaissance facade that remained unfinished. Descending beyond the city walls we reach Piazzale Cacciatori del Tevere, breached by **Porta Romana** (1882). The parapet affords a splendid view of the valley, crossed in a straight line by the **medieval aqueduct** (13C), a masterpiece of hydraulic engineering that started at the springs of the Alfina hills, traversing Settecamini, from where the water was channeled to the town through lead conduits. Further up stands **Palazzo del Comune**, built in 1216-19 in Piazza della Repubblica and completely remodeled in 1573-81 to designs by Ippolito Scalza. The building has a series of arches supporting a broad terrace with large windows. The site upon which the **collegiata di S. Andrea/collegiate church of S. Andrea*** ⑫ stands was chosen back in Etruscan times for the construction of a temple, as testified by the walls of massive blocks of tufa brought to light. A place of worship founded here in late Roman times (see fragments of geometric mosaics) was followed by the early Christian church. Next to the facade rises the ponderous **twelve-sided tower***, whose walls are covered with coats of arms; the tower culminates in an embattled crown. The tower gave hospitality to some illustrious

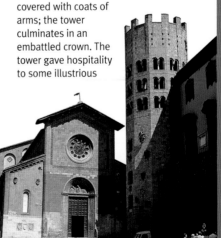

The collegiate church of S. Andrea, with its twelve-sided tower.

personalities, such as Pope Innocent III, who proclaimed the Fourth Crusade (1201), Martin IV, crowned pope (1281) in the presence of Charles I of Anjou. It is divided into a nave and two aisles by monolithic columns of oriental stone (2C) and has frescoes by the school of Signorelli (15C). In the neighboring Piazza dell'Erba stands **Palazzo Mancini**, one of the few 15th-century palaces left, which can be recognized by its four cross-mullioned windows. **Via Loggia dei Mercanti** 🔞 stands in the medieval quarter of Serancia, which bristles with noble family towers (the only ones still intact are *Torre Polidori* and *Torre Ranieri*). On the street stand the remains of the former Gothic **church of S. Giovanni**, which belonged to the Order of Malta, with its memorable ogival doorway. At the end of the street, the **church of the Carmine** is the outcome of remodeling (1308) by the Carmelites of the 13th-century Loggia dei Mercanti: the archways were filled in and a pointed basalt doorway was added. The church was decorated between the 14th and 16th centuries with wall paintings. In Piazza de' Ranieri stands the baroque **church of S. Lodovico**, with the medieval *tower* of the same name. The **chiesa di S. Giovanni Evangelista/church of S. Giovanni Evangelista** 🔞 stands in the old square in one of the more characteristic medieval neighborhoods of the city. Founded in the year 916, the church was rebuilt (1704) on a smaller scale and was reoriented. The single, octagonal nave develops round a marble stoup from the 1400s, supported by a 4th-century column. Before reaching **Porta Maggiore**, the main gate to the Etruscan part of the city, visitors should stop to look at the crenellated wall that follows the western border of the cliff, a point from which one can admire several religious buildings belonging to the Orvieto diocese on the hills opposite the town. We then leave from the city gate which bears a marble *statue* of *Pope Boniface VIII*, dated 1294. The sturdy tower that occupies the facade of the **chiesa di S. Giovenale/church of S. Giovenale*** 🔞, reflects a past in which the church was fortified to justify its strategic position at the edge of the precipice. Rebuilt in the year 1004 on the site of an earlier religious building, the

church has a nave and two aisles, supported on columns of tufa and covered in fine frescoes (13-16C).
Via Malabranca 🔞 runs along the edge of the rock past buildings such as **Palazzo Caravajal**, remodeled in the 1500s by Ippolito Scalza and decorated with Latin mottoes on the lintels of the windows and on the bands below them, or the 15th-century **Palazzo Filippeschi-Simoncelli** with its elegant little courtyard of Renaissance columns. Sloping down sharply toward Porta Maggiore, **Via della Cava**, excavated from the tufa cliff, runs past an archaeological area with a view of an imposing bastion and the remains of an Etruscan gate which was part of the city walls.
On the way down, in one of the shops one can visit a *reverberating furnace*, once used for processing ore (late 14-mid-16C). Where the road divides, on the left stands the small *church of the*

The three-light windows on the facade of Palazzo del Popolo.

Madonna della Cava; on the right is the entrance to the *Pozzo della Cava* (36m deep) dug out from the tufa by Etruscans and adapted by Pope Clement VII to guarantee the supply of water in the event of a siege (1527).
At the end of the 13th century, the **Palazzo dei Sette** 🔞 was designated as the seat of the magistracy of the Signori Sette, the councilors representing the guilds. Consequently the building became the cardinal point for all further urban renewal. From here, the "new" streets spread out towards the cathedral and Palazzo del Popolo. In the second half of the 16th century, the L-shaped palazzo was completely reworked, with the addition of the

rusticated doorway and the monumental staircase. Today the palace is used for exhibitions and cultural events. Excavation in the cellars has revealed a series of cisterns and tunnels dating back to Etruscan times. In the corner rises a **Torre Civica**, known as the *Torre del Moro*, perhaps owing to the coat of arms on a doorway near the tower. At the top hangs a bell bearing the symbols of the 24 guilds (1316).

Piazza del Popolo ⑱ was conceived as the fulcrum of the 13th-century town. In addition to the public palace of the same name (see below), the square contains the **church of S. Rocco**, which has an apse decorated with frescoes. The other major building in the square is *Palazzo Bracci-Testasecca*, now a hotel. In 1281 **Palazzo del Popolo*** makes its first appearance in the annals of the commune. The building was built of basalt and tufa, intended to symbolize the new independent power of communes. The initial project envisioned an arcade along the street, and a large hall on the first floor. However, while it was being built, the plan was enlarged to contain the residence of the Capitano del Popolo (mayor), and by 1308, a bell tower had been added. Having lost its original function, the palazzo underwent numerous alterations – some radical – until its current function of venue for cultural events and conventions. The large hall, known as the *Sala dei Quattrocento*, contains remnants of frescoes that illustrate the feats of the various Capitani del Popolo and popes from the 14th to the 17th centuries. Between 1230 and 1233, friars settled in the town and took over an existing chapel. In 1260-80 the **chiesa di S. Domenico/ church of S. Domenico** ⑲ was erected, originally designed as an oblong block with a nave and aisles. At the end of the 17th century, the church was given a baroque face-lift and, in 1934, the nave was completely demolished. Among the main features inside is the **monument to Cardinal Guglielmo de Braye*** by Arnolfo di Cambio (1285); beneath the tribune is the **Petrucci chapel*** (1516-18), a harmonious Renaissance work which can be accessed by a symmetrical interplay of vestibules and flights of stairs.
Having reached **Corso Cavour** ⑳ from Via Cavallotti, level with *Palazzo Guidoni*,

we find the **Teatro Civico** (1866), decorated inside with grotesques, putti and festoons in the Roman style. Opposite stands the unfinished *Palazzo Petrucci*. Beside it is the vast *Palazzo della Greca-Alberi,* the so-called *Palazzaccio* (ugly palace), which is the result of alterations in various periods. Continuing our descent we come to **S. Michele Arcangelo**, a modern-looking church but actually of early origin, as proved by the remains of the 12th-14th century recently discovered in the sacristy. Beyond the little Romanesque **church of S. Stefano,** which contains fragments of 15th-century frescoes, our path leads to the **church of S. Maria dei Servi**, founded in 1259 and completely transformed in neoclassical style. Here we are at the end of the corso, which leads away from the medieval walls to become the tree-lined street leading to Piazza Cahen. The valley surrounding the peak is dotted with interesting archaeological and natural sites to visit. At 1.6km from Orvieto, by following the SS 71 road, we reach the **necropolis of Crocifisso del Tufo*** (8-3C BC), which is of special interest for its irregular, carefully planned layout. On the south side of the rock we find some chamber burials. This is the **necropolis of the Cannicella**, which was in use from the 7th to the 3rd century BC. Still on the state road, on the right, after 3 km we come to the monastic complex of the **abbey of Ss. Severo e Martirio***, founded in the early Middle Ages. The abbey building and the atrium of the church date from around 1240; the west wing from 1260. Today the abbey is a hotel, but this does not prevent visitors from seeing the *Oratory of Crocifisso*, an ancient refectory with 13th-century frescoes, and the ruins of the *Aula Capitolare*, which afford a superb view of the rock and the cathedral. The old *Casa Abbaziale*, in Cistercian style, is now a restaurant; the **church** (12C) which is still intact, with reinforced masonry, has a handsome Cosmatesque floor.
Two kilometers beyond the abbey we come to the so-called **Etruscan tombs of the Settecamini** (2nd half of the 4C to early 3C BC). Many of the wall paintings were detached and are conserved in the Museo Archeologico Nazionale.

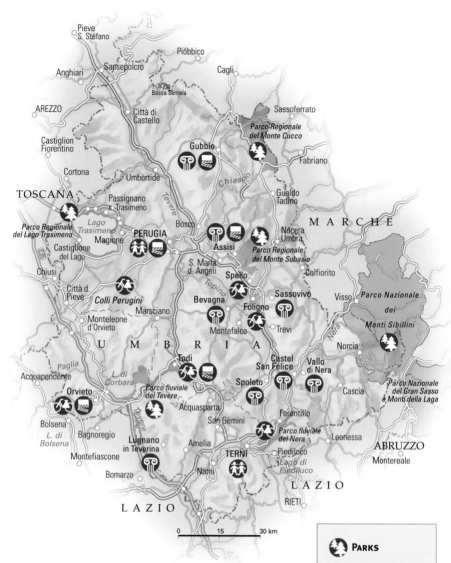

Map Labels

Pieve S. Stéfano

Anghiari

Sansepolcro

Pióbbico

Cagli

AREZZO

Città di Castello

Sassoferrato

JC730 Bocca Serriola

Castiglion Fiorentino

Parco Regionale del Monte Cucco

Fabriano

Cortona

Umbèrtide

Gubbio

Chiascio

Gualdo Tadino

TOSCANA

Passignano s. Trasimeno

Bosco

M A R C H E

Lago Trasimeno

Nócera Umbra

Parco Regionale del Lago Trasimeno

Magione

PERUGIA

Assisi

Parco Regionale del Monte Subasio

Colfiorito

Castiglione del Lago

S. Maria d. Angéli

Spello

Chiusi

Città d. Pieve

Colli Perugini

Bevagna

Sassovivo

Visso

Parco Nazionale dei Monti Sibillini

Marsciano

Foligno

Tevere

Topino

Montefalco

Trevi

Monteleone d'Orvieto

U M B R I A

Norcia

Paglia

L. di Corbara

Todi

Castel San Felice

Vallo di Nera

Parco Nazionale del Gran Sasso e Monti della Laga

Acquapendente

Orvieto

Parco fluviale del Tevere

Spoleto

Cascia

Bolsena

Acquasparta

San Gèmini

Ferentillo

L. di Bolsena

Bagnoregio

Lugnano in Teverina

Amelia

Parco fluviale del Nera

Leonessa

ABRUZZO

Montefiascone

Bomarzo

Narni

TERNI

Piediluco

Lago di Piediluco

Montereale

Nera

L A Z I O

RIETI

L A Z I O

0   15   30 km

Legend

PARKS

CHILDREN

CINEMA

ST FRANCIS – MEDIEVAL UMBRIA

BIKING ROUTES

I n his *Song of the Creatures*, Francis praises God in the sweetest, most profound way possible. He speaks of all God's creatures, including stars, wind, water, fire, humble men and death itself, telling how the inseparable link is "our sister, Mother Earth". Umbria, where Francis was born and spent much of his life, is still imbued with the "sense" of nature that inspired the saint. This section gives you ideas to explore these places and discover the wondrous nature. This is the "green heart" of Italy, home to part of the Parco Nazionale dei Monti

Sibillini and 6 regional parks. Some of the trails are suitable for children, although they are by no means only for children. There is also the amazing Dunarobba fossil forest, a unique place with nearly 50 tree trunks that are over 2 million years old, but that are still rooted to the ground.

Highlights

- Follow St Francis' footsteps to the hermitage of the Carceri and the Basilica of S. Maria degli Angeli.

- Stroncone, Castel San Felice, Ponte, Sassovivo and Cerreto di Spoleto all remain tied to the Middle Ages.

- Cycle through the Umbra valley, around Assisi and Spello or on the Colli Perugini, discovering the artistic heritage of these towns and hamlets immersed in a natural environment.

- Geolab is a superb place for children and adults to explore science.

Inside

PARCO NAZIONALE DEI MONTI SIBILLINI/MONTI SIBILLINI NATIONAL PARK

PROVINCES OF ASCOLI PICENO, MACERATA (MARCHE) AND PERUGIA

AREA: 69,722 HECTARES. LIMESTONE OF THE APENNINES IN UMBRIA AND MARCHE.

HEADQUARTERS: ENTE PARCO NAZIONALE DEI MONTI SIBILLINI, LARGO G.B. ANTINORI 1, VISSO (MACERATA) TEL. 0737972711.

VISITORS' CENTERS: CASA DEL PARCO DI NORCIA, PIAZZA DUOMO 1, NORCIA (PERUGIA), TEL. 0743817090.

CASA DEL PARCO DI PRECI, VIA DI PRECI, PRECI (PERUGIA), TEL. 0743937000.

WEB: WWW.SIBILLINI.NET

This bewitched, fatal place once drew the attention of wizards and necromancers, even causing access to be banned for a time. It is a land of bare mountain tops ravaged by the wind. Over 50 peaks soar above the 2,000m barrier, with rocky cliffs, moraine, sinkholes and sweeping slopes. In spring, these areas are covered in Apennine flora, attracting hundreds of butterfly species. The most unusual of these, known as *Erebia pluto beelzebub*, is found on the highest mountain, at nearly 2,500m.

Legend

S Park headquarters | Park Visitors' Center

TCI HIGHLIGHTS

THE SYBIL'S CAVE

The Sibillini Mountains are the dominion of the Alcina Sybil, the "illustrious prophet" who had a magic garden of delight there. According to the legend, anyone who reached the garden, which lay at the end of incredible trials and tests, could only stay for a maximum of a year, after which that person would be eternally damned. It is said that the Sybil, along with her maidservants, would turn into snakes for three days a week before returning to their bewitching forms. Numerous humanists visited the area and were inspired by the famous legend. Wagner recorded this ancient myth in *Tannhauser*. In 1953, an expedition from the Royal Belgium Academy recovered traces of this ancient past. The field around the Sybil's cave is home to a rare, magical flower: the trumpet gentian with its large blue petals.

Lake Pilato, a mysterious, isolated expanse of water.

Where the Apennines become spectacular

The Sibillini Mountains are one of the parts of the Apennines with the most limestone, forming a sort of prelude to the highest peaks in the chain in Abruzzo. The mountains are rough in these parts, tending to lie in parallel bands, but mainly, they tower solemnly above the hills of Marche and the valleys and rises that flank the Tiber. The landscape is less rolling here, becoming much harsher at times, as can been seen in the impressive section of the park that juts out above Piano Grande at Castelluccio. The geographical terms "plateau" and "mount" are just about perfect for this zone. Piano Grande, amazingly green in spring and blotted by the colors of cultivated fields, especially lentils, comes as something of a surprise to just about every visitor because of its enormity and the altitude of the plateau – standing at 1,500m it is remarkably high for the Apennines. This sense of

 TCI HIGHLIGHTS

THE PARK'S TRAILS

To Lake Pilato (2h30; change in altitude, 790 m). From Foce to Piano della Gardosa (1,150m) by car. Then on foot, through a valley shaped by ice to the spring and lake (1,940m).

To the Ambro springs (3h15; change in altitude 562m). From the forecourt of the Sanctuary of the Madonna dell'Ambro (683m) to 2km from Piedivalle, you cross the beech wood beneath Balzo Rosso and then head to Casale di San Giovanni Gualberto and Fonte del Faggio (1,243m). By going back through the beech wood, you come to Fonte Feletta (1,192m) and Roccacce, which lie before the lovely springs.

Infernaccio gully (2h30; change in altitude 521m). From the parking lot (919m), at the end of the Montefortino road, you head along the gully to Capotenna (1,183m); on the way back, you can pass by the hermitage of San Leonardo.

Mt Vettore (2,476m) from Pian Grande (6km long and 3km wide).

Pian Perduto or lost plateau, Parco Nazionale dei Monti Sibillini. The name recalls a battle on 20 July 1522 in which the people of Norcia took this land from those of Visso.

size is added to by the Vettore ridge, which rises for nearly 1,100m above the plateau. At first, the slope of the ridge seems passable, largely because of the layout of the detritus, but as you look further up, it seems to become an impenetrable mass. Visitors often speak of a sense of disorientation as the setting is so unexpected that it is easy to lose oneself both in what one sees and what one imagines.

Exploring the park

The diversity of the park habitats ensures that any exploratory walk is the opposite of monotonous. To start, there are the riverside areas of the Nera, Fiastrone, Tenna and Ambro rivers. Here, a combination of tectonic ruptures and erosion has created awe-inspiring gullies, such as the one

named *Infernaccio*, where you can find medieval hermitages or unusual trees and plants, such as the turpentine tree, a local form of ephedra and *Drypis spinosa*. The Canatra valley, in the heart of the park, is like a storybook of the relationship between wood, pasture and cultivated field. The balance between man and nature is one of dialogue rather than imposition and this probably explains the return of the wolf. The Castoriana valley, slightly north of Norcia, is a world unto itself where medieval notions such as brotherliness and community still ring true. This is so at the abbey known as Guaita di Sant'Eutizio, named after a Syrian monk who founded the first monastic settlements here and encouraged the study of local medicinal herbs.

 ## TCI HIGHLIGHTS

THE BEGINNING OF TIME

Lake Pilato is the only natural lake in the Sibillini Mountains. It is well known among naturalists for a tiny, yet exclusive resident: a tiny fairy shrimp with a shell that is about 10mm long. It is known as the Marchesoni fairy shrimp (*Chirocephalus marchesonii*). It is part of a truly ancient group – although it was only discovered in 1953 – and it seems likely that it has lived in this small glacial lake for millions of years, surviving an incredible number of natural disasters and changes in the environment.

The tops of the valleys are crowned by extensive beech woods, like the Macchia Cavaliera or Frondosa woods. These expanses of trees are a mix of new trees and age-old trunks that are practically botanical monuments. In these woodlands, you might well hear the call of the eagle-owl or even catch a glimpse of the elusive marten or wild cat. Above the tree line, you find the wide open spaces of glacial valleys, such as the Lago or Panico ones. These are like repositories of geomorphologic phenomena, with moraine steps, cirques and sinkholes. Finally, it is necessary to mention the highest peaks in the Sibillini Mountains, Mt Vettore (2,476m) and Mt Bove, which is a wonderful natural limestone climbing wall with its two peaks (each just over 2,000m) separated by a glacial cirque. This is very much a nature reserve, but not one where man is forgotten. Many old centers bring an element of nobility to this protected area: Visso, home to the park's headquarters, is wedged between the confluence of the Nera and Ussita rivers, and has numerous noble buildings, mansions and religious structures;

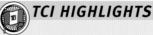

TCI HIGHLIGHTS

BEWARE THE QUILLS

The Romans probably brought the porcupine here from Africa because of its meat, then a delicacy. The result was that the porcupine (*Hystrix cristata*) acclimatized superbly in Italy and today this is the only European country where this rodent with long, pointed quills can be found naturally. The quills are actually the most reliable sign of its presence since they easily detach. Otherwise, it is hard to track this nocturnal animal. This once endangered animal is now a common feature of parks in central and southern Italy.

Norcia, with its stylish piazza; Castelluccio di Norcia, on Piano Grande, a magnificent mountain settlement; Montemonaco, a hamlet on the Ascoli Piceno slope with some Romanesque architecture, which overlooks the surrounding land and districts; and finally, Amandola, perched on the remnants of its three old castles.

Piano Grande, a plateau of colors created by the cultivation of lentils, barley and rye.

Parks

PARCO NATURALE REGIONALE COLFIORITO/COLFIORITO REGIONAL NATURE PARK

PROVINCE OF PERUGIA

AREA: 338 HECTARES. KARST PLATEAU, WETLAND.

HEADQUARTERS: CONSORZIO PARCO COLFIORITO, VIA ADRIATICA, COLFIORITO, FOLIGNO, TEL. 0742681011.

WEB: WWW.PARKS.IT/PARCO.COLFIORITO

SERVICES: MARKED TRAILS (POSSIBLE FOR DISABLED PEOPLE); OBSERVATION HIDES.

The Colfiorito plateau, lying on the border between Marche and Umbria, consists of seven flattish depressions that were once lakebeds and now stand at 750-800m above sea level. The most

The Colfiorito swamp, one of the few Ramsar sites on the peninsula.

important aspect of the park, though, is the Colfiorito swamp. This lake where the water level varies is a stopover point for various migratory birds (herons, bitterns, waterfowl).
It also has two other notable features, the Molinaccio swallow hole, a karst formation through which the swamp waters drain, and the Selva di Cupigliolo wood, where the eagle-owl nests.
The actual stretches of water are rich in plant life, with water lilies, pondweed and bladderwort along with some typical swamp features such as reeds and rushes. The main architectural and historical elements are the Monte Orve *castelliere* (a 10th-cent BC fortified settlement), the Roman municipium, the sanctuary built on the early-Christians ruins of Plestia, various hermitages and the Colfiorito castle.

PARCO NATURALE REGIONALE LAGO TRASIMENO/LAKE TRASIMENO REGIONAL PARK

PROVINCE OF PERUGIA

AREA: 13,200 HECTARES.
LAKE FORMED THROUGH TECTONIC MOVEMENT.

HEADQUARTERS: PARCO DEL LAGO TRASIMENO, VIALE EUROPA 4, PASSIGNANO SUL TRASIMENO, TEL. 075828059.

WEB: WWW.PARKS.IT/PARCO.TRASIMENO

SERVICES: MARKED TRAILS WITH STOPOVER POINTS FOR WALKING, HORSE-RIDING AND CYCLING; BIRD-WATCHING HIDES. THE ISLANDS AND MAIN CENTERS ARE CONNECTED BY A FERRY.

INFO: IAT DEL TRASIMENO, CASTIGLIONE DEL LAGO, TEL. 0759652484-0759652738.

Lake Trasimeno, covering 128 km², is the fourth-largest lake in Italy. The ecosystem is relatively fragile (especially since the lake is only 3.5-6.2m deep), suffering from pollution, overdrawing of water from the lake and human settlement. The park covers the water, the three islands (Polvese, Minore and Maggiore) and the shores.

 TCI HIGHLIGHTS

ITALIAN TULIPS

Holland might be the place most commonly associated with the garden bulb known as the tulip. However, yellow tulips are a natural part of the splendid Italian landscape. Cultivated fields, vineyards and olive groves provide the ideal habitat – right across the Italian peninsula, except for Lazio, Emilia and Veneto – for the wild tulip (*Tulipa sylvestris*), which flowers in mid-Spring. Dry, sunny fields in the mountains (up to 1,800m above sea level) are home to the *Tulipa australis*, which flowers in May or June. Both of these rare tulips can cover entire fields, turning patches of nature into large natural flowerbeds worthy of a garden.

Isola Minore, near the north shore of Lake Trasimeno.

The park covers a section in the upper Chiascio valley between the Apennines and the ancient Via Flaminia, a road built on the orders of the Roman statesman Gaius Flaminius in 220BC to connect Rome with the lands along the northern Adriatic coast.

The zone is mainly mountainous, dominated by the summit of Mt Cucco (1,566m), with plenty of forests and mountain pastures as well as some age-old beech woods in the higher reaches. The lower sections are characterized by a hilly zone with coppice woods that slowly run down to the valley floor and the Sentino and Chiascio rivers. The near absence of humans and the pristine state of the

An age-old beech (*Fagus sylvatica*) in the Rango valley, on the slopes of Mt Cucco.

The shores tend to be home to cane and sedge-grass beds as well as clumps of bent grass. The plants and trees just beyond the shore tend to be willows, black alders and elm.

These shores are often inhabited by migrating birds (storks, egrets, bitterns, pochards, black-winged stilts and grebes), but there are a number of permanent residents too. The most common animals – perhaps even too common – are the cormorant, wild boar and coypu.

Fish also abound, including some prized species: chub, rudd, tench, dace, carp, eel, pike, smelt, grey mullet and perch.

The numerous tourists, who also come to see the medieval hamlets and monuments that are an integral part of the park, and the consumption of the water are the two greatest dangers for this fragile ecosystem that has no real tributaries and is located in a relatively low rainfall area.

PARCO NATURALE REGIONALE MONTE CUCCO/MONTE CUCCO REGIONAL NATURE PARK

PROVINCE OF PERUGIA

AREA: 10,480 HECTARES. APENNINES.

HEADQUARTERS: CONSORZIO PARCO MONTE CUCCO, VIA GIACOMO MATTEOTTI 50, SIGILLO, TEL. 0759177326.

WEB: WWW.PARKS.IT/PARCO.MONTE.CUCCO

SERVICES: CENS - THE ITALIAN NATIONAL CAVE EXPLORATION SOCIETY (EDUCATIONAL, SPORTING AND RECREATIONAL OPTIONS AVAILABLE), COSTACCIARO, TEL. 0759170400; PICNIC AREAS AND MARKED TRAIL; MUSEUM ON THE CAVES AND

environment has enabled the return of animals that are rare or extinct elsewhere, such as the wolf, golden eagle, eagle-owl and the freshwater crayfish. There are also plenty of fallow deer, wild cats, porcupines, martens, kingfishers, Grey partridges and trout. The park is close to Gubbio and Gualdo Tadino and so has its own remnants from the past: stretches of basalt where the road ran, medieval hamlets, and Benedictine hermitages and abbeys, such as the one of Sant'Emiliano at Isola Fossara and the hermitage of San Girolamo at Pascelupo.

The mountainous section of the park is crossed by the Sentiero Italia (trail across Italy) as well has having 120km of trails, some of which can be covered on horseback or mountain bike.

PARCO NATURALE REGIONALE MONTE SUBASIO/MT SUBASIO REGIONAL NATURE PARK

PROVINCE OF PERUGIA

AREA: 7,442 HECTARES. LIMESTONE APENNINES.

HEADQUARTERS: ENTE PARCO, CA' PIOMBINO, ASSISI, TEL. 075815181.

WEB: WWW.PARKS.IT/PARCO.MONTE.SUBASIO

SERVICES: GEO-PALEONTOLOGICAL DISPLAY ABOUT MT SUBASIO AT THE PARK HEADQUARTERS; TRAILS WITH STOPOVER POINTS AND REFUGE HUTS; "LITERARY PARK" WITH TEN TRAILS, EACH INSPIRED BY ST FRANCIS' *SONG OF THE CREATURES*.

A young boar (*Sus scrofa*) with its characteristic stripes.

Standing at 1,290m, Mt Subasio overlooks Assisi. Indeed, over the centuries, this mountain has literally provided wood from its forest and pink stone to the Umbri, the Romans and, later, the friars of the best-loved religious order in the world.
The summit is actually flattish, with karst phenomena, but it becomes steeper on the eastern side. Olives are grown on the lower slopes; Turkey oaks, hornbeam, manna-ash, maple and durmast grow further up; and conifers reach up to the summit. The hermitage of the Carceri is near two lovely beech woods and an ilex wood. The wolf is occasionally spotted, but more usually Italian woodland species are the norm (porcupine, fox, badger, wild boar, weasel and so on) with the addition of the grey partridge and the wild cat. One of the key elements of the park is its historical and artistic heritage: there are obviously the wonders of Assisi and Spoleto, but there are also many "lesser" abbeys, castles and fortified hamlets dotted about the area.

PARCO NATURALE REGIONALE NERA/NERA REGIONAL NATURE PARK

PROVINCE OF TERNI

AREA: 2,120 HECTARES. RIVER ENVIRONMENT.

HEADQUARTERS: CONSORZIO PARCO FLUVIALE DEL NERA, VIA S. FRANCESCO, BUONACQUISTO, TEL. 0744389966.

WEB: WWW.PARKS.IT/PARCO.FLUVIALE.NERA

SERVICES: CENTRO CANOA E RAFTING LE MÀRMORE, WWW.RAFTINGMARMORE.COM; CENTRO TREKKING C/O THE MONTERIVOSO HOTEL, TEL. 0744780772/780725 (FREE CLIMBING, HIKING AND MOUNTAIN BIKING).

The park covers the middle and lower section of the Nera River as far as its confluence with the Velino at Cascata delle Màrmore (a waterfall).
As such, water is a dominant element, influencing both the landscape and man's activities, such as the bridge built in Augustan times or the hydroelectric plant that was built, causing changes to the course of the river. Nonetheless, the lower section of the Valnerina is still genuinely beautiful, with mountains covered in beech woods and pastures that come alive with violets, gentians and asphodels. The riverside vegetation is also notable, with willows, poplars and black alders forming a green band marking the river's path. The list of animals has a few rarities in it, such as the lanner falcon and the wild cat.

PARCO NATURALE REGIONALE TEVERE/TIBER REGIONAL NATURE PARK

PROVINCES OF PERUGIA AND TERNI

AREA: 7,295 HECTARES. RIVER AND SWAMP (LAKE ALVIANO).

HEADQUARTERS: CONSORZIO PARCO FIUME TEVERE, PIAZZA UMBERTO I 16, CIVITELLA DEL LAGO, TEL. 0744950732.

WEB: WWW.PARKS.IT/PARCO.FLUVIALE.TEVERE

The Tiber River could be called the backbone of Umbria as it runs across

After passing the Todi hill and heading towards the Forello gully, green with hornbeam and ilex and rich with grottoes inhabited since earliest times, the Tiber runs into the manmade Lake Corbara.

the entire region from north to south. The park protects 50km of this famous river in the provinces of Perugia and Terni, between the towns of Todi and Orvieto. This is by no means a monotonous stretch of the river, especially as it starts with plenty of white water at Montemolino, where it is called "the Furious", then calms somewhat near Todi, becoming the so-called "dead Tiber", before picking up speed in the Forello gully and then flowing gently into the manmade Lake Corbara. After this, the Paglia River flows into the Tiber, before reaching the Alviano wetland, which was created by man to allow the river some overflow space in times of flood. The flora and fauna tends to follow the mood of the river: parts are bordered by alders and willows, while some steeper stretches are home to ilex, hornbeam, heather and gentian. The swamp areas are filled with reeds.

All this creates an ideal habitat for birds, ensuring a rich array of species, with buzzards, kites, kingfishers, egrets, herons and a range of waterfowl. The main nature sites are the meanders at "Cul del Monte" near Monte Castello Vibio, the Forello gully between Orvieto and Todi, the Piana caves at Titignano, the Guardea ravines, the ilex woods of Melezzole and Croci di Serra, the Oasi di Alviano (special protected areas) and Lake Corbara. Signs of archaeology abound, including

the Umbri-Etruscan necropolises at Montecchio, the villa and kiln from the 3rd century at Scoppieto (many vases from here, identifiable by the maker's stamp, have been found in North Africa) and the Roman river port at the confluence of the Tiber and the Paglia rivers. These sites have often provided a wealth of material and objects for local archaeology museums, such as the Antiquarium at Scoppieto, where you can also learn how an ancient kiln worked. Signs of human activity are even more numerous, ranging over many centuries: there are plenty of medieval hamlets and castles (Baschi, Montecchio, Guardea, Alviano), the splendid town of Todi, which is actually in the park, and Orvieto, which is just outside.

The dipper stays close to the rapids, where the water is cold and full of oxygen.

103

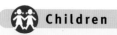
CISTERNE ROMANE/ ROMAN CISTERNS

AMELIA (TERNI)

GETTING THERE

BY CAR: FROM PERUGIA AND TERNI E45 FREEWAY, AMELIA EXIT.

BY TRAIN: NARNI-AMELIA OR ORTE TRAIN STATIONS.

INFO: CISTERNE ROMANE, PIAZZA MATTEOTTI, AMELIA (TERNI), TEL. 0744978436.

WEB: WWW.AMELIASOTTERRANEA.IT

OPENING TIMES: APRIL-SEPTEMBER, SATURDAYS 4.30-7.30PM, SUNDAYS AND HOLIDAYS ALSO 10.30AM-12.30PM; OCTOBER-MARCH, SATURDAYS 3-6PM, SUNDAYS AND HOLIDAYS ALSO 10.30AM-12.30PM.

ADMISSION: € 3; REDUCED € 2; FREE FOR CHILDREN UNDER 11.

DISCOUNTS: TCI 33% OF ENTRANCE PRICE.

When the ancient Umbri city of Amelia became a Roman municipium, numerous public works projects were undertaken, including the creation of an ingenious system to provide water. One way to really see and understand how it worked is to book a guided tour of Amelia Sotterranea (Underground Amelia). A few steps below the surface, the massive cisterns are giant rooms with vaulted ceilings that once filled with rain water (the capacity was 4,400 cubic meters). Surface wells then made this water available to the city. Some of these wells can be seen on the squares and in the courtyards of the town.

The Roman cisterns at Amelia.

FORESTA PIETRIFICATA/ FOSSIL FOREST

DUNAROBBA (TERNI)

GETTING THERE

BY CAR: A1 HIGHWAY (TOLL ROAD), ORTE OR ATTIGLIANO EXITS; ORTE-TERNI HIGHWAY LINK, AMELIA EXIT.

BY TRAIN: NARNI-AMELIA, ORTE OR ATTIGLIANO STATIONS.

INFO: FORESTA PIETRIFICATA, DUNAROBBA (TERNI), TEL. 0744940348.

WEB: WWW.FORESTAFOSSILE.IT

OPEN: APRIL-OCTOBER.

OPENING TIMES: SUNDAYS AND HOLIDAYS 9.30-11.30AM AND 3.30-5.30PM; JULY, AUGUST AND SEPTEMBER ALSO SATURDAYS 3.30-5.30PM.

ADMISSION: € 4.13; REDUCED (6-12 YEARS) € 2.58.

The Foresta Fossile di Dunarobba (Dunarobba fossil forest) is an unusual, charming site with some amazingly large tree trunks (over 1.5m in diameter) that stand vertically. Amazingly, these upright trunks are the fossilized remnants of a forest that once stood by a river. Worldwide, there are only a few such areas, especially ones that are this old. To protect the area and obviously the invaluable trees, the only way to see the area is as part of tour with a guide from the University of Perugia. The tour takes roughly an hour and includes a stop in the paleontology museum at the edge of the forest.

CITTÀ DELLA DOMENICA

PERUGIA

GETTING THERE

BY CAR: PERUGIA LINK ROAD (FROM THE HIGHWAY), PERUGIA-FERRO DI CAVALLO EXIT.

INFO: CITTÀ DELLA DOMENICA, VIA COL DI TENDA 140, PERUGIA, TEL. 0755054941.

WEB: WWW.CITTADELLADOMENICA.COM

OPEN: EVERY DAY FROM 29/3 TO 14/9; UNTIL 2/11 ONLY SATURDAYS AND HOLIDAYS; FROM 3/11 TO MARCH, ONLY THE REPTILE HOUSE AND GAMES AREA ARE OPEN

(REDUCED OPENING HOURS).

OPENING TIMES: 10AM-7PM.

ADMISSION: WEEKDAY € 9; HOLIDAY € 10; REDUCED (4-10 YEARS) € 8.

DISCOUNTS: TCI ENTRANCE TICKET REDUCTION FOR CHILDREN AND ADULTS.

Città della Domenica is an amusement park 2km outside Perugia. It has numerous aspects of interest for adults and children in a setting that reproduces a natural Apennine habitat. The park, on the summit of Mt Pulito (with disabled access), was originally inspired by fairytales, but over the years it has grown with the addition of new attractions and a movement more towards nature. A little train, leaving from the entrance, takes visitors through the enchanted forest, past elf houses and stone monsters living in underground tunnels. This is followed by Pinocchio's village, the castle of Sleeping Beauty in the forest, Little Red Riding Hood's house and Snow White's house, the witches' wood and the Trojan horse. After the crazy bridge, you come to an Indian camp. Throughout the park, you can also find some more classic items, such as a merry-go-round, a maze, slides and a reproduction of a missile. There are some motorized boats to explore the little lake. The covered areas have video games and dodgem cars. The baby-park area has a pool of balls and various jumping castle-like games. The nature section of the park can be visited along a special path that allows you to see nearly 100 animals – including various foreign species and some local endangered ones - roaming freely. There is also an indoor marine area, with sharks, turtles and a shell collection. In winter, you can see the reptile house, which remains open from November to March. Here, you can admire an anaconda, boa, pythons, albino cobras, mambas, rattlesnakes, African vipers, iguanas, alligators and various species of lizard.

GEOLAB

SAN GEMINI (TERNI)
GETTING THERE

BY CAR: FROM ROME, A1 HIGHWAY, ORTE EXIT, ORTE-TERNI LINK ROAD, SAN GEMINI NORD EXIT; FROM FLORENCE A1 HIGHWAY, VALDICHIANA EXIT, PERUGIA-BETTOLLE LINK ROAD, AFTER PERUGIA TAKE THE E45 ROAD TO TERNI-ROMA, SAN GEMINI NORD EXIT.

INFO: GEOLAB, VIA DELLA MISERICORDIA 1, SAN GEMINI (TERNI), TEL. 0744331293.

WEB: WWW.SISTEMAMUSEO.IT

OPENING TIMES: OCTOBER-MAY: SATURDAYS AND SUNDAYS 10AM-1PM AND 3-6PM; JUNE-SEPTEMBER: SATURDAYS AND SUNDAYS 10AM-1PM AND 4.30-7.30PM.

ADMISSION: € 3; REDUCED ADULTS (15-25 YEARS) € 2.50; REDUCED CHILDREN (6-13 YEARS) € 2; UNDER 5S FREE; FAMILY TICKET (2 ADULTS AND MAX. 3 CHILDREN UNDER 14) € 7.

DISCOUNTS: TCI REDUCED TICKET.

Geolab is an excellent source of scientific knowledge. This museum and laboratory gives visitors the chance not only to watch but also to be actively involved. It is centered on the theme of the "history of the planet", looking at this issue through the lens of various disciplines: geology, biology and paleontology. The first room has a game that allows you to disassemble and reassemble the world as it was 150 million years ago. The second room has an interactive model that shows how mountains form, why earthquakes happen and how volcanoes are born. Another exhibit is the Wheel of Time, which makes it possible to jump 200 million years into the past to see the Atlantic ocean being created. Then there is the Rain Machine, a diorama of San Gemini and surrounds that explains how the famous local mineral waters came to be. Finally, the Quadrisphere is a corner with numerous monitors where you can watch nature in all its incredible forms, colors and roles. A visit to the center is also a good time to take in the medieval heart of San Gemini, which is normally – and unreasonably – left off tourist itineraries. The park has mini golf, a bowls court, tennis and ping-pong, an exercise trail and some fenced areas where fallow deer can be seen. In summer, the park is open from 8am to 7pm.

Saints and poets in the green heart of Italy

This green land of rolling hills has been home to important men and women of the church, men of letters and saints. Umbria is also a region that has inspired Italian and foreign filmmakers, often to make films set in the Middle Ages or movies about saints, although a notable number of existential road movies have also come from here. Every corner of the region seems to be filled with a quiet sense of hope, from the calmness of the mountains to the old farmhouses with dovecots, and the simple residences of the Pro Civitate Christiana di Assisi, where Pier Paolo Pasolini found a copy of the Gospel that he used for his *Vangelo Secondo Matteo* (known in the USA as *The Gospel According to St Matthew*; 1964). Umbria's heart has deep roots, like the poetry of Jacopone da Todi or even St Francis. This poetry is often and willingly mixed with prayer, originating in a land filled with revered and well-known saints: Francis of Assisi, Benedict of Norcia, Rita of Cascia and Angela of Foligno. As such, it is no surprise the local art – so deeply influenced and tied to this deep religious fervor – draws deeply on the panoramic views of such medieval gems as Perugia, Gubbio, Orvieto and Spoleto, making it a form of art that often tells stories of a journey and focuses on the importance of "simple things".

The elegance of Perugia and Assisi, the beauty of medieval Gubbio, Todi and Orvieto

This imaginary, idyllic journey through the history of film in Umbria starts by entering the region from the north, at Città di Castello, birthplace of Monica Bellucci, an Italian icon who managed to make the move from the world of top fashion to become a sought-after actress in Italy, France and the United States. Heading down the valley where the Tiber flows, near Lake Trasimeno, you come to Perugia, where another elegant lady of the house is waiting. Valeria Ciangottini, an actress of Raphaelesque beauty, became a part of film history as a symbol of purity. She is the girl in the finale of Federico Fellini's *Dolce vita* (1960), at dawn on the beach, whose innocent gaze meets the disillusioned look of Marcello Mastroianni. Gubbio lies to the north east of Perugia, which was a stopover for Laura Morante, Fabrizio Bentivoglio and Diego Abatantuono, as artists on the road in *Turné* (1990) by Gabriele Salvatores. By heading back past Perugia and around Mt Subasio, you come to the stunning, famed and picturesque Assisi. Pier Paolo Pasolini used this city for some scenes in his magnificent *Uccellacci e uccellini* (The Hawks and the Sparrows, 1966), an extraordinary rereading in the form of a fairytale of the Franciscan soul, the contradictions of pacifism and the role of the intellectual. And what about Assisi? How many films have been made about St Francis, the patron saint of Italy, and St Clare To name just the main pictures from the age of sound, we have *Francesco giullare di Dio* (The Flowers of St. Francis; 1950) by Roberto Rossellini, which is a series of vignettes told using a combination of neorealism and spirituality, and where the austerity of the direction matches the humility of the friars. This list must also include *Francis of Assisi* by Michael Curtiz (director of *Casablanca*) in 1961. This film went to great lengths, especially in terms of technology, to reproduce as accurately as possible the real places in the saint's life. In 1989, for *Francesco* (St Francis of Assisi), which was largely filmed in Perugia, the director Liliana Cavani used the American star Mickey Rourke, then at the height of his popularity, for Francis and Helena Bonham Carter for Clare. This version, with its soundtrack by Vangelis, takes the essence of "Francisism" and adapts it to the 1980s. Rourke's Francis is a sidelined, solitary hippy. The most successful of all the Francis films was Franco Zeffirelli's *Fratello sole, sorella luna* (Brother Sun,

Sister Moon, 1972), which was largely filmed at Pian Grande di Castelluccio. Our journey then continues to Foligno, where you can head to Norcia. There, you can pay homage to a comment made by Vittorio Gassman in *Armata Brancaleone* (For Love and Gold; 1966) by Mario Monicelli. This film is a masterpiece of Italian comedy and was shot at, among other places, Arrone and Ferentillo. In its original language version, it is made more intriguing and thrilling via the protagonists' use of a mix of Latin and the local dialect. The result is wonderful and, indeed, the very language used seems to account for some of the witty, memorable lines associated with this film. The next place on our trip is Spoleto, home to the Festival dei Due Mondi and setting for various films. The Frenchman, Louis Malle visited the city in 1961 for the finale of *Vie privée* (A Very Private Affair) with Marcello Mastroianni and Brigitte Bardot, who dies in the film as a result of the paparazzi.

The next place is Terni. Nearby, the dramatic spot where the Velino River "falls" into the Nera River, known as the Màrmore waterfall, appears in Federico Fellini's *Intervista* (Fellini's Intervista; 1987), featuring a young Sergio Rubini who delves into the world of Fellini's memories. Terni, both the central section and the outlying parts, has been used in numerous films,

including Luchino Visconti's *La Caduta degli Dei* (The Damned; 1969), a story about the rise of Nazism told through the events of a German industrial dynasty, and *Le Coppie* (1970), a series of period comedies by Vittorio De Sica, Alberto Sordi and Mario Monicelli. The most recent additions to this zone are the film facilities at Papigno, which have even managed to compete with Cinecittà, hosting complex sets for *La Vita è Bella* (Life is Beautiful; 1997) and *Pinocchio* (2002) by Roberto Benigni.

A short deviation to the north west takes you to Todi, a place often used by Pupi Avati in his films, from his early horror works to his pieces set in the Middle Ages. Perhaps the most memorable of his works featuring Todi is *Cavalieri che Fecero L'Impresa* (The Knights of the Quest; 2001), an adventurous saga about five young knights who journey to Thebes in Greece to recover the Holy Shroud in 1271.

Todi was also used in *The Agony and the Ecstasy* (1965) by Carol Reed, with Charlton Heston as Michelangelo, the tormented Renaissance artist.

 ## TCI HIGHLIGHTS

L'ARMATA BRANCALEONE

The action-filled journey of Brancaleone da Norcia (Vittorio Gassman) and the rogues who accompany him on the road to possess the Aurocastro feud in Puglia is set in the Umbrian countryside near Arrone and Ferentillo, which is turned into genuine, bloody medieval countryside.

L'armata Brancaleone (For Love and Gold), one of the most successful films in the history of Italian cinema, dealt a hard blow to the polished armor, mystical abnegation and the sense of honor typical of Hollywood's representations of the Middle Ages. The film is particularly interesting because of the wonderful dialect spoken by the main characters, a combination of Latin and the Viterbo dialect.

In the footsteps of St Francis

"In the city of Assisi, in the Spoleto valley area, there once lived a man by the name of Francis, whose bad upbringing by his parents had since his very first days taught him the vain ways of worldly life….". These words, seemingly the start of a fairytale, open the oldest known account of the life of St Francis, written by Thomas of Celano between 1227 and 1229 on the orders of Pope Gregory IX. Francis had died in 1226, bringing to an end a life during which he was revered and praised by the poor and the powerful alike. He was solemnly buried and, a mere two years later, gloriously canonized. The story of St Francis' life is a human tale with a deep element of mysticism. He embodied simplicity and peace, revolutionizing Christian thinking through his being and his actions. In the context of the age, this was an even more amazing feat. In the Middle Ages, Italy was a place scarred by war and crusades, and marked by the troubles and upheaval that comes with deep, lasting social and cultural change. Ironically, the saint of happiness and joy - as he is nearly always remembered - was in reality torn by deep spiritual crises. Perhaps the best-known event marking his troubled inner life was the crisis he went through at the La Verna sanctuary that ended with him receiving the stigmata. For St Francis, though, this conflict was a deeply private matter that he did not even share with his companions. Indeed, he was reported to have said to a companion who asked about the bloody wounds on his feet, "mind your own business", at least according to Thomas' account (XCVIII, 135).

A journey in Umbria in the footprints of St Francis must begin in Assisi, in the very heart of the old city where his merchant father, Pietro di Bernardone, owned a house. The remnants of that house were incorporated in the Chiesa Nuova (new church) on the orders of Philip III of Spain, supposedly in memory of the "prison" where the young, rebellious Francis was held by his parents to prevent him from doing scandalous things such as visiting the needy or lepers. According to accounts by his closest friends, Angelo, Rufino and Leone, Francis (baptized in the baptismal font of S. Rufino) went to a school on Piazza S. Chiara that adjoined the hospital of S. Giorgio. The ruins are still visible in the crypt of the basilica named after the saint. You can also see the crucifix that spoke to him in the church of S. Damiano, saying, "Go, and repair my house, which as you see is falling into ruin."

So Francis went, traveling Italy and the world as few men of his time did, to bring his revolutionary message of peace. This young and cultured man traveled as far as Damietta. There, the crusaders besieging the town had little time for Francis, but he was received courteously by the Muslim sultan. After renouncing worldly goods at the Bishop's Residence in Assisi, he took refuge in Gubbio, with the Spadalonga family (their drapery is visible in the church of S. Francesco). Here, Francis tamed the wolf he had come across near the out-of-town church of the Vittorina. Indeed, the wolf was known to sometimes take refuge in the church of S. Francesco, where you can still see the stone on which the saint stood when praying.

During his travels, the saint stopped at Cannara (church of the Buona Morte, where he is said to have founded the Third Order), Bevagna (the stone from which he preached to the birds at Pian d'Arca is in the local church of S. Francesco), Vecciano near Montefalco

St Francis preaching to the birds, a fresco in the Basilica of S. Francesco in Assisi by Giotto.

S. Francesco in Umbria

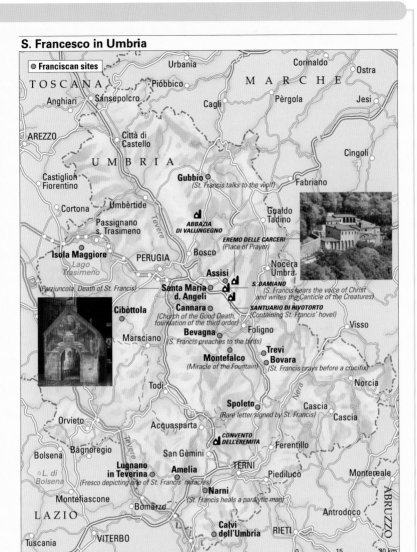

Franciscan sites

TOSCANA · Urbania · Corinaldo · Ostra
MARCHE
Anghiari · Pióbbico · Cagli · Pèrgola · Jesi
Sánsepolcro
AREZZO · Città di Castello
Cìngoli
U M B R I A
Castiglion Fiorentino · Umbèrtide · Gubbio (*S. Francis talks to the wolf*) · Fabriano
Cortona · Passignano s. Trasimeno · Gualdo Tadino
ABBAZIA DI VALLINGEGNO
Isola Maggiore · PERUGIA · Bosco · **EREMO DELLE CARCERI** (*Place of Prayer*)
Lago Trasimeno · Nocera Umbra
(*Porziuncola, Death of St. Francis*) · Assisi · **S. DAMIANO** (*S. Francis hears the voice of Christ and writes the Canticle of the Creatures*)
Santa Maria d. Angeli
Cibòttola · Cannara (*Church of the Good Death, foundation of the third order*) · **SANTUARIO DI RIVOTORTO** (*Containing St. Francis' hovel*) · Vìsso
Marsciano · Bevagna (*S. Francis preaches to the birds*) · Foligno
Montefalco (*Miracle of the Fountain*) · Trevi · Bovara (*St. Francis prays before a crucifix*)
Todi · Norcia
Spoleto (*Rare letter signed by St. Francis*) · Cascia · Cascia
Orvieto · Acquasparta
CONVENTO DELL'EREMITA · Ferentillo
Bolsena · Bàgnoregio · San Gèmini · TERNI · Montereale
L. di Bolsena · Lugnano in Teverina (*Fresco depicting one of St. Francis' miracles*) · Amelia · Piediluco
Montefiascone · Bomarzo · Narni (*St. Francis heals a paralytic man*) · Antrodoco
LAZIO · Calvi dell'Umbria · RIETI
Tuscania · VITERBO
0   15   30 km

ABRUZZO

(where he is said to have caused water to gush forth from a rock), S. Francesco di Bovara near Trevi (home to the Crucifix in front of which the saint prayed), Lugnano in Teverina (one of his miracles is depicted in an old fresco in the 13th-cent. church of S. Francesco), Narni (where he healed Peter, who was paralyzed), Isola Maggiore on Lake Trasimeno and the Sanctuary of Monteluco near Spoleto.

The cathedral in the latter town conserves a letter signed by Francis and written to his friend Leone, who was with him at La Verna.

Still following St Francis' footsteps, you return to Assisi and the places where he "happily" chose to die and was buried: Porziuncola ("this place – said Francis as he lay dying – is truly sacred, the House of God; [...] whosoever prays here with devotion will receive that which they ask"); the Transito chapel in the Basilica of Santa Maria degli Angeli; and the Basilica of S. Francesco, housing his tomb and relics.

The wonderful cycle of frescoes in the upper church "fixed" the image of the saint, passing on the stories and lessons of his life as told in his "official" biography (*Legenda maior*) by the

S. Francesco ad Assisi

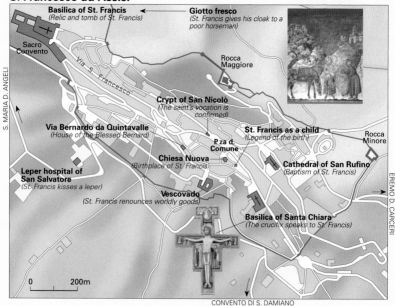

Basilica of St. Francis
(Relic and tomb of St. Francis)

Giotto fresco
(St. Francis gives his cloak to a poor horseman)

Sacro Convento

Via S. Francesco

Rocca Maggiore

S. MARIA D. ANGELI

Crypt of San Nicolò
(The saint's vocation is confirmed)

Via Bernardo da Quintavalle
(House of the Blessed Bernard)

St. Francis as a child
(Legend of the birth)

P.za d. Comune

Rocca Minore

Chiesa Nuova
(Birthplace of St. Francis)

Leper hospital of San Salvatore
(St. Francis kisses a leper)

Cathedral of San Rufino
(Baptism of St. Francis)

EREMO D. CARCERI

Vescovado
(St. Francis renounces worldly goods)

Basilica of Santa Chiara
(The crucifix speaks to St. Francis)

0   200m

CONVENTO DI S. DAMIANO

Order of St Francis, compiled in 1263 by Bonaventure of Bagnoregio, minister general of the Friars Minor of St Francis. Francis himself always cautioned against too much longing for books although he was certainly not behind the decision, and meticulous execution, of the order to search every last convent and destroy all previous biographies and documents of the saint.

The places of St Francis

To find the places where St Francis sought out and found his spirituality, you need to head into the countryside around Assisi. The lovely convent of S. Damiano stands 2.5km from Porta Nuova, or the new city gate. Porta dei Cappuccini is the starting point for the second highly recommended outing to the hermitage of the Carceri, which lies at the end of 3.8km of scenic road. After the hermitage, you can head into the Parco Naturale del Subasio towards Collepino and Armenzano.
The last suggested outing

is 5km from Largo S. Pietro: the famous Basilica of S. Maria degli Angeli, below Assisi.

S. Damiano

After leaving Assisi through Porta Nuova, it is a lovely walk amid the olive groves to the convent. According to various biographies of St Francis, this is where, in 1205, the Crucifix (now in the Basilica of S. Chiara) spoke to the saint, asking him to refurbish the building that, in 1212, housed St Clare (Santa Chiara) and her first companions. Here, in the winter of 1224-25, Francis

The hermitage of the Carceri near Assisi in a lovely wood of ilex and oak trees.

composed the *Song of the Creatures* and, following the death of St Clare, her companions continued to live there until 1260, when they moved into Assisi, ceding the convent to the cathedral chapter. Inside, the apse is decorated with 14th-century frescoes.

The wooden choir (1504) now covers part of a small window that the Poor Clares used to communicate with each other. By heading through the vestibule, you reach the tiny garden, known as St Clare's garden, with an excellent view of the plain.

Eremo delle Carceri

The path to one of the most lovely and memory-filled places associated with St Francis initially takes you through olive groves and then uphill along the slopes of the S. Rufino hill, passing oak and ilex trees. This is where St Francis and his companions would retreat in prayer, to a small church surrounded by grottoes that had long been used by hermits. The convent you see now was built by St Bernardine of Siena (1400) and has a triangular courtyard and a 15th-century church. Some steps and a series of small doors lead to the Grotta di S. Francesco (St Francis' cave), where the saint would relax and meditate. The so-called Viale di S. Francesco is a path through the wood that is well-worth doing, both for the nature and the grottoes once used by hermits.

S. Maria degli Angeli

In 1205, the saint chose the abandoned chapel of Porziuncola (10-11C) to be his base. In those days, the chapel stood deep in the woods and Francis restored it and then founded the Franciscan Order. This is where the saint most often resided, where he gave the habit to Clare and where he held the "Chapter of Mats", attended by over 5,000 friars. It is a simple

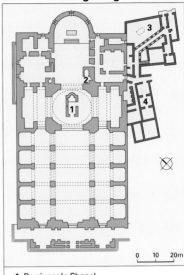

Santa Maria degli Angeli: Basilica

1 Porziuncola Chapel
2 Transito Chapel
3 Roseto Chapel
4 Museum

rectangular building with 14th- and 15th-century frescoes. From 1569 to 1679, a grand basilica with a nave and two aisles was built around the original structure. The basilica's slender dome, with latticework added in 1832, is a genuine landmark for surrounding areas. The building houses a collection of 16th- and 17th-century Umbrian paintings. The Transito chapel, the old hospital 'ward' where Francis died, stands at the beginning of the presbytery. It is adorned with some frescoes and glazed terracotta (another notable glazed terracotta work is the altar-frontal in the crypt). You should also see the rose garden with its many thornless roses. Just beyond the chapel lies the area known as the Roseto, which consists of three parts, including the oratory of St Bonaventure, frescoed in 1506. Some rooms next to the basilica house a museum with religious art and liturgical objects, including a Crucifixion on a panel (ca. 1236) and a St Francis.

S. Maria degli Angeli: chapel of Porziuncola.

The wonders of Medieval Umbria

Umbria has an enormous wealth of natural beauty, art and history, and perhaps more importantly, there are many ways to explore it. Much of the exceptional artistic heritage is found in the hamlets and towns, while many churches are dotted across the picturesque landscape, where the atmosphere is imbued with a sense of time past. The Middle Ages was a flourishing time for Umbria, causing a growth in artistic and political activity. From the 11th century through to the mid-14th century, it was a time of rebirth and glory for the walled settlements. From the 13th century on, these towns became places where the mendicant orders built churches and other structures, leaving a mark on local architecture. At the forefront of this was the Order of St Francis, which often built in a combined Umbrian Romanesque and International Gothic style. What follows is a selection of some of the best examples of medieval Umbrian architecture. Of course, all this architectural beauty lies against a backdrop of gently rolling hills and harsh, steep mountains, often topped by small treasures from the Middle Ages.

Abbey of S. Eutizio

It is said that the grottoes near the abbey were once home to hermits who would occasionally meet under the guidance of Spes and later of Eutitius. By the 10th century, the abbey (elev. 720m) was the political and economic hub of the region and, until the 12th century, the Benedictine monastery increased its estates and influence over the surrounding areas. Yet, this glory was followed by a slow but notable decline, with the estates gradually falling under other ownership until the final assets of the monastery were given to the Commune of Norcia in 1259. Interestingly, the Abbey of S. Eutizio was the origin of one of the oldest known documents (late - 11C) written in early Italian (rather than Latin, which was the language of writing in those days). The entrance courtyard is surrounded by various monastic buildings, which are now home to a small Benedictine community, and leads to the church, built in 1190 by Maestro Pietro, as is indicated on the lunette. The church doorway has a double arched lintel and a rose window decorated with two rows of small columns (1236). The bell tower is from the 17th century, although it stands on the site of a medieval structure.

Abbey of S. Salvatore

The Abbey of S. Salvatore or Montecorona, near Umbèrtide, is one of the most important Benedictine abbeys in Umbria. It was a cradle of the Order of Camaldoli and was probably founded by the creator of the order, St Romuald, in 1008-09. The crypt was part of that original Romanesque building. It consists of five aisles and three apses, with groin vaults supported by Roman columns that were probably part of an earlier pagan structure. The upper church, altered in the baroque period, has some 14th-century frescoes by the Umbrian school, an 8th-century ciborium and a Gothic apse.

Bettona

This ancient Umbrian settlement was an autonomous city-state during the Middle Ages. As a result, various private buildings and houses are from that period, especially the 14th century. The collegiate church of S. Maria Maggiore is from the 13th century, with its simple, rough facade and single-nave interior. Palazzo del Podestà is from 1371, while the church of S. Crispolto, with a small Romanesque bell tower topped by a spire, was built in the 13th century and altered in the late 18th.

Castel San Felice

The old settlement of Castel San Felice lies not far from Sant'Anatolia di Narco. It stands surrounded by an oval ring of walls on a hill by the church of S. Felice. The latter was founded in the Dark Ages, probably by the Benedictines who were busy reclaiming land in the swampy areas. It was then remodeled in 1194. The building is one of the most interesting examples of Romanesque architecture in the Spoleto area. The lovely facade is topped by a tympanum with a dentil band and decorated with blind arches and pilaster strips. The rose window is surrounded by a decorative frame (once colored) filled with shapes and figures (the Evangelists) in full relief. The bottom of this frame has a frieze depicting the legend of Sts Felix and Maurus. The combination of these elements is a clear reference to the farming and land reclamation efforts of the local Benedictine monks as well as to their evangelical mission.

Cerreto di Spoleto

Cerreto di Spoleto sits like a sentinel guarding the most rugged part of the Valnerina. It once had a castle, but only parts of the 13th-century fortifications remain along with a tall tower. The parish church has some frescoes by Felice Damiani (*Our Lady of the Rosary*, 1583) and the so-called Painter from Poreta (*Adoration of the Magi*). The town hall houses a *Virgin Mary with Child and Sts Anthony Abbot and Lucy* by Felice Damiani and a *Visitation* by Camillo Angelucci (1573). The lower section of the town is home to the fortified monastery of S. Giacomo. This 14th-century complex was refurbished, at least internally, in the 16th century. Fortunately, the

Montone: the roads and houses of this old town follow the unusual elliptical shape of the hamlet.

wonderful 15th-century frescoes were kept. One of the rooms nearby, perhaps a presbytery of an earlier church, has some paintings by an artist from the school of Foligno (15C). The monastery houses the Center for Documentation and Anthropological Research in Valnerina (CEDRAV), which has an interesting ethnographical collection.

Montone

This wonderful, elliptical hamlet still has much of its medieval layout intact. Montone lies between two "centers", the political one and the religious one, each located on a hill. Here, the Dark Ages were dominated by the Colle and Del Monte families and then, from the 13th century, by Andrea Fortebraccio, known as Braccio da Montone, a mercenary leader and Lord of Perugia. His residence, now Palazzo Comunale, is in the heart of the hamlet, near the Gothic church of S. Francesco (14C), at the end of some steps from where the view is quite superb. Both the church and the adjoining Franciscan convent have partially been turned into a museum (Museo Civico) and picture gallery. In the church, there are some frescoes, generally votive, by the Umbrian school on the walls and in the apses. Note, especially, the frescoes in the Gothic-style apse depicting the *Life of St Francis*. Just outside the hamlet lies a lovely little country church (11C) dedicated to St Gregory. In Romanesque-Byzantine style, it has a nave, two aisles and some frescoes by the Umbrian school.

Ponte

This former Lombard *gastaldato* (a type of administrative district that is not unlike a viceroyalty) was the local military and economic power during the Dark Ages. It ruled an area running as far as what are now the Norcia and Cascia zones. Some ruins from this period can be seen atop the rocky outcrop (441m). The next dominant local force was the parish church of S. Maria. As late as the 14th century, this church still commanded notable influence over the surrounding area. The actual church building is 12th-century and is in Romanesque style, with a rectangular facade decorated with an ornate rose window framed by mosaics and symbols of the Evangelists. The single-nave interior is decorated with frescoes from the Umbrian school (14C and 15C) and the baptistery's font is a reused large, monolithic Roman slab. The design cut into the wall to the right of the entrance replicates the rose window on the facade.

Sassovivo Abbey: the convent is set around the lovely Romanesq cloister of twin columns.

The main road continues through a lonely landscape, passing Rocchetta (elev. 793m) and the Sanctuary of the Madonna della Stella, which was founded in 1308 as the hermitage of S. Croce by the Augustinians. It was then abandoned in 1630 but rebuilt and refurbished in 1833. Interestingly, part of the church is cut into the rock and it is surrounded by nearly 20 monks' cells that were chipped into the mountain. The sanctuary also has some frescoes from the 14th-century.

Sassovivo

The Abbey of Sassovivo lies in front of a thick ilex wood and was built around the middle of the 11th century, using an old, fortified residence as the basis. The abbey rose to prominence soon after it was completed, eventually controlling an impressive 92 monasteries, 41 churches and 7 hospitals. It continued to dominate the area under the Benedictines, who occupied the complex from the mid-15th century until the Napoleonic suppression in 1860. The church was

rebuilt in 1832 following an earthquake. The Romanesque cloister, created by a Roman maestro called Pietro De Maria, is from 1229 and is the undoubted highlight. It has 128 coupled and spiral columns supporting 58 arches in a classic trabeated system that is made more lively through the use of colored marble. It was created using single pieces that were actually carved in Rome by the artist and his collaborators who came from Como in the north of Italy. In the center of the cloister stands a cistern that was built in 1340. The cloister also leads to the monastery, with its lovely vaulted dormitories from the 13th century. Next, you should head down to the inner courtyard to see the Loggia del

Paradiso, with the remnants of some single-color frescoes (early 15C.). After that, continue to the 11th-century crypt, also known as the chapel of Blessed Alano. This is the final one of structures that remain from the original construction.

Stroncone

This evidently age-old town lies on a hill covered with olive trees and is still partly enclosed by a 10th-century ring of walls. Before reaching there, you should visit the church of S. Francesco, which is said to have been founded along with the adjoining convent by the saint in 1213. A chapel on the left of the porch has a fresco by Tiberio d'Assisi from 1509. The entrance to Stroncone is marked by a 17th-century fountain and the old hamlet gate, which leads onto a small, charming piazza. Here, you find the church of S. Giovanni Decollato, a 1604 enlargement of a building from 1435. The church of S. Nicolò dominates from above, with its Romanesque portal (1171) decorated with a Byzantine-style low relief. A flight of steps leads up to the 13th-century Palazzo Comunale (town hall), with nine choir parchments originally from the churches of

S. Michele and S. Nicolò, including 6 with illuminated capital letters.

Vallo di Nera

The hamlet, located roughly 20km from Spoleto, is still relatively medieval in appearance. The streets are narrow and, often quite steep because the hamlet lies on a hill and is enclosed by a ring of walls. The roads are such that foot is the only viable means of transport. The houses are linked by arched bridges that make it possible to go directly from one house into another across the street. The ring of walls, protected by towers, was created in the 12th century by the feudal lord Corrado di Spoleto.

The 13th-14th-century parish church of S. Giovanni Battista was altered in the 16th century. The church of S. Maria, from the late 13th century, still has clear Romanesque Gothic elements. The simple facade is enlivened by a Gothic portal with small columns that reach up to leafed capitals. The apse has frescoes from the schools of Umbria and Marche with the *Stories of Christ, the Virgin Mary and the Saints* (late-14C.).

A typical hill-top town in the Valnerina.

THE UMBRA VALLEY

ROUTE: 24KM (18.5KM PAVED, 5.5KM UNPAVED): FOLIGNO - TORRE DI MONTEFALCO - BORGO TREVI - CAMPELLO SUL CLITUNNO. ON SECONDARY ROADS.

DIFFICULTY: VERY EASY AND FLAT, IDEAL FOR FAMILIES WITH CHILDREN.

BIKE + TRAIN: THE AREA IS COVERED BY THE TERONTOLA-FOLIGNO AND ANCONA-ROME LINES. YOU CAN GET BACK FROM CAMPELLO SUL CLITUNNO BY TAKING ONE OF THE REGIONAL TRAINS THAT ALLOW BICYCLES.

BIKE SERVICE: CICLI BATTISTELLI, VIA XX SETTEMBRE 88, FOLIGNO; TEL. 0742344059. CICLI CLEMENTI, VIA XVI GIUGNO 36, FOLIGNO; TEL. 074223085.

BICYCLE HIRE: TESTI CICLI, STRADA TRASIMENO OVEST 287, PERUGIA; TEL. 0755172123

TOURIST INFORMATION

IAT FOLIGNATE, CORSO CAVOUR 126, FOLIGNO; TEL. 0742354459-0742354165.

Along the watercourses

An enjoyable ride along the Marroggia stream to the Clitunno springs.
Leave Foligno through Porta Firenze and head along Via XVI Giugno towards the stadium until you reach the San Magno bridge. After crossing the bridge, head right towards Montefalco.
This takes you past Corvia and to Torre di Montefalco (6.4km from the start). Just before the bridge over the Marroggia stream, you need to head left onto the road running along the bank of the watercourse. 3.4km down this road, head left, thus leaving the stream and going towards Casevecchie. After crossing the bridge over the Clitunno, take the unpaved road to the

Trevi in the Umbra valley.

Legend

- Train station
- Point of departure and arrival
- Museum
- Viewpoint
- Stop en route
- Spring
- Tourist information
- Monuments, ruins

right that follows the watercourse. Next, you pass the Foligno clay-pigeon shooting club and the Casco dell'Acqua district, while remaining on the road by the stream.

Eventually, near a farmhouse, the road becomes a cattle-track. Keep going and you come to the paved road in Pietrarossa.

When you reach the bridge, head right and continue for 400m until you come to the road, where you need to go left and follow the course of the Marroggia. After about 800m, you come to another crossroads at Borgo Trevi. This time, turn left and, after 500m – after the bridge over the Clitunno – you need to head right off the paved road and along the bank of the watercourse. The next place is Faustana.

Keep cycling, past the Clitunno mill, the Trevi paper mill and the washhouses along the stream, until you reach a crossroads (about 700m).

Turn left back onto the road running along the Marroggia stream. Stay on this little road for 3.7km (the end of the road) and then head left going over the bridge across the railway near the Campello sul Clitunno train station. Continue until the road joins the Strada Statale Flaminia (main road) at Settecamini, where you need to head left to the Fonti del Clitunno (springs). The route ends near the Tempio del Clitunno (Clitunno temple). To get back to Foligno, you can take the train (from Campello sul Clitunno) or stay on the bike. From Tempio, follow the signs for the pedestrian crossing (*passaggio pedonale*). After 500m, continue downhill to the right and head past Clitunno, going through the tunnel that leads onto the road you came on. To get back to Foligno, follow the bank of the Marroggia to Torre di Montefalco.

MOUNT SUBASIO

ROUTE: 35KM: ASSISI - COSTA DI TREK - ARMENZANO - SAN GIOVANNI - COLLEPINO - SPELLO - VIA DEGLI ULIVI - ASSISI. MAINLY PAVED ROAD, WITH SOME UNPAVED STRETCHES. A MOUNTAIN BIKE IS RECOMMENDED.

DIFFICULTY: A MODERATELY DIFFICULT ROUTE, WITH SOME FAIRLY STEEP SECTIONS: THE FIRST STRETCH TO COSTA DI TREK,

THE CLIMB (1.8KM) TOWARDS ARMENZANO AND THE FINAL STRETCH BEFORE ASSISI.

BIKE SERVICE: CICLI BATTISTELLI, VIA XX SETTEMBRE 88, FOLIGNO; TEL. 0742344059. CICLI CLEMENTI, VIA XVI GIUGNO 36, FOLIGNO; TEL. 074223085.

BICYCLE HIRE: TESTI CICLI, STRADA TRASIMENO OVEST 287, PERUGIA; TEL. 0755172123.

TOURIST INFORMATION

IAT ASSISI, PIAZZA DEL COMUNE, ASSISI; TEL. 075812534.

Between Assisi and Spello

This is a really lovely route that works its way around Mt Subasio and enters the most mystic and charming part of Umbria. The start is from Piazza Matteotti in the upper part of Assisi. Head out of the city by following the signs for Gualdo Tadino and the SS444 road. After about 1km, you need to head right towards Collepino. The road starts to climb relatively sharply, eventually reaching Costa di Trek (4km). The next stretch is mainly flat, with some slightly sloping sections, as it follows the contours of the mountain. A few kilometers further on, though, the road starts to climb once more and for just

View of the medieval hamlet of Spello.

under 2km, the going is quite tough as the average slope is 10%. You then head down off the slopes near the hamlet of Armenzano (9km from Assisi). From Armenzano, you stay at roughly the same altitude until San Giovanni (3.9km), where the road starts to head down to Collepino (4km), a wonderful stone hamlet with many stone buildings and an ideal place for a quick break and some refreshments. From here on, the road follows a scenic route immersed in greenery as far as Spello (5km). Head up to the upper part of this town, near the Bastiglia hotel, and take the road to Assisi. After heading down a tree-lined

road (only a few hundred meters), you need to be ready not to miss the turn. Head right onto Via degli Ulivi, a secondary road that runs along the slopes of Mt Subasio. The road continues at roughly the same altitude. After about 5km, ignore the road to Capodacqua di Assisi on the left and take the next road to the right. The next stretch is about 1km along a fairly steep, unpaved road. After this, you join another dirt road. Head left and stay on this road, halfway up the mountain, until you come to the paved road to Assisi (4,5 km), which winds its way through wide bends to Piazza Matteotti (2km).

BETWEEN TODI AND ORVIETO

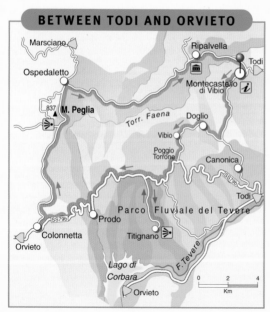

ROUTE: 68KM: MONTECASTELLO DI VIBIO - DOGLIO - TITIGNANO - MT PEGLIA - OSPEDALETTO - RIPALVELLA - MONTECASTELLO DI VIBIO. A THIRD OF THE ROUTE (22,6KM) IS ON UNPAVED ROADS AND SO IS BEST DONE ON A MOUNTAIN BIKE. ALL OF THE ROADS HAVE VERY LITTLE TRAFFIC ON THEM.

DIFFICULTY: THE LENGTH AND CHANGE IN ALTITUDE (ABOUT 1.1KM) MEAN YOU NEED TO BE IN GOOD PHYSICAL CONDITION. THE TOUGHEST STRETCHES ARE THE CLIMB UP MT PEGLIA, WHICH IS NOT THAT STEEP BUT IS QUITE LONG (ABOUT 13KM), THE UP-AND-DOWN STRETCHES ON THE DIRT ROAD TO RIPARVELLA AND THE FINAL TAXING CLIMB TOWARDS MONTECASTELLO DI VIBIO.

BIKE SERVICE: RUSPOLINI CICLI, VIA XXV APRILE, 1, TODI; TEL. 0758942030.

BICYCLE HIRE: SACCARELLI CICLI, VIA TUDERTE 6, MARSCIANO; TEL. 0758743421.

TOURIST INFORMATION

IAT TUDERTE, PIAZZA DEL POPOLO 38/39, TODI; TEL. 0758945416-0758942526.

The tour of Mt Peglia

This route takes you through some genuinely beautiful landscapes along Mt Peglia and the valley of the Faena Stream, passing some hamlets and other little places of the main tourist path. From Montecastello di Vibio, follow the signs for Doglio.
You come to the hamlet after 8km and a touch of climbing. From Doglio, head to the Vibio farm, which is clearly signed. A little further on, the road becomes unpaved and, after 3.8km, you come to the old Orvietana (79bis), a lovely road with little traffic that meanders through the countryside. When you come to the intersection with the old Orvietana road, head left towards Orvieto. After 3.9km, it is best to take the road to the left towards Titignano, a magnificent hamlet that lies at the end of a 3.4km unpaved road. From the viewpoint, you can see Lake Corbara.
After this, you need to head back to the Orvietana and on to Prodo (7km), where the road heads downhill before starting to climb again as it heads to Colonnetta (6.3km). Here, you need to head right following the signs for Marsciano.
The road continues to climb consistently without any particularly steep sections. After 10.2km, the road starts to go back downhill near Mt Peglia,

at the highest point on the route (about 800m). The descent is towards Ospedaletto (2.2km). When you reach the road to Ripalvella, head right along a lovely unpaved road that heads down to the valley of the Faena stream. The downhill section continues for about 5km, then climbs for 900m before another stretch of downhill that is about

Cyclist at Doglio.

4km long. This brings you to a paved road near the intersection to Ripalvella (a few meters further on).
Head across the small town and, after about 400m (near the nursery school), turn right and follow the signs for Montecastello di Vibio. The paved road soon ends and, after a steep descent, you come to the valley floor near the Faena stream (about 2.5km).
Here, on the last part of the route, you come to the final climb of 2.4km, once again on a dirt road, that leads to the intersection for Montecastello di Vibio, which you come to after a further 1.3km and thus complete the circuit.

The Torrone farm on the slopes of Mt Peglia.

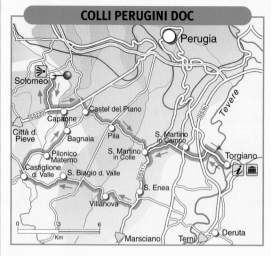

COLLI PERUGINI DOC

ROUTE: 48KM: SOLOMEO - CAPANNE - CASTEL DEL PIANO - SAN MARTINO IN COLLE - TORGIANO - SAN MARTINO IN COLLE - SANT'ENEA - SAN BIAGIO DELLA VALLE - CAPANNE -SOLOMEO. YOU CAN GET TO THE START BY TAKING THE FREEWAY FROM PERUGIA TO BETTOLLE, GETTING OFF AT THE CORCIANO INTERCHANGE AND FOLLOWING THE SS75BIS ROAD TOWARDS ELLERA AND THEN SOLOMEO. IF YOU WISH, YOU CAN MAKE THE ROUTE EVEN MORE INTERESTING BY FOLLOWING THE VARIATION THAT INCLUDES DERUTA, A TOWN FAMOUS FOR ITS CERAMICS.

DIFFICULTY: A MODERATELY DIFFICULT ROUTE ALONG PAVED ROADS. THERE ARE NO MAJOR CLIMBS, ALTHOUGH IT IS UNDULATING.

BIKE SERVICE: PUNTO BICI, VIA G. BRODOLINI 9, PERUGIA, TEL. 0755171847. IT IS ON THE ROAD TO SOLOMEO, JUST AFTER THE CORCIANO INTERSECTION.

TOURIST INFORMATION

IAT PERUGIA, LOGGIA DEI LANARI - PIAZZA MATTEOTTI 18, PERUGIA; TEL. 0755736458.

The cashmere and wine route

The route takes in many vineyards along the hills south of Perugia, starting from Solomeo, a delightful medieval hamlet that was turned into a factory town producing famous colored cashmere. The start is in Solomeo and you immediately meet an enjoyable downhill to Via Pievolana (SS220 road from Perugia to Città delle Pieve), which is about 3km away. You need to head left onto this road and go past Capanne before turning right towards Castel del Piano. Here, you need to head right and then immediately left towards Pila, as

the road climbs steadily. Continue, first downhill and then uphill (but not steep), to San Martino in Colle. At the T-junction with the SS317 road from Perugia to Marsciano, turn left and then immediately right to reach Torgiano, in the wide valley where the Tiber runs. You need to cross the train tracks and the 4-lane freeway (SS3bis road Perugia-Terni). After crossing the bridge over the Tiber, you come to Torgiano: welcome to the Umbrian wine capital! From Torgiano, you need to head back along the same road to San Martino in Colle. Continue by following the signs for Marsciano. After about 4km, you come to Sant'Enea and then, immediately afterwards, you need to head right on the road that heads to Villanova. After passing this small town, you come to a T-junction where you must head left and then immediately right, thus heading past San Biagio della Valle. At the next intersection, keep right and continue to Castiglione della Valle. From here, you should head to Capanne, thus passing Pilonico Materno and Bagnaia. In Capanne, take Via Pievolana (SS220 road) left and then, immediately afterwards, head right and back up the hill where Solomeo sits.

The hamlet of Solomeo.

PARCO FLUVIALE DEL NERA/ THE PARK AROUND NERA RIVER

ROUTE: 12KM: ARRONE (REST AREA) - PALOMBARE - PRECETTO - FERENTILLO - ARRONE. A MIX OF PAVED AND UNPAVED ROADS. YOU CAN REACH THE START BY TAKING THE SS209 VALNERINA DA TERNI ROAD. AFTER THE MÀRMORE WATERFALL, CONTINUE FOR 12KM AND THEN TURN RIGHT, FOLLOWING THE SIGNS FOR ARRONE. AFTER CROSSING THE NERA RIVER, TAKE THE FIRST LEFT (VIA DELLE PALOMBARE) TO REACH THE CENTRO ESCURSIONI - SCUOLA DI CICLISMO FUORISTRADA.

DIFFICULTY: THE LENGTH MEANS MOST PEOPLE CAN DO THIS ROUTE AND THERE ARE NO MAJOR CLIMBS, ALTHOUGH ONE OR TWO STRETCHES ARE A LITTLE TAXING.

BIKE SERVICE: MASSARUCCI CICLI E MOTOCICLI, VIALE OBERDAN 12, TERNI; TEL. 0744409769.

TOURIST INFORMATION

CONSORZIO PARCO FLUVIALE DEL NERA, VIA S. FRANCESCO, BUONACQUISTO; TEL. 0744389966.

IAT TERNI, VIA CASSIAN BON 1, TERNI; TEL. 0744427259-0744423047.

Between Arrone and Ferentillo

The Parco Fluviale del Nera protects the middle and lower section of the river, from the border with the province of Terni to the confluence with the Velino River, best known for being the watercourse with the Màrmore waterfall. Park the car at Arrone, in the parking lot with camper facilities,

and then head off down the road. After a short cycle, you come to a bend in the river where the current is calm and welcoming – and a swim might be in order. After this, the road starts to climb as you head up for about 1km to Palombare. Here, you need to head right about 20m before the little fountain. After the turn, the road becomes a contour road halfway up the hill, amid cultivated fields, olive groves and coppice woods. About 2.8km from the start, you come to a crossroads where four dirt roads meet. This marks the toughest part of the route, with a descent down a slightly uneven track with a drainage ditch to the side that means one must take extra care. This downhill only lasts for about 200m, when you come to another dirt road that is more even.

Turn right and continue amid the fields. This section has various short uphill and downhill stretches. Keep going straight, following the same road, as you pass by fields and drainage ditches in the heart of the Parco Fluviale del Nera. If you are lucky, you might see pheasants, greenfinches, falcons, squirrels, weasels and badgers.

A little further on, the route is paved once more and climbs gently to the spring at Precetto, a typical medieval hamlet that is well worth the visit. To leave here, take the road by the spring to the Ferentillo cemetery. The road initially descends, but then it climbs constantly. At the top of the climb, you need to head off the road and onto the cart track to the right. The view here is lovely and the road heads through pretty thick vegetation, eventually reaching a fork. Keep right and head downhill until the road ends.

Head right down the short (100m) but steep and uneven path. After this, you need to head right onto the cart track that leads to a crossroads. Head left, staying on the main road. You come to the unpaved road you were on earlier and should follow that back to the road to Palombare. Head right, downhill, and after the bend in the river, you come to the starting point in Arrone.

Pieve S. Stéfano
Anghiari
Sansepolcro
Pióbbico
Cagli
AREZZO
Bocca Serriola 730
Città di Castello
Sassoferrato
Castiglion Fiorentino
Gubbio
Fabriano
Cortona
Umbèrtide
Chiascio
Fossáto di Vico
TOSCANA
Passignano s. Trasimeno
Gualdo Tadino
Lago Trasimeno
Bosco
Nocèra Umbra
M A R C H E
Magione
PERUGIA
Assisi
Castiglione del Lago
Colfiorito
Chiusi
Torgiano
Spello
Città d. Pieve
Topino
Foligno
Visso
Parco Nazionale dei Monti Sibillini
Marsciano
Bevagna
Montefalco
Monteleone d'Orvieto
Trevi
Nera
Norcia
U M B R I A
Paglia
L. di Corbara
Todi
Spoleto
Cascia
Parco Nazionale del Gran Sasso è Monti della Laga
Acquapendente
Orvieto
Acquasparta
Ferentillo
Avigliano Umbro
Bolsena
San Gèmini
Leonessa
L. di Bolsena
TERNI
Piediluco
ABRUZZO
Montefiascone
Amelia
Lago di Piediluco
Montereale
Bomarzo
Narni
L A Z I O
L A Z I O
RIETI

0   15   30 km

PASTA

HAMS AND SALAMI

CHEESE

OIL

WINE

CAKES

This is a land of hills and mountains, covered in vineyards, olive groves and woods, where water flows by, sometimes gently and sometimes rapidly, and the great expanse of Lake Trasimeno is like an "inland sea". The countryside is dotted with towns and farmhouses. All this is the setting for age-old Umbrian cuisine. The local products are inevitably linked to the range of landscapes. Traditional Umbrian gastronomy is dominated by olive oil, roasted pork and a range of precious ingredients, such as truffles, which are the

Food

pride of the land. Raw materials are used in the most natural state possible. Three elements are needed to prepare any Umbrian dish: a fire burning, either in a grill or an oven, local ingredients and sufficient time, since "cooking and eating is an art" in these parts.

Highlights

■ The famous cured meats from Norcia, at the heart of a renowned culinary tradition.

■ Tasty, thick soups that make superb use of the delicious lentils from Castelluccio.

■ The cheeses made with milk from the pastures in the Sibillini Mountains, perhaps lightly smoked or flavored with herbs or truffles.

■ Some truly superb wines, with two outstanding options: Forgiano Rosso Riserva and Montefalco Sagrantino.

Umbria, where eating is an art

Umbria, lying in the heart of the Apennines, is covered in mountains that lie next to the valleys carved by the Tiber River, and its tributaries and that rise up around Lake Trasimeno. This ancient landscape, loved by travelers of every age, is delightful both where the natural, deep green vegetation still abounds and where the cultivated fields, often filled with vineyards and olive groves, have taken over. This poetic beauty is added to by the various buildings: from the hamlets, wrapped tightly around old churches and mansions, to the farmhouses scattered across the undulating countryside. This is a land where the past has not been forgotten, especially in the kitchen, where raw materials and traditional methods are favored. A typical Umbrian table is filled with simplicity and covered in simple pasta dishes, thick soups, cold meats, cheeses and meat roasted on the spit or in the oven. One of the most used ingredients is the truffle, normally black in Norcia and Spoleto, but white in the Gubbio-Gualdo Taldino area. This delight has infused a whole range of cooking – from toasted bread to risottos and from pasta to stuffed game – and is the heart of numerous products that exalt its aroma, including sauces, pâtés and even cheeses. To all of this, you must add the golden olive oil, which is produced in the mountains and is of exceptional quality and goodness, and some of the best Italian wines, with the whites having a long, established tradition and the reds being newer, but still a source of pride.

Country cuisine

Perugia is the start of a journey into a world of images and flavors from another age. The hamlets recall the Middle Ages as does the food. To start, there is a type of homemade pasta, *strangozzi*, where the dough is made without eggs and kneaded on a pastry board before being sliced and stretched, piece by piece, to form crude shapes just large enough to soak up the sauce. Each

Trevi is one of the main regional olive producers.

town has its own culinary treasure, such as the *Prosciutto di Norcia*, which is the highlight of this town that is synonymous with cured meats. In a similar line, there are lentils from Castelluccio and spelt from Spoleto, raw materials used to make strong-flavored soups. Cannara is known for red onions, Trevi for black celery and Colfiorito for red-skinned potatoes. The meat in the zone is exceptional, with pork leading the way and reaching its climax in roasted pig with fennel, which actually originated in Umbria. Pork is also the basis for various pasta sauces. Then, there is the white veal from Chianina cows, often sumptuously grilled. The game is also notable: hares stewed in white wine and flavored with black olives; woodcock stuffed with sausage and truffle before being cooked on the spit; and wild pigeons basted with a mix of fat, red wine, herbs and spices . Last, but not least, is the fish, ranging from the large carp caught in Lake Trasimeno and cooked stuffed with lard, fennel fronds and other spices, to the trout found in the Nera River that is rather unusually combined with black truffle. The relatively small size of the territory makes the amount of wonderful oil produced in the region somewhat unexpected. Local olives predominate, giving the oil a distinct fruity flavor that ranges from strongly bitter and spicy to notably less so. On a similar level to the olive is the vine, providing a fitting crown to all the wonderful goodness on the table. There are some noted, excellent reds, such as the Torgiano and Sagrantino di Montefalco, but there is also the white Orvieto, favored by popes and emperors. The sweet finale, and it really is true, is chocolate. This is a recent tradition in the Perugia zone, with a history of less than a hundred years, but the notoriety suggests a much longer past. First and foremost, the Baci company has become a true symbol of Italian romance across the globe. Today, this fame is furthered by an annual festival, Eurochocolate, that draws larger crowds than many major art events.

TRADITIONAL DISHES

First Courses

Ciriole
Typical of Terni, *ciriole* are homemade tagliatelli pasta that are boiled and then dressed with some garlic fried in oil or combined with a minced meat and fresh tomato sauce.

Impastoiata
This is a now rare peasant dish where beans are boiled and then sautéed in a pan of tomato sauce before being added to a standard polenta.

Risotto alla norcina
This is the Umbrian version of the plain risotto with parmesan cheese, and grated black truffle at the end.

Spaghetti al tartufo
In this tasty dish, the spaghetti is dressed with a sauce made of oil, truffle, garlic and anchovies.

Main and side dishes

Beccacce alla norcina
This dish is common in Norcia and across the whole Nerina valley. Woodcocks are cooked on skewers after being stuffed with a mixture of their giblets, sausage, butter, marjoram, thyme and other herbs and spices. The stuffing also has some grated black truffle.

Cardi al grifo
A famed peasant dish. The cardoons are cut into pieces of the same size, boiled until half done, dipped in egg and then covered in bread crumbs before being fried. They are then placed on a baking tray with layers of chopped veal and chicken livers sautéed in butter. Finally, they are wet with some tomato sauce and then cooked in an oven.

Frittata al tartufo
A truly simply recipe that originated in Norcia and the Nera valley. Some black truffle is grated over a beaten egg, potentially adding in some parmesan cheese, and then cooked in a pot. Sometimes, to make the omelet richer, cubes of *scamorza* cheese and ham are added.

Lepre alle olive
A hare is chopped into pieces and then covered in lard so the meat can tenderize a bit. It is then stuffed with a mixture of herbs, white wine and meat cooking broth. When it is nearly cooked, some black olives and a touch of vinegar are added.

Palombacci
This is one of the most traditional Umbrian dishes thanks to the abundance of migrating wild pigeons. The bird is cooked on a skewer and basted regularly with a mixture of red wine, oil, capers, sage, chopped ham and some other ingredients. It is then cooked in a pan, basting continually with the fat that drains off the meat. Sometimes, a touch of extra flavor is added by including a handful of black olives. In Todi, the wild pigeons are first cooked until half-done on the skewer and then finished in a pan with some ham, red wine and other ingredients.

Porchetta al finocchio
Umbrians claim they created this pork and fennel dish. A 40kg pig is stuffed with a mix made with the animal's liver, heart and lungs that is cooked with wild fennel, pepper, garlic and other herbs. It is then roasted on the spit.

Regina in porchetta
This is a large carp that is stuffed with herbs and cooked in wood-fired oven. This is a specialty from Lake Trasimeno, like *tegamaccio*, which is somewhere between a fish soup and a rich stew.

Norcia, a shop selling cured meats and truffles.

PASTA

This is the "green heart" of Italy where the mountainous landscape is a backdrop for medieval, stone-colored towns filled with intriguing history. It is a land with powerful mystical ties and the food tends to be from the peasant tradition, using simple raw materials with uncomplicated flavors. In Umbria, this simplicity is immediately evident in the pasta: it is generally made with soft wheat flour and water, with eggs rarely being used. *Ciriole*, *strangozzi*, *umbrici* and *picchiettini* are types of pasta made using a very simple dough that has been molded into interesting shapes over the years by peasants' imagination and skill. The consistency is relatively rough, making it ideal both for strong-flavored sauces based on meat and lighter ones, based on vegetables and tomatoes, perhaps with a touch of garlic Umbria, and especially Norcia, is a land of butchers and cured meat specialists. This love of meat, especially pork (from sausages to pancetta) is the basis of many sauces, although it is not the only common ingredient, with pulses and truffles being used liberally as well. Cheese is another ingredient used unsparingly, especially if it is pecorino, a ewe's milk cheese that is often combined with sausage and egg to make a sauce for *stracinati* pasta.

Ciriole or Ceriole

A long pasta with a square or rectangular cross-section. Typical of the Terni area, *ciriole* is rather like a homemade version of fettuccine made with soft wheat flour and water (a common variant uses 2/3 soft wheat flour and 1/3 semolina). *Ciriole* is traditionally handmade, but can also be made using a machine. The dough made by mixing the ingredients on a pastry board or in a pasta machine is rolled to about 3mm high, then rolled up and cut into strips about 3mm wide and 15-20cm long. This pasta is traditionally combined with garlic fried in oil, with the pasta also being fried briefly after being cooked in boiling water.
These days, the pasta is often served with a tomato and basil, truffle, mushroom or meat sauce.

Pappardelle

A long pasta with a rectangular cross-section. *Pappardelle* is the Umbrian name for the pasta used to make lasagna. The egg-pasta dough is

generally rolled out until it is about
2-2.5mm thick and cut into pieces that
are 5-6cm long. The sizes and widths
vary somewhat from zone to zone,
with the pasta squares sometimes
having 8cm sides. The unique feature
of Umbrian *pappardelle* is the addition
of a drop of dry white wine. The best
dressing for this pasta is the cooking
liquid that comes from cooking game,
especially hare or wild boar. As a matter
of fact, the meat used to obtain the
cooking liquid is often served as the
next course. *Papapardelle* pasta goes
well with strong-flavored sauces and
can be superbly combined with a
mushroom sauce.

Pasta for soups

Frascarelli, *passatelli* and *quadrucci*.
Frascarelli pasta is found all across
Umbria. This dough is made with eggs
and soft wheat flour; then broken up
into grains and pushed through a sieve
before being cooked in hen broth.
Quadrucci pasta is also found in all
the provinces in the region. The square
pieces of dough (usually made without
eggs) are often used in broths and
lentil soups, another common Umbrian
food. *Passatelli* is typical of the Perugia
area. This small, cylindrical-shaped
pasta has a rough texture. The dough is
made of breadcrumbs, Grana Padano
cheese (similar to parmesan), egg,
nutmeg, lemon and salt. This mixture is
kneaded until a smooth dough is
obtained, which is then forced into
shape using a special machine,
creating cylinders that are from 1-10cm
long. This pasta is generally served in
broth, although in some areas it is
served with a cheese, mushroom or
truffle sauce.

Picchiettini

A short pasta with a square cross-
section. *Picchiettini* pasta is typical
of the Ferentillo and Valnerina (Terni)
zones. The dough, made with water
and flour, is rolled out until it is about
as high as a matchstick, then left to dry
before being cut into strips. The result
is small sticks that are about 7-8cm
long. Traditionally, *picchiettini* pasta is
served with a sauce of chopped tomato
with some garlic, marjoram and chili
pepper.

Strangozzi or Stringozzi

A long pasta with a square or
rectangular cross-section. *Strangozzi*
pasta is typical of the Foligno and
Spoleto (Perugia) zones. It is one of
the many pastas from the peasant
tradition that is made without eggs
(even today, only the egg white is used).
Not unlike *ciriole* from Terni, this pasta
differs from the latter in that it is less
thick (only 2mm) and a different size.
The dough, made of water and soft
wheat flour (a variant uses some
semolina instead of all soft wheat
flour and some more modern variants
include a touch of dried porcini
mushrooms in the actual dough), is
rolled into sheets and then
cut into 3-4mm wide strips that are
about 20-30cm long. In Umbria, this
pasta is sometimes called *strozzapreti*
or *strangolapreti* (literally meaning
priest strangler) and in the Narni area,
manfricoli. The favored sauce to go
with it is a tomato one with a touch of
chili pepper to add some tang. The
rough texture, that allows sauces to
stick to the pasta, makes *strangozzi*
ideal for more delicate sauces.

Strascinati

This is the name given to one of the
oldest regional types of pasta that is
particularly common in the Spoleto

**Strascinati is sometimes called penchi and has
age-old origins.**

zone in the province of Perugia. In
essence, this pasta is like a rough or
homemade version of the pasta used
to make lasagna. It is served with a
sauce consisting of sausage fried in a
pan combined with an egg and some
pecorino cheese (these days, parmesan
cheese is a popular substitute for the
pecorino). The pasta is initially boiled in
salted water but it is removed from the

Strangozzi, a typical local shape of pasta.

and is sometimes called *pici*. The preparation is relatively tiresome and time-consuming: the dough is rolled until it is 5-8mm thick; it is then cut into strips about 10cm wide, which are then cut into smaller strips (about 1cm wide) and rolled more until they resemble spaghetti that are 25-30cm long. The other preparation method uses a special, indented rolling pin; the strips created like this are then stretched by hand. *Umbricelli* pasta is normally served with a tomato or meat sauce.

water a few minutes before it is completely cooked. It is then sautéed (*strascinata*) in a pan until the cooking is complete.

Umbricelli or Umbrici

A long pasta with a circular cross-section. This pasta is like spaghetti, but it is rolled by hand rather than with a special pasta machine. The dough does not include any egg (like so many of the local types of pasta), but only soft wheat flour, water and salt. It is typically of the Castiglione del Lago and Città di Castello zones

PERUGIA

Pastificio Bacoccoli Giulio
Via Bartolo 39, Tel. 0755725878
This pastry house is also called "La Bolognese", clearly indicating that it specializes in fresh, homemade pasta.

GUALDO TADINO
Pasta Fresca Gastronomia
Via Flaminia 296, Tel. 0759145035
Fresh pasta, pasta and various ready-made pasta dishes in the deli area.

 TCI HIGHLIGHTS

THE TRUFFLE, A COMMON DELICACY IN UMBRIA

Many places in central Italy "harvest", in autumn and winter, notable amounts of the black Périgord truffle, but none of them match Norcia. Indeed, it is often called the Norcia truffle not because it is exclusively found there, but because of the quantity collected there and the numerous products made from it.
The skin is black and rough with tiny bumps; the flesh is a blackish-purple with fine white veins when ripe. The smell is obviously delicate and pleasant. Although excellent when eaten raw, perhaps on a good piece of fillet, the black truffle is best when cooked, especially with ingredients commonly used to stuff meat. Norcia is the best place to test this as you can try

truffle on toasted bread, in omelets, with spaghetti and *strozzapreti* pasta, or even trout from the Nera River covered with a truffle sauce. Although associated with Norcia, the black Périgord truffle is found across Umbria, from Spoleto to Città di Castello and on to Orvieto.
There is also the white truffle, which is plentiful around Gubbio and in the upper

GUBBIO
Pasta Fresca - Punto Pasta
Casamorcia 47, Tel. 0759255704
The Fondacci e Rosini pasta
house makes homemade pasta,
only using soft wheat flour.
The various egg pastas include
tagliatelle, *umbricelli* and *gnocchi
di patate*. There is some
colored pasta: red (tomato)
and green (spinach).

SPOLETO
Pasta Antica Tradizione
*Via Martiri della Resistenza 139,
Tel. 074346504*
This fresh pasta is homemade
and includes many traditional types,
such as *tagliatelle*, *strangozzi*
and *spaghetti*. The highlight is probably
the ravioli filled with lemon or porcini
mushrooms.

TREVI
La Pastaia di Egidio Pasta Fresca Gastronomia
*Loc. Pigge, Via Chiesa Tonda 2/a,
Tel. 0742781079*
This pasta house has various types

of homemade fresh pasta as well
as green spinach pasta and red
tomato or chili pepper pasta.
It has a deli section, with an excellent
strangozzi in a vegetable
sauce.

TERNI
L'Angolo della Pasta
Via Narni 192/D, Tel. 0744811230
A pasta house with traditional Umbrian
types of pasta, such as *ciriole*. There is
also a deli section with some ready-
made sauces.

A typical farmhouse in the Umbrian countryside.

Pasta all'Uovo La Casareccia
Via Podgora 6, Tel. 0744273953
At this artisan pasta house, you can
buy the most popular Italian and
Umbrian types of pasta, including
ciriole. There is also a deli section
where you can find, among other
things, some good sauces to go with
the pasta.

AMELIA
Pasta all'Uovo
Via Farrattini 14, Tel. 0744982619
This artisan pasta house has
many different types of fresh egg
pasta from all the regions across
Italy. However, the Umbrian varieties
are favored, with some especially
good *ciriole*.

ORVIETO
La Campagnola Pasta Fresca
*Via Angelo Costanzi,
Tel. 0763305742*
This artisan pasta house has
various forms of Italianand Umbrian
pastas, including *umbricelli*.

Chiasco valley. It has a smooth, light-
yellow or greenish skin (without the
bumps of the black truffle), hazelnut-
brown flesh and a pleasant aroma.

In **Norcia** you can buy Norcia truffles,
truffles from other parts of Italy and
various local products, such as
lentils, oil, sauces and mushrooms.
Diosi Tartufi
Via Madonna Bella 374,
Tel. 0743816222,
www.diositartufi.com

In **Terni** you can buy truffles from the
Nerina valley, which are fresh when in
season or preserved in oil or sauces
out-of-season.
Massarini Tartufi
Via Biblioteca 8, Tel. 0744405286.

Umbria has a range of truffle
festivals, see pages 146/147.

Umbrian towns and hamlets, perched on hills, outcrops and rises, and protected by rings of walls, with magnificent views out across this undulating land, are imbued with a sense of archaic simplicity. As such, the landscape seems to recall the regional cuisine, which is simple but tasty and dominated by the spit, grill and oven. In essence, the methods favored are those that preserve natural flavors, rather than those that combine ingredients to make something totally new. Umbria is a fertile land covered with an abundance of wheat fields and silvery olive groves.Pigs are still fed on acorns, giving the hams a strong, wild flavor. Norcia is at the very heart of this renowned culinary tradition and is famed for its black truffle and *castaldo* (ewe's and cows' milk cheese), but especially for its age-old tradition of cured meats, including such interesting items as *budellaccio*, *corallina*, *prosciutto antico* and *capocollo* with plenty of garlic and pepper. One tasty dish, *spaghetti alla perugina*, is a particularly good example – or even summation – of this tradition from Norcia: spaghetti is combined with a sauce made of fried onion, dried sausage and pieces of salami.

Capocollo

Made across the region, *capocollo* is a large, cylindrical sausage made entirely with pork. On average, it weighs between 2.5 and 3kg. It is made using pork shoulder and a section of the neck. This meat is cut into pieces that are about 30cm long, then trimmed and seasoned with salt, pepper, crushed garlic and coriander. The pieces are then rubbed by hand for quite a long time to allow the salt to soak in well and the meat and muscles to lose some blood and water. It is then washed in dry white wine, before being stuffed into natural sausage casings, tied and placed in a cellar to cure for somewhere between 30 and 60 days. Sometimes, it can be smoked for 4 months. It is reddish when cut, with fatty veins.

Coglioni di Mulo

The literal translation of this salami - mule balls - might be slightly surprising and even a touch alarming, but it is actually a lean pork salami that has a piece of lard in the center. It is made across the entire region, but like many cured meats, it is commonly associated with and found in the Norcia area. After being stuffed into the casing, the meat is stewed and then cured for 30 days.

Coppa di Testa

Found all across the region, *coppa di testa* is made of boiled pork (head, ears, nose, muzzle and rind) that is seasoned with pepper, salt, a touch of garlic, and lemon and orange rind. It is somewhat rectangular in shape when ready to eat.

 TCI HIGHLIGHTS

PRODUCTS WITH THE DOP AND IGP LABELS

Protecting food production is the first step to safeguarding a heritage which is not only of economic significance, but also, and more importantly, of cultural importance. It is an act which confirms and aims to preserve the quality of a product. The DOP and IGP labels protect a product's environment, the human input and its quality. Products carrying the DOP (Protected Designation of Origin) label are products which, first, must comply with a strict set of production regulations, based on the local tradition, which specify what raw materials must be used and how they are processed. Secondly, they must be produced in a particular geographical area, although the "typical production area" may extend beyond the territory of a town and refer to a whole region. Products carrying the IGP (Protected Geographic Indication) label are protected in a similar way to DOP products (in terms of complying with production regulations and the particular area in which it may be produced) but the processing and packaging may be conducted in a wider area. The IGP label is the form of protection most often applied to fruit and vegetable products and their derivatives.

Corallina di Norcia

Named after the town in Umbria, this is a pure pork salami made with a medium-thick paste. The *corallina* is made using finely minced shoulder meat and trimmings from ham, with the addition of lard cubes. The paste is seasoned with salt, finely and coarsely ground pepper and pieces of garlic that have been soaked in dry Marsala or red wine. When the paste is ready, it is stuffed into a natural pig-gut casing and tied to form long salamis. It is then cured in a well-ventilated room heated with a wood-fired oven burning to reduce moisture before being moved to a cooler, damp room for 3-5 months. It is bright red when cut.

Guanciale or Barbozzo

Produced across the region, this cured meat is made from the cheek muscle of pigs that have been reared in a free or semi-free range state. The meat is salted, seasoned with some garlic and wine and then covered with pepper. After this stage, it is seasoned for somewhere between 60 and 90 days. In the end, it has a triangular shape.

Lombetto

This cylindrical, fat-free salami weighs about 2kg and is reddish when cut. It is cured for a week with salt, pepper and garlic, before being washed and dried. This stage is followed by the addition of more pepper, garlic and some wine. It is then cured for 30 to 40 days. This curing and seasoning makes the meat last for quite a long time and so it does not need to be eaten immediately afer being produced.

Mazzafegati

These small sausages have a strong, rustic flavor and are made across the region with a paste of liver, heart, spleen, lungs, some fresh cheek meat and pork fat. The meat is minced and seasoned, for the spicy version, with pepper, salt, orange rind and spices, or for the sweeter version, with pine seeds, cinnamon, wine, raisins and sugar. It is then stuffed into a natural casing that is tied to form little sausages. These are then kept in well-ventilated, hot rooms for a few days, after which they can be eaten. There is also a cured version, where the sausages are then placed in cool, damp rooms for 6-7 months.

Prosciutto di Norcia IGP

The highlight of local pork butchers, this seasoned raw ham has a characteristic spicy flavor. It is exclusively made in the Norcia, Preci, Cascia, Monteleone di Spoleto and Poggidomo municipalities at an altitude over 500m using haunches from Pesante Nazionale pigs. The haunches are trimmed to given them the characteristic pear or violoncello shape and then cured with salted, pepper and garlic for about a month. The seasoning stage is next, taking place in well-ventilated rooms for at least a year. Over this period, natural enzymes and bacterial processes give

The unique taste of Prosciutto di Norcia is best eaten with pit-aged pecorino.

the ham its definitive color and taste. When ready, these hams must weigh more than 8.5kg. It is reddish tending to red when cut.

PERUGIA

Magazzini Gio
Via R. D'Andreotto 19, Tel. 0755726953
Here, you can find the best types of cured meat from Umbria. It also has local cheeses, cereal-crops used for thick soups, truffles and mushrooms.

ASSISI

Bottega del Papa
Via S. Gabriele dell'Addolorata 6, Tel. 075812264
Traditional cured meats made using meat from pigs and cows that graze naturally in the Umbrian mountains.

FOOD

Gambacorta Gastronomia Bottega del Buongustaio
*Via S. Gabriele dell'Addolorata 17,
Tel. 075812454, www.ilbuongustaio.com*
A wide range of food products,
with a good cured meat section:
capocollo, corallina and wild
boar salamis, carefully chosen by
the owner.

CITTÀ DI CASTELLO
Macelleria Fratelli Giulietti
*Corso Cavour 13, Tel. 0758554371,
www.giulietti.it*
Here, you can buy traditional cured
meats, including *capocollo*
and *lombetto*.

FOLIGNO
Norcineria Di Biagio
Piazza Repubblica 26, Tel. 0742350560
This shop and butcher in the
town center produces local
cured meats.
Norcineria Olivieri
Via Garibaldi 74, Tel. 0742340690
The highlight of this butchery is the
coppa di testa, but you can also buy a
range of other pork products.

GUBBIO
Macelleria Pompeo
*Via Cavour 6, Tel. 0759273850,
www.gubbiosalumi.it*
This is the sales outlet for the
butchery with the same name.
You can find: *mazzafegati, capocollo*,
salami with figs, *coppa di testa*, sausage
with truffle and wild boar.

NORCIA
La Boutique del Pecoraro
Via S. Benedetto 7, Tel. 0743816453
Located on the main square,
this small shops sells cured meats,
including some rare specialties.
L'Artigiano dei Salumi
Opaco, Tel. 0743816010
This traditional butchery only
uses pork from Umbria, making
excellent ham, sausage, *capocollo*
and *pancetta*.
Norcineria Fratelli Ansuini
Via Anicia 105, Tel. 0743816643
In the town synonymous with
cured meats, a series of craftsmen
continue the local tradition.
The highlight is the lovely taste

of the local ham, made using Umbrian
pork cured with salt and pepper before
being seasoned for 2 years.

TERNI

Enzo e Adriana
Via Nobili 8, Tel. 0744407065
In addition to local and traditional
cured meats, this butchery offers
the rare salted intestine.
In this age-old recipe intestines,
seasoned with salt, pepper and
fennel, are dried before being
eaten raw or roasted.
Gastronomia Galli
Via C. Battisti 44, Tel. 0744403276
This excellent deli seasons its own
cured meats in grottoes: *capocollo*,
sausage, scented ham and *coglioni
di mulo*. It also has some rare cheese,
products preserved in oil, sauces
and ready-made dishes.

ORVIETO
Azienda Agricola Urbevetus
*Tamburino 81, Tel. 3292720029,
www.urbevetus.it*
The owner's passion has led
to the rebirth of the Cinta Senese pig
breed, reared in a free range state.
The meat is used to make excellent
hams and sausages.
Norcineria Oreto
Orvieto Scalo, Tel. 0763301817
The products from the butchery
are worth trying, including the
lombetto, capocollo and *coppa*.

The unique feature of the local capocollo is the
addition of coriander to the mix of spices.

CHEESE

This is the center of Italy, far from the sea and, for much of the territory, mountainous. It would seem to be a region with a lone destiny. Yet, it has been a truly universal and brotherly place, with integration between peoples of different origins. It is also a mystic region, even in the austere harmony of the landscapes and the harsh, medieval nature of the towns. If you exclude the Renaissance courts, opportunities for banquets were few, meaning the food tends to be simple and rooted in peasant traditions. Grilled meat is common, especially lamb and, in the past, game (although one should not exclude pork or beef). This land is also a place of olive oil, spelt, and basic pulses, like lentils and chickpeas. Finally, it is a cheese zone, especially pecorino and ricotta from Norcia and from the high-mountain pastures in the Sibillini Mountains, where the cheese is smoked using chimney smoke, sometimes with the addition of herbs or truffles. The Easter cake, a complex, time-consuming item to make that is found all across Umbria, is a cake with cheese that is still placed in the middle of the table, the symbol of the feast.

Caciotta

Caciotta, sometimes called *formetta*, is made across the region. This cheese, which can be sliced, is made from cows' milk and has a semi-soft texture and a firm consistency. The taste is sweet and the cheese weighs 1.5-3kg. The cheese is steamed in special molds, then placed in brine for 12 hours and finally aged for 15-20 days in storage rooms. It is then dried with warm air before being sold. *Caciotta al tartufo* is made in exactly the same way as normal *caciotta*, but grated black and/or white truffle is added to the curd.

Umbria is the only area in Italy where truffle-scented cheese is officially made.

Formaggio Farcito

This cheese, which can be sliced, is made with ewe's or cows' milk. The weight varies from 1-3kg. Once you have a clean break of the curds, various additions can be made: truffle, chili pepper, olives, herbs, onions or garlic.

Formaggio Misto

Also known as *caciottone*, this tasty, aromatic cheese is made with a mixture of cows' and ewe's milk. The molds, about 3kg, are immersed in brine for about 36 hours. Ageing takes place in damp, non-ventilated storage rooms and lasts at least 2 months. The cheese molds are then washed and cleaned with a brushing machine to remove the mold on the crust. There is evidence of ewe's milk cheese in the region from 1586.

Pecorino di Norcia

This cheese is from the extraordinarily rich, in culinary terms, little town of Norcia in the upper Nerina valley. The town's gastronomic fame is tied to the wonderful local black truffles and a tradition of cured meats that is so known that the local butchers are a symbol of an entire category. Cheese-making is also well known, producing both cheeses to slice and to grate. The cheese, know locally as *cacio*, is made with untreated milk from ewe that graze high in the mountains. The finished product is rounded, weighing roughly 3kg. The fresh version, which takes 60 days to make, is quite spicy, while the more aged versions, 8-12 months, are less strong and can be grated. This cheese is actually made in an area that includes Norcia as well as a zone between the provinces of Perugia and Terni. *Pecorino di Norcia del Pastore* is a variant that is made in similar ways and places to the main version.

Pecorino Stagionato in Botte

This barrel-aged cheese is made in the same way and the same places as *pecorino di Norcia*; but it is aged in wooden barrels for 45-60 days. It is then dried for 10 days, wrapped in jute paper and sold a month later.

FOOD

Pecorino Stagionato in Fossa

Pecorino aged in a *fossa* (pit) or grotto is produced in various municipalities in the provinces of Perugia and Terni and is made with ewe's milk from the Eugubino-Gualdese area. The cheese molds are irregular, weighing from 1-3kg. These molds are dry salted, rubbed with olive oil and flavored with herbs before being kept in a refrigerated storage room for 3-4 months. They are then oiled again before being aged in a pit (100 days) or a grotto (45-60 days).

Pecorino Umbro or Subasio

Made across the entire region, this ewe's milk cheese has a strong flavor that tends to be a touch spicy.

Raviggiolo

Also known as *cacetto*, *giuncata* or *tomino*, this very fresh cheese is only made with raw cows' milk. It is a soft, creamy cheese, rich in enzymes. It is slightly sweet and milky white. It is often made in biscuit-like shapes weighing 250g.

Ricotta Salata

The salted ricotta, made from the whey of boiled ewe's milk, comes in small, truncated-cone shapes that are, traditionally, sprinkled with bran or semolina. It takes 10-20 days to make the version that is eaten, while the grating version takes 4-6 months. It is made in various municipalities in the provinces of Perugia and Terni.

PERUGIA

Gastronomia Gaggi & Gaggi
Piazza Dalmazio Birago 49,
Tel. 07532315, www.gaggiegaggi.it
A deli selling pecorino with truffles, pecorino flavored with Cascia saffron and goat's milk cheese sprinkled with Apennine herbs. Cured meats available.

ASSISI

Caseificio Ubaldo Brufani
Santa Maria degli Angeli,
Via Los Angeles 31, Tel. 0758041916
This cheese maker uses only local milk to make *caciotta*, fresh or matured pecorino and *caciottina* flavored with truffles, chili pepper or olives.

FOSSATO DI VICO

Golosità Umbre
Via Eugubina 75, Tel. 075919936
A wide array of pecorino, cows' milk and mixed cheeses, including some of the pit-aged types and some flavored with truffle, pepper, chili pepper or walnuts. The organic section has lentils, chickpeas and spelt.

NORCIA

Azienda Agricola Graziosi
Campi, Via dei Casali 43,
Tel. 0743820082
The milk from the farm's ewe is used to make *pecorino umbro* and fresh or salted ricotta.

Severini Alimentari
Via Mazzini 12, Tel. 0743817291
A cheese shop specializing in *caciottina di Norcia* and pecorino. It also sells local cured meats, Castelluccio lentils (IGP) and truffles.

SIGILLO

Caseificio Facchini
Le Pezze 1, Tel. 0759177090
A wide range of flavored cheeses: pit-aged pecorino and cheese aged in ashes, cheese matured in wheat, marc and fig and walnut leaves. Also produces its own cured meats.

TERNI

ORVIETO

Gastronomia Carraro
Corso Cavour 101, Tel. 0763342870
A shop where you can find some rarities, including *formaggio cenerino* (cheese aged in the ashes of walnut leaves). Truffles, cured meats, mushrooms and other local products are also on sale.

Only a few parts of the Apennines have so many flavors: cheeses, cured meats, pulses, truffles...

OIL

Umbria is a relatively small, compact place with plenty of history and culture, and a focus on value. This is also true of the oil, which places quality ahead of quantity. The oil making tradition is both ancient and illustrious, with olive groves dominating the hilly landscape between 250 and 450m above sea level. Indeed, 90% of the region's olives fall into that band, with the remaining 10% often being higher up (600m). The majority of the olive groves are on the slopes of the Martani hills and along the Umbra valley, which is also worth visiting to see the treasure trove of art and towns located there. Olives cover these hills, up to the turreted tops, surrounding towns and leaving an indelible mark on the landscape. The other olive regions are the upper Tiberina valley, the hills around Lake Trasimeno, the mountains around Norcia and Cascia, the Orvieto area in the province of Terni and the Nerina valley.

A charming view of one of the many hamlets surrounded by olive groves.

The two hallmarks of Umbrian oil: quality and distinctiveness

In contrast to much of the country, the majority of the oil (90%) produced in Umbria is extra-virgin and has prized, unusual qualities, fragrances and tastes. Various elements combine to make this the case. First, the location of the olive groves along an area at the foot of the Apennines where the soil is quite soft allowing the roots to penetrate easily. This, with the special climatic conditions, allows the fruit to ripen quite slowly, ensuring that the natural level of acidity in the oil is quite low. Secondly, there is the contribution made by man, who has managed to wisely combine innovation with tradition. The tradition of collecting the olives by hand, called *brucatura*, has been maintained, although there is now a degree of experimentation to find mechanical methods that do not damage the fruit. Immediately after the harvest, the olives are sent to the press to ensure they remain as fresh and as whole as possible. The extraction of the oil is only done using mechanical and

FOOD

TCI HIGHLIGHTS

TORRE DELL'OLIO

This is name, literally olive tower, of one of the towers near Porta Fuga, symbol of Spoleto's resistance against Hannibal's troops in 217 BC when the famed general from Carthage was marching on Rome following his victory at Lake Trasimeno. This episode took hold in the popular imagination, becoming a legend. The army from Carthage was defeated, they said, and forced to flee from a solitary and "invaluable" weapon: the boiling oil of Spoleto that was thrown over the walls at the enemy soldiers.

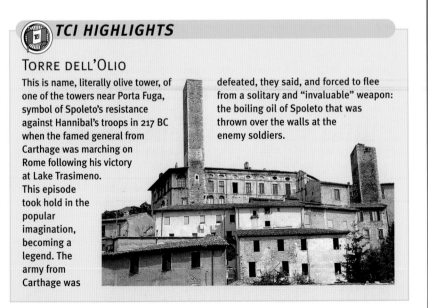

physical methods, guaranteeing the oil keeps, as far as is possible, the unusual characteristics of the fruit. In addition, the local tradition of olive pressing has helped to instill a degree of pride and knowledge in the locals about the quality of the product.

Extra-virgin olive oil from Umbria PDO

The PDO (or *DOP* in Italian) label covers various geographic sub-regions: Colli Assisi-Spoleto, Colli Martani, Colli Amerini, Colli del Trasimeno and Colli Orvietani. Umbrian oil is yellow, with touches of green. The aroma is fruity, with the smell of the leaves discernable. The taste is fruity and harmonious and it leaves you with a slightly bitter, spicy sensation.

PERUGIA

SPELLO
Azienda Agricola Cianetti
Via Bulgarella 4,
Tel. 0742652834
On the Spello hills, this artisan produces small amounts of oil. Only cold pressing is used, ensuring the extra-virgin olive oil has a strong, fruity flavor.

TERNI

TREVI
Agricola Trevi
Torre Matigge, Via Fosso Rio,
Tel. 07423917631, www.oliotrevi.it
Numerous local farmers bring their olives here. This company, located in the central part of the Colli di Assisi-Spoleto PDO region, then produces various types of extra-virgin olive oil.

 TCI HIGHLIGHTS

Museo della civiltà dell'ulivo
The Museo della Civiltà dell'Ulivo di Trevi, located in the monumental complex of S. Francesco, gives a good overview of the culture of olives and oil. It covers the history of this fruit, looking at man's attempts to "domesticate" it from Stone Age times right up to modern extraction techniques. There is also plenty of archaeological material linked to the symbolism of olives and the use of oil. Visitors can taste, and try to identify, various types of oil. A computer supplies a range of recipes.

The Olive trail
This trail is about 70km long, running from Spoleto to Assisi via Trevi and Spello. It follows the eastern ridge of the Umbra valley, passing through a landscape rich in olive groves. This walk, between 500 and 600m above sea level on gentle slopes, is good for panoramic views, but there are also points of botanical and geological interest. Of course, medieval castles, hamlets and historical and artistic monuments abound. The walk is an excellent chance to admire how the olive groves have been adapted, by man, to the lie of the land through the use of terraces or *lunettes*, a no longer used method for growing olives on steep hills.

WINE

In the heart of central Italy, along the valley where the Tiber runs on its way to Rome and around Lake Trasimeno, the landscape is adorned with the wonderful, clear cut lines and colors of the numerous vineyards. In this area, wine is only produced in limited quantities, but the excellent quality easily makes up for this. Evidence of vineyards in Umbria reaches as far back as the Etruscan necropolises, which have proved a fertile ground for a range of wine-related items and clearly suggest that the Etruscan were au fait with good wine. Roman chroniclers speak of famous wines and in the Middle Ages, the wine farms around Orvieto came into their own. This wine tradition is comparable to the modern situation, where Umbria is starting to increase the quantity, but is already at the forefront of quality, with two truly excellent wines, Torgiano Rosso Riserva and Montefalco Sagrantino, which have both earned the prestigious controlled and guaranteed denomination of origin (DOCG) recognition. There are also a number of controlled denomination of origin wines (DOC), often touted by wine experts. "Little" Umbria is thus one of Italy's leading wine regions. This is the only Apennine region without a coastline, with seven tenths covered in hills and the rest mountainous. The focal point for the lie of the land is largely the Tiber valley. The hills around this river, along with the series of adjoining valleys, make this place very suitable, in terms of soil and climate, for vineyards. The area around Lake Trasimeno is more like a micro-environment, especially as this is Italy's fourth-largest lake, but it is also a very good wine area.

Neat rows of vines in the Umbrian countryside.

FOOD

Sagrantino, the great Umbrian vine

Over three quarters of Umbrian grapes are either Trebbiano or Sangiovese, thus ensuring that these form the basis of most regional wines. Nonetheless, the local grapes, partly thanks to notable experimentation, are the basis for some superb wines: this holds true for Grechetto, used to make some of the best DOC whites, and is especially true for Sagrantino, which comes from the Montefalco area and lends its name to a DOCG red. Traditionally, vines were grown using a fan training system, but this has gradual lost ground to the more evolved cordon training.

Montefalco Sagrantino DOCG

Sagrantino di Montefalco, made exclusively using the precious Sagrantino grape, is one of the flagships of Umbrian wine-making and has a tradition traceable right back to ancient times. It is a red wine with a deep ruby color that has a dry, harmonious taste and a delicate nose with evident traces of mulberry. Ideally, it goes with red meat dishes, roasted meat and tasty, aged cheeses. The Passito version, made using raisins, is quite sweet and best served at the end of the meal or even by itself.

Torgiano Rosso Riserva DOCG

A red wine made with a mixture of Sangiovese and Canaiolo grapes, it has a delicate, winey nose and a dry taste that is harmonious and nicely bodied. It is best served with red meat or game.

Assisi DOC

Made in the Assisi, Perugia and Spello municipalities, it comes in red, white and rosé. The version made with Grechetto is white with a dry, fresh and fruity flavor and, as such, it is best served with fish dishes.

Colli Altotiberini DOC

There are three types under this label: red, rosé and white. The white is a light wine with a hay yellow color and a delicate, floral nose. It goes well with starters and fish dishes. The rosé has a fruity nose, combining well with appetizers and roast meat. The red has a deep, winey nose and is best served with meat or a local specialty, *mazzafegati*.

Colli Amerini DOC

Produced in 12 municipalities of the province of Terni, including Terni itself, it comes in white, red, rosé and malmsey. The latter is dry and full-bodied with a slightly velvety aftertaste, making it particularly good with shellfish. The red is also worth trying, especially in the *novello* or new version.

Colli del Trasimeno or Trasimeno DOC

This wine is produced on the hills around the lake, where the microclimate is excellent. There are many varieties of this wine, some of which vary notably. Some of the most loved are the whites made with Grechetto grapes (and best with fish) and the Vin Santo (holy wine) that is superb with dry desserts. The best red is the Gamay, which can be drunk with most types of food.

Colli Martani DOC

This label combines wines made with Grechetto and Trebbiano, creating whites that are ideal with appetizers or fish dishes, and Sangiovese, which is used for a red. The red wine should ideally be served with red meat or some hard cheeses.

Colli Perugini DOC

Colli Perugini DOC comes in three types, white, with Trebbiano grapes, rosé and red, made with Sangiovese grapes. All of these wines can be drunk with most types of food.

Lago di Corbara DOC

Generally, this only comes in red versions: Merlot, Pinot Nero, Cabernet Sauvignon and Rosso. These wines have a winey, pleasant nose and are full-bodied and velvety. They are best combined with red meat, cured meats and hard cheese.

Montefalco DOC

Produced as a red and a white, this wine truly is a top quality product. The white, dry and fruity, is ideal with appetizers and meals with fish, while the red, dry and full-bodied, is recommended with red meat dishes. It is worth trying the Rosso Riserva, aged for 30 months, while eating some roast meats or aged cheese.

Orvieto DOC

The first wine made in Orvieto was made by the Etruscans, who used a simple technique that left some of the sugar unfermented. This was the birth of that enjoyable taste that made Orvieto wines famous enough to be included in the meals of the popes. Hay yellow in color, the Secco (dry) variety has a delicate nose and a slightly bitter aftertaste, making it best with light or fish meals. Some of the sweeter versions can also be drunk with dessert.

A wonderful view of Todi.

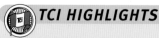
WINE CATEGORIES
Three labels define Italian wines according to quality. The top label is DOCG (Guaranteed and Controlled Origin Denomination); there are around 20 DOCG wines in Italy. DOC (Controlled Origin Denomination) indicates conformity to regulations for a given area of origin, and production and maturation procedures. IGT (Typical Geographic Indication) guarantees vine cultivation according to certain regulations. VDT is for table wine with an alcohol content of at least 10%.

Orvietano Rosso DOC
This wine comes in a range of types, including Aleatico, to be drunk after a meal, Cabernet, possibly drunk throughout a meal, Canaiolo, Merlot and Pinot Nero.

Torgiano DOC
This DOC label actually refers to a range of different wines: Bianco, Chardonnay, Pinot Grigio and Nero, Riesling Italico, Rosato, Rosso, Cabernet Sauvignon and Spumante. The highlights, in terms of the whites, are the Chardonnay, dry and fruity, the Pinot Grigio, fragrant and tasty, and the Riesling Italico, which is pleasantly sharp. These all go with fish dishes. As for the reds, there is the Cabernet Sauvignon, with an intense nose and dry taste, and the Pinot Nero, which has a full, persistent bouquet and a full-bodied taste. Like most reds that are fairly full-bodied, they are both best served with roasted meat or seasoned cheeses.

PERUGIA

FOLIGNO
Terre de' Trinci
Via Fiamenga 57, Tel. 0742320165, www.terredetrinci.com
- ● DOCG Montefalco Sagrantino
- ● DOCG Montefalco Sagrantino Passito

MONTEFALCO
Antonelli - San Marco
San Marco 59, Tel. 0742379158, www.antonellisanmarco.it
- ● DOCG Montefalco Sagrantino
- ○ DOC Colli Martani Grechetto

Caprai
Torre, Tel. 0742378422, www.arnaldocaprai.it
- ● DOCG Montefalco Sagrantino
- ○ DOC Colli Martani Grechetto

Madonna Alta
Pietrauta, Tel. 0742378568, www.madonnalta.it
- ● DOCG Montefalco Sagrantino
- ○ DOC Colli Martani Grechetto

A view of the old center of Montefalco.

Rocca di Fabbri
Fabbri, Tel. 0742399379,
www.roccadifabbri.com
- ● DOCG Montefalco Sagrantino
- ○ DOC Colli Martani Grechetto

Tabarrini
Turrita, Tel. 0742379351,
www.tabarrini.com
- ● DOCG Montefalco Sagrantino
- ○ IGT Umbria

SPOLETO
Spoleto Ducale Casale Triocco
Petrognano 54, Tel. 074356224,
www.casaletriocco.it
- ● DOCG Montefalco Sagrantino
- ○ DOC Colli Martani Grechetto

TORGIANO
Lungarotti
Via Mario Angeloni 16, Tel. 075988661,
www.lungarotti.it
- ● DOCG Torgiano Rosso Riserva
- ○ DOC Torgiano
- ● DOCG Montefalco Sagrantino
- ● DOC Torgiano

WINE LEGEND

Wines are listed with symbols which indicate their type
- ● red
- ○ white
- ◉ rosé
- ◖ sweet or dessert

TERNI

ORVIETO
Cardeto
Sferracavallo, Tel. 0763341286,
www.cardeto.com
- ● IGT Umbria Rupestro
- ○ IGT Umbria Grechetto

La Carraia
Tordimonte 56, Tel. 0763304013
- ● IGT Umbria Sangiovese
- ○ DOC Orvieto

Palazzone
Rocca Ripesena 68, Tel. 0763344921,
www.palazzone.com
- ○ DOC Orvieto

 TCI HIGHLIGHTS

THE LUNGAROTTI MUSEUM IN TORGIANO

The Museo del Vino is in the outbuildings of Palazzo Graziani-Baglioni, a 17th-century summer residence. The museum tells the story of local winemaking and the evolution of techniques using a wide array of items: archaeological finds, equipment and tools used

in growing vines and making wine, ceramic pieces from the Middle Ages, the Renaissance, baroque times and the contemporary age, engravings and drawings from the 15th to 20th centuries, old and antique documents, items used by goldsmiths, fabrics and other related articles. All of these items also show the importance of the vine and wine in Western culture, the numerous ways in which they are used, and the ways in which they are perceived by the "collective imagination" of the Mediterranean peoples.

The Museo dell'Olivo e dell'Olio has sections with disabled access. It examines the techniques used to grow olives and turn them into oil, the uses of the oil and olives, and the importance of olives and oil as cultural symbols of Western countries. It is located in a part of a series of medieval buildings that once housed a hydraulic olive press (*see photo*). A visit to this museum shows how ancient man's ties to the olive is. It does this with a series of displays that include equipment for growing olives, machines, archaeological finds, silver, glass and ceramics and various examples of applied art.

MUSEO DELL'OLIVO E DELL'OLIO - Via Garibaldi 10, Torgiano
MUSEO DEL VINO - Corso Vittorio Emanuele 31, Torgiano
Tel. 0759880300-0759880200, www.lungarotti.it

CAKES

In terms of the Italian peninsula, this region is uniquely isolated and mountainous. Over the centuries, for things to reach here, whether intellectual or material, they had to cross the surrounding regions. The result was a melting pot that forged a unique tradition that is austere like the landscape, but rich in meaning. The Middle Ages, with the rule of city-states, was the golden age for Perugia and other hamlets, with the following centuries under conservative Church rule being largely a time of stagnation. In culinary terms, this means that an enormous number of the traditions are linked directly to the Middle Ages. This holds true for the desserts, cakes and sweets, which includes *pampepati*, a sweet leaven *focaccia* (type of bread) filled with spices and soaked in raisin wine – a product filled with history – perhaps in the Sagrantino di Montefalco variety. The exception that proves the rule is Perugia, a company founded in the early 20th century and now known across the

Baci chocolates are known across the world.

world because of its Baci chocolates. This company is also one of the key reasons behind an annual festival held in Umbria, Eurochocolate, which takes place every autumn (normally in late October), bringing together hundreds of the best chocolate-makers and many of the most dedicated chocolate lovers in an unequalled culinary setting. Finally, a word or two needs to be said about a new and unusual delight: chocolate truffle from Nero di Norcia. The name says it all.

Attorta

This puff pastry dessert is typical of Spoleto and is filled with drops of alkermes, sugar or almonds covered in various colors of sugar coating. The dough is made with flour, olive oil, eggs, sugar and rum before being rolled into elongated strips. The filling (apricot jam, cooked slices of apples with sugar, bitter cocoa, grated dark chocolate, grated lemon rind, chopped walnuts, pine-seeds and almonds, rum and/or alkermes, olive oil) is spread on the pastry, which is then

 TCI HIGHLIGHTS

THE KISS OF SUCCESS

Imagine the following scene: a jumbo jet parked at Osaka airport and surrounded by a throng of photographers fighting to get the best shot of a strange airplane painted blue and silver, with thousands of small stars on the wings and fuselage. Painting a plane like a packet of Baci Perugina chocolates (*see photo*) might have been a publicity stunt, but it also
shows just how dynamic this major Italian company is. Perugina is a hundred years old: it was founded in 1907 by a group of entrepreneurs, including Annibale Spagnoli, Francesco Andreani and, most importantly, Francesco Buitoni, the heir of a famed pasta-making family from Sansepolcro. The company was christened "Perugina cioccolata & confetture" (*see photo*) and was based on a small, existing chocolate factory. The famous Bacio chocolate was created in 1922. During the period between the wars, the company invested in modern technology and organizational methods,

wound in a spiral, placed in a greased pan and baked in the oven.

Brustengolo

This simple, rustic cake with age-old origins is found across Perugia. It is dry and quite low, with a rounded or rectangular shape. Made with maize flour and milk, the first stage is to produce a soft polenta and then add in apple slices, raisins, pine-seeds, grated lemon rind, sugar, walnut kernels and aniseed or anisette seeds. A 2cm-high layer of the mixture is then placed in a greased pan and baked in the oven at 180°C/356°F for 20-30 minutes.

Castagnole

These are a bit like fried gnocchetti pasta and come in two forms: soft and hard. The dough is made with soft wheat flour, eggs, anisette or rum, grated lemon rind, seed (or olive) oil and baking powder. Once made, the dough is left covered for 15 minutes before spoon-sized pieces are fried in boiling lard. The *castagnole* are then placed on kitchen towel before being sprinkled with alkermes, honey or sugar.

Ciaramicola

This cake, typical of Perugia, is like a large doughnut topped by a cross and five balls made of dough, and covered in icing sugar or meringue. This traditional Easter cake, hence the cross, is also symbolic of the city: the five spheres represent Piazza Grande and the four city gates, while the colors (red inside, covered in white, with blue, yellow and green coated almonds) stand for the five city districts. The ingredients are simple, but the result is quite unusual.

Cresciole di Ciccioli or Torta 'ch'i ciccili

A rounded or braided dessert in various sizes. The dough is made with soft wheat flour, water and yeast.
When it has risen to twice the original size, the dough is kneaded once more, this time adding in scraps of pork fat, milk, olive oil, a touch of flour, eggs, sugar, lard, candied or diced lemon rind, raisins, cinnamon or nutmeg and pine-seeds. This dough is then shaped as desired, allowed to rise for 45-60 minutes and, finally, baked in an oven at 180°C/356°F for about an hour.

Crescionda

This flattish dessert with three layers is found across Spoleto and is associated with Carnival. The bottom layer is made of almond biscuits and flour; the middle one is light-colored and soft like a pudding; the upper one, a dark brown, is chocolate. Ingredients: milk, whole eggs, sugar, crumbs of almond biscuits, soft wheat flour, lemon rind and grated dark chocolate.

FOOD

reaping the benefits of rapid growth and becoming a market leader. The Bacio Perugina, a true little delicacy, has a gianduja and hazelnut filling coated in dark chocolate – as simple as it is poetic. The idea behind the product is traditionally set to have come from Luisa Spagnoli, wife of Francesco Buitoni and a well-known fashion stylist. Indeed, it is said to have been the result of the search to find a practical use for processed hazelnuts and the intuition to include a little message with each chocolate. As Emily Dickinson said, "That love is all there is, is all we know of love". The commercial success of the product is, though, the merit of the husband, who started things off superbly by commissioning a timeless drawing from Seneca of two lovers under a starlit sky, inspired by Grancesco Hayez's work *The Kiss*.

The Museo Storico Perugina, Via Pievaiola, San Sisto, Tel. 0755276796, www.perugina.it, at the San Sisto plant, covers the history and importance of these chocolates.

Fave dei Morti are common in early November and at feasts and festivals.

Fave dei Morti

Generally associated with the province of Perugia, and especially with the Nerina valley, these biscuits are often found at feasts in early November (especially on 2 November, the Day of the Dead in Italy). The name roughly means "beans of the dead" and seems to be a reference to the classical world, where beans became associated with death as the flowers are white with black marks. The biscuits are dry and oval shaped, and are made with either sweet or bitter almonds that have been peeled, toasted and chopped. These almonds are made into a dough with egg whites, sugar and grated lemon rind. This dough is then shaped into small, squashed balls that are baked on a greased, floured baking tray at 180°C/356°F for 10-15 minutes.

Mostaccioli

Found across the region, these dry must biscuits are either shaped like doughnuts or squashed "flat". Ingredients: soft wheat flour, white grape-must, sugar and aniseed. This is leavened for 2 hours before being baked for 30 minutes. A variant sees the addition of raisins, olive oil, brewer's yeast and diced orange rind.

Pammelati

This is a typical Christmas cake in Deruta and Torgiano (Perugia). Bread crumbs, walnuts, cinnamon, orange rind and pine-seeds (optional) are mixed over a gentle heat. It is then turned out on a marble surface, rolled using one's hands, cut into pieces and shaped into little balls.

Pampepato

This is a typical Christmas cake that is rounded and common in Massa Martana, Todi, Marsciano, Deruta (Perugia) and the province of Terni. Ingredients: walnuts, raisins, cocoa, honey, almonds, hazelnuts, cooked must, candied fruits, pine-seeds, lemon, pepper, anisette or dry Marsala, coffee, cinnamon, cloves (optional), a touch of flour, a little sugar and, if you want, jam. It goes especially well with Aleatico di Orvieto wine.

Pinolate

These are rounded, dry almond biscuits with pine-seeds. The mixture is made with potato starch, chopped almonds, sugar and egg white. This is shaped into slightly squashed balls that are baked on a baking tray covered with pine-seeds.

Pinolate are one of the more inventive biscuits found in Umbria.

Rocciata

This cake is a typical of the province of Perugia. It is a baked, filled puff pastry cake that is either spiral or horseshoe shaped. The name (seemingly linked to the word rock) is not a reference to the consistency, but actually indicates 'rounded' as that is the meaning of *roccia* in the local dialect. The filling is made of apples, fig jam, walnuts, sultanas, pine-seeds, almonds, cinnamon, lemon, vanilla and, sometimes, cocoa. It is made from autumn to January and is eaten fresh, especially on All Saints' Day.

Stinchetti

Typical of Perugia, these dry biscuits are shaped rather like a shinbone, hence the other name, *Ossi dei Morti* or bones of the dead. White on the outside (sugar, egg white and fish-glue), the inside is dark (sugar or honey, cocoa, toasted and chopped sweet and bitter almonds, cinnamon, vanilla, grated lemon rind and egg whites).

Torciglione

Found across the province of Perugia, these dry biscuits are made with equal amounts of sweet almonds and sugar, which is mixed together with whipped egg whites.
They are shaped like twisted snakes and are decorated with whole almonds or pine-seeds – to look like scales – candied citron (the ears) and coffee beans (the eyes).

Torcolo di San Costanzo or Torcolo al candito

This is a type of doughnut that is common in Perugia. The surface is marked with small cuts representing the city gates. This symbolic cake is linked to St Constantius the Martyr, patron saint of Perugia.

Torta di Orvieto

A sweet bread that is traditionally eaten around Easter, it can easily be found at other times of the year.
Wide, flat and very soft, the dough has cherries, raisins and candied citron.

Zuccherini di Bettona

The name is linked to where they are made, but it does not really explain what they are: sweet, small doughnuts filled with raisins, pine-seeds, aniseed and pieces of candied citron.

The torciglione is an eye-catching cake that looks like a snake.

torciglione, pinoccata, pinolata, stinchetti and mostaccioli.

ASSISI

Marinella
Santa Maria degli Angeli, Piazza Porziuncola 8/D, Tel. 0758041826, www.pastmarinella.it
A wonderful pastry house that has been selling traditional cakes for over fifty years.

FOLIGNO

Beddini
Via Rutili 28/30, Tel. 0742350767, www.beddinipasticceria.com
Located in the old center of Foligno, it produces traditional cakes, including *rocciata*.

Muzzi Antica Pasticceria
Via Mazzini 7, Tel. 0742352243, www.pasticceriamuzzi.com
A famous, small and elegant pastry house that sells a wonderful array of regional specialties, chocolates and biscuits.

PERUGIA

Pasticceria Sonia
Ponte Felcino, Via L. Mastrodicasa 13, Tel. 0755913128
Traditional homemade cakes: *pinoccata*, *ciaramicola* and *torcolo di S. Costanzo*.

Sandri
Corso Vannucci 32, Tel. 0755724112
This is a small, famous and old pastry house. Dating from 1860, it is worth a visit just to see the furniture. On sale:

TERNI

Carletti
Via Ippocrate 51, Tel. 0744220307
This elegant place is much loved for the cakes made with good basic ingredients. A member of the Consorzio Pampepato Ternano.

ORVIETO

Montanucci
Corso Cavour 21, Tel. 0763341261
This lovely, elegant place is well cared for and offers a fanciful range of homemade cakes.

FOOD

145

Food festivals

JANUARY

↘ **29 January**
SAGRA DEL TORCOLO DI SAN COSTANZO
Perugia
Tourist information:
Tel. 0755736458
During the feast of the patron saint, the city's pastry houses display this typical, ring-shape cake that is a symbol of union for all engaged couples who bring the saint gifts of sultanas, pine-seeds and aniseed.

FEBRUARY

↘ **Last weekend in February**
MOSTRA MERCATO DEL TARTUFO NERO E DEI PRODOTTI TIPICI DELLA VALNERINA
Norcia (Perugia)
www.valnerinaonline.it
This feast-market is centered on typical products from the Nerina valley. It is an ideal time to try some truffle and other products from the Norcia area, such as cheeses, lentils from Castelluccio, trout from the Nera and red fruits.

FEBRUARY/MARCH

↘ **Last Sunday before lent**
FESTA DELL'OLIVO E SAGRA DELLA BRUSCHETTA
Spello (Perugia)
Pro Loco, Tel. 0742301009,
www.comune.spello.pg.it
This festival marks the end of the olive harvest. Olive harvesters parade through the streets on tractors holding olive branches, a symbol of the *benfinita* (the end of the harvest). The *Sagra* della Bruschetta (or bruschetta festival) is filled with singing and dancing. *Bruschetta*, a classical Italian snack of toasted bread sprinkled with oil and salt, is handed out in the streets so locals can taste the olive oil. Traditional local inns are open and the piazzas come alive with stalls selling local products.

↘ **Last weekend of February/first of March**
MOSTRA MERCATO DEL TARTUFO NERO DI NORCIA
Norcia (Perugia)
www.italianodoc.com

There have already been 44 of these black truffle festivals. This annual event takes place over two weekends at the end of February and the beginning of March. Gourmets and tasters from across the world flock here for the famous black truffle from Norcia, as do lovers of ham, cured meats, fresh and aged cheeses.

JUNE

↘ **Early June**
FIOR DI CACIO
Vallo di Nera (Perugia)
www.fiordicacio.it
This delightful medieval hamlet at the entrance to the Nerina valley becomes the setting for shepherds and cheese makers to reveal the secrets of making the famed local ewe's and goats' milk cheeses.

JUNE/JULY

↘ **Last week of June/first of July**
SAGRA DEL FIORE DI ZUCCA
Loc. Nera Montoro Narni (Terni)
www.terniforum.it
There are food stalls where you can taste tagliatelle with zucchini flowers, a dessert made of zucchini flowers or fried zucchini flowers.

↘ **Last week of June/first of July**
SAGRA DELLA RANOCCHIA
Loc. Selci, San Giustino
www.umbriaonline.com
This festival has been going for over 25 years and it is an excellent opportunity to try some very tasty dishes, such as frogs covered in maize flour and fried.

JULY

↘ **Second half of July**
FESTA DEL GIACCHIO
Magione (Perugia)
Comune, Tel. 075847701,
www.comune.magione.pg.it
Held near San Feliciano, this festival lasts about 10 days and gets its name from the typical fishing net used until about the 1950s by fishermen plying their trade on Lake Trasimeno. This form of fishing was banned

as it damages the lake bed, but it is re-enacted during this event as fishermen compete to see who throws the net the best. In the evening, the menu is obviously centered on lake fish: *tegamaccio* is a local specialty, but there are plenty of other traditional dishes on offer.

AUGUST

↘ **Final 10 days of August**
FESTA DELLA PADELLA
Passignano sul Trasimeno
www.paesaggi.umbria2000.it
Every year, and only for this event, the world's largest frying pan is used. It can fry 200kg of fish in an hour! All the dishes are enhanced by the excellent local wine.

↘ **Week of 15 August**
SAGRA DELLA PATATA ROSSA
Colfiorito di Foligno (Perugia)
www.comune.foligno-pg.it
Red potatoes have been grown for a few decades on the Colfiorito plateaux. It is not a local variety, coming from Holland, but it has acclimatized excellently. During the festival, the culinary aspects are flanked by cultural initiatives, sports events and musical performances.

↘ **Third weekend of August**
SAGRA DELLA PECORA
Loc. Morra, Città di Castello (Perugia)
www.grandieventi.
umbria2000.it
Here, you can taste local mutton-based dishes as well as buy various local products. Games and folklore events enhance the atmosphere.

SEPTEMBER

↘ **First ten days of September**
FESTA DELLA CIPOLLA
Cannara (Perugia)
Tourist information:
organising committee,
Tel. 0742681230,
www.prolococannara.it
This annual event is a good opportunity to taste some of the best and most popular Umbrian dishes. Onions (called *cipolle* in Italian,

hence the name of the festival) are used to make absolutely delicious thick soups as well as to give other dishes a special, unique flavor. The area has an abundance of high quality onions because of the nature of the soil and the local climate.

SEPTEMBER/OCTOBER

↘ **Late September-Early October**
I PRIMI D'ITALIA
Foligno (Perugia)
www.iprimiditalia.it
This festival is all about Italian starters (*primi piatti*), with tastings of some delicious dishes on the squares and in the local inns.

↘ **Late September-Early October**
SETTIMANA ENOLOGICA
Montefalco (Perugia)
Tel. 0742378490,
www.montefalcodoc.it
This wine week is like a homage to the Sagrantino di Montefalco DOCG. There are tastings of the latest wine (3 years after the harvest) and theme dinners.

OCTOBER

↘ **Last weekend of October**
MOSTRA MERCATO DELLO ZAFFERANO DI CASCIA
Cascia (Perugia)
Tel. 074371147,
www.cascianet.it
The local saffron (*zafferano*) is on display to buy and taste. There are also other local delicacies from the Cascia area.

↘ **Early October**
ORVIETO CON GUSTO
Orvieto (Terni)
www.orvietocongusto.it
This event is all about eating well and good culinary traditions. Each year, a different theme is chosen (spices, bread, flavors from the vegetable patch).

↘ **Third weekend in October**
SAGRA DELLA CASTAGNA
Loc. Morra, Città di Castello (Perugia)
www.cittadicastelloonline.it/eventi/
There are food stalls serving lunches and dinners filled with local dishes based on chestnuts (*castagne*). Various other traditional dishes are also available.

↘ **First weekend in October**
SAGRA DELLA CIACCIA FRITTA
Fighille (Perugia)
www.ciboviaggiando.it
Fried *ciaccia* is a type of pizza, made with water, salt, flour and brewer's yeast. The ingredients are combined and shaped into little round pizzas that are fried in boiling oil, filled with local cured meats and served with a good, young red wine.

OCTOBER/NOVEMBER

↘ **Late October-early November**
FRANTOI APERTI
Giano, Spello, Montefalco, Trevi, Spoleto, Isola Polvese
Tel. 0742344214,
www.frantoiaperti.net
The oil presses are opened to the public so that they can learn more about the art of making oil. This initiative is accompanied by tastings of Umbrian extra-virgin olive oil.

↘ **Late October-early November**
MOSTRA MERCATO DEL TARTUFO BIANCO E DEI PRODOTTI AGROALIMENTARI
Gubbio (Perugia)
www.gubbio-altochiascio.umbria2ooo.it
This big event is centered on the white truffle, but there are plenty of other local products as well (meats, cheeses and oil).

NOVEMBER

↘ **First weekend in November**
MOSTRA MERCATO DEL TARTUFO BIANCO E PRODOTTI DEL BOSCO
Città di Castello (Perugia)
IAT Città di Castello,
Tel. 0758554922,
www.cdcnet.net
This event is centered on the excellent local white truffle and other products from the forest.

↘ **Last two weekends in November**
MOSTRA MERCATO NAZIONALE DEL TARTUFO
Valtopina (Perugia)
www.bellaumbria.net/valtopina
This national truffle festival and market offers tastings accompanied by many related events that bring the town to life.

FOOD

 ## TCI HIGHLIGHTS

EUROCHOCOLATE

The Eurochocolate Festival is an annual event held in mid-October that is dedicated to the culture of chocolate. The heart of the event is the old center, with Rocca Paolina, various piazzas and a number of other areas. In the space of just a few years, it has won over the public's affection, becoming the chocolate festival par excellence and making Perugia the European chocolate capital. For nine days, the capital of Umbria becomes a giant, open-air pastry house where you can taste, browse and buy. It is also a wonderful chance to discover some of the more hidden corners of the old medieval center and to enjoy famed Umbrian hospitality.

For further information: www.eurochocolate.it

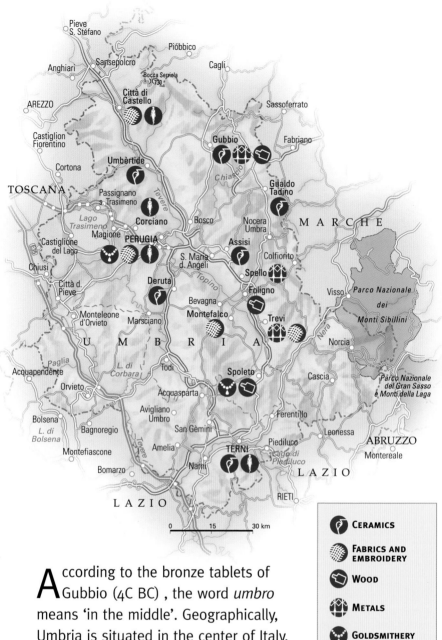

	CERAMICS
	FABRICS AND EMBROIDERY
	WOOD
	METALS
	GOLDSMITHERY
	FASHION

A ccording to the bronze tablets of
Gubbio (4C BC) , the word *umbro*
means 'in the middle'. Geographically,
Umbria is situated in the center of Italy,
surrounded by Tuscany, Marche and Lazio.
In this area there are many workshops
where traditional crafts are still practiced. Products
made here are the result of the enthusiasm and
manual dexterity of generations of artisans with
natural flair and long experience. In Umbria, this
superior level of craftsmanship is being further
enhanced through exhibition facilities and workshops,

the aim of which is to promote the vast local craft heritage. But Umbria also means fashion: factory outlets offer high-quality, top-brand goods at bargain prices. Finally, the small street markets of Umbria will delight collectors hunting for antiques and second-hand books.

Highlights

- The ancient art of working clay is alive and well in Deruta, Perugia, Gubbio Orvieto and Umbèrtide.
- Fairs and markets are held across the region, often in charming towns like Città di Castello and Todi.
- Fabrics, embroidered objects and lace with geometric or animal motifs are made in Assisi, Panicale and Orvieto.
- Wood, wrought-iron and copper products are still made in the region employing traditional processes in use since the Middle Ages.

Inside

ARTS AND CRAFTS

In Umbria, the production of objects for everyday use has always run parallel to artistic production of extremely high quality which, at the same time, helped to raise the esthetic level, as the ceramics and textiles still made here today show. On the other hand, even back in the Middle Ages, the creation of craft guilds which kept a stern eye on the quality of the output of the workshops, shows how important art and crafts had become from a cultural and economic point of view. Although this legacy has been partially rescaled as a result of increasing industrialization, in this region it has been jealously preserved and is being promoted today through the study and recovery of traditional techniques and iconography, with the aim of preventing this extensive technical and creative heritage from being lost, and providing new avenues for development.

Pottery

In Umbria, the art of working clay flourished in many Umbrian towns (Deruta, Perugia, Gubbio, Gualdo Tadino, Orvieto, Città di Castello and Umbèrtide) and is continued today by artisans who never cease to research and protect the original techniques and forms, to highlight and exploit the quality and specific characteristics of the pottery of each town. Deruta possibly has the most ancient tradition. The ceramics tradition here certainly dates from the 13th century and reached its height in the 16th century, when the local pottery was glazed with very white enamel decorated with orange, blue and yellow. During the same century, majolicas produced in Gubbio became very popular. Giorgio Andreoli, Umbria's greatest 16th-century ceramicist, was famous for having achieved results which have yet to be equaled, using a technique of Arabic origin to decorate his pieces with golden highlights. At Gualdo Tadino, artisan workshops still produce ceramics with highlights "from the third firing", which local potters have been proud of for centuries, whereas industrially produced pieces tend to reproduce shapes and decoration based on medieval artifacts. The pottery made in Orvieto also stems from a tradition about a thousand years old, now consolidated into an unmistakable style dominated by plant and animal motifs. The artistic ceramics produced at Umbèrtide is distinctive on account of its metallic luster, obtained by applying the so-called luster pigment, while, at Città di Castello, ceramic products are usually decorated with heraldic motifs and relief decoration.

TCI HIGHLIGHTS

THE MUSEO REGIONALE DELLA CERAMICA AT DERUTA

Deruta is associated with the production of artistic majolica. This art form dates from 1290. This is termed the archaic period, when objects were produced for everyday use: pouring jugs, basins and bowls decorated with geometric and zoomorphic patterns. The dominant colors used then were copper-speckled green and manganese-brown. In the centuries that followed, majolica from Deruta reached its greatest splendor. It was traded throughout the 16th century and exported all over Europe. There were many different kinds of original decoration: floral, zoomorphic and grotesque. Meanwhile, the range of colors was enhanced with the addition of orange, blue and yellow, and the metallic luster technique appeared, resulting in splendid gold highlights. As the centuries passed, style and decoration evolved into the "compendious" style of quick strokes, and the "calligraphic" style based on Moorish techniques, with interwoven flowers, leaves, arabesques, birds and animals. Today, you can tell that the artistic output here is enormous just by wandering around the streets of Deruta, with its shops, workshops, factories and

Fabrics

The earliest examples of hand-woven fabric in Umbria date from the 12th century, when Perugia became famous for its *tovaglie perugine*, veritable works of art which are still made to this day. At Città di Castello there are still some artisans weaving cloth on old wooden looms, adhering rigorously to ancient techniques, designs and colors. These fabrics are distinctive for their original depictions of

Table-cloths made in Perugia.

the griffin, the symbol of Perugia, and their Renaissance-style geometric patterns in blue, golden yellow and red which are applied to linen, woven using the "partridge eye" technique with colored stripes, or fine linen decorated with brocade motifs or with the classic *quadruccio umbro* (Umbrian checks).

Embroidery and lace

In the 14th century, some artisans in Assisi adapted a technique of Coptic origin to decorate fabrics with dense geometric embroidered patterns which they used to create motifs and imaginary animals. This is how "punto Assisi" began. The technique is still commonly used in Assisi today. The origins of the delicate, renowned lace made in Orvieto, on the other hand, are quite recent. It was invented in the early 20th century by applying an Irish pillow-lace technique. However, the original embroidery technique was soon enhanced with Renaissance-style motifs based on the low reliefs on the facade of the Duomo, resulting in original creations which were extraordinary as much for their symbolism as their delicate beauty. Orvieto lace is still produced and is very popular. The same technique, together with that of bobbin lace, is very common in the Lake Trasimeno area, while, at Panicale, for centuries, they have been embroidering tulle, using techniques which have brought the prices of this fine pillow-lace to the level of the more famous lace from Florence, Brianza or Venice.

Wood

In Umbria, there are two parallel branches of wood-working: a rural branch which originated from the need for objects for everyday use, and a more "cultured" branch, which raised marquetry techniques to the outstanding levels of the wooden decoration we see in churches and palazzi from the Renaissance and baroque periods. Nowadays wood-working is mainly a service activity and is conducted all over Umbria, taking the form of a vast range of expertise, from processes to prepare wood for industrial applications to the creation, repair or restoration of a vast

showrooms. The Museo Regionale della Ceramica was conceived as a collection of models for people working with majolica, or conducting research into the history of ceramics, and to promote and raise awareness about local production. Situated in the former monastery of San Francesco, it has more than 6,000 pieces, including Greek and Roman pottery, and examples of local ceramic production from medieval times to the present day. The two rooms off the cloister are used for temporary exhibitions. The displays of Deruta pottery pottery are upstairs, arranged in chronological order, including areas devoted to special themes, from the archaic period to the early 20th century. An old pharmacy has been reconstructed with its typical majolica storage jars, used throughout Italy between the 15th and 19th centuries.

Museo Regionale della Ceramica, Largo S. Francesco 1, Tel. 0759711000, www.museoceramicaderuta.it

SHOPPING

VOTIVE OFFERINGS

There are some forms of craftsmanship which ignore the rules of the market and are rarely noticed. The 17th-century sanctuary of Madonna del Bagno, set in a pleasant corner of the Umbrian countryside, not far from Deruta, is a good example. You step over the threshold and are suddenly confronted with the world's finest and most diverse collection of votive majolica

tiles. The first votive offering, an image of the Madonna painted in reds and blues on the fragment of a cup, was placed in the cavity of an oak tree in 1657, and is now incorporated in the central wall of the church. The cup in the oak tree was commissioned by a pedlar from Casalina who was worried about the fate of his ailing wife. The miracle recovery of the woman gave rise to a tradition which continues to this day, and led to a form of craftsmanship where the manual expertise of the craftsman is secondary to the depiction of an image conveying the feelings of joy and amazement of someone who has seen their faith rewarded in a moment of despair. In the sanctuary of Madonna del Bagno, all the votive offerings are made of majolica and the thousands of votive tiles which have been placed there over three centuries provide a fascinating insight into local styles, culture and the people who commissioned them.

spectrum of objects, work-tools and furnishing accessories. Città di Castello, Todi, Assisi and Perugia are the towns where skilled wood craftsmen are still active, with a considerable number of workshops belonging to marquetry workers, wood-carvers and sculptors. Gubbio deserves a special mention as the town which has succeeded in preserving not only its craft traditions but also its cultural traditions, so that there is still a technical school where carpenters, shoemakers and tailors can learn their trade.

Wrought iron and copper

The fact that wrought iron is very common, as a structural feature, a functional feature or for decoration in the old palaces and ordinary houses proves that this craft skill was already very common in the Middle Ages. This ancient trade is still being plied today in the many wrought iron workshops dotted around the region, especially at Assisi, Città della Pieve, the small towns near Lake Trasimeno and near Spoleto. The workshops are nearly always located in old town centers, small places which emphasize the close relationship which once existed between the place where people worked and where

they lived. Here the iron artisans tended to produce tools for everyday use. In addition to this main form of production, smaller businesses grew up producing specialized, more unusual objects, like the old weapons industry in Gubbio, or the files and rasps made in Villamagina and the surgical implements made in Norcia since the 16th century. There is also a large number of workshops making beaten copper, the best of which are located at Magione, on the Perugia side of Lake Trasimeno. Here master coppersmiths excel in the production of copper objects using hammering, carving or embossing techniques to make pots, pans and jugs.

PERUGIA

FABRICS AND EMBROIDERY
Bottega d'Arte Ceccucci
Strada di Prepo 115,
Tel. 0755051966
JEWELRY
Oro degli Etruschi
Corso Vittorio Emanuele 10,
Tel. 075985466

ASSISI
ARTISTIC CERAMICS
Feba Ceramiche Artistiche
Santa Maria degli Angeli

Via Protomartiri Francescani 90,
Tel. 0758043901

CITTÀ DI CASTELLO
FABRICS AND EMBROIDERY
Tela Umbra Società Cooperativa Arl
Via S. Antonio 3, Tel. 0758554337

DERUTA
ARTISTIC CERAMICS
Ceramiche Artistiche G. & P.
Via Tiberina 300, Tel. 075972016
Fratelli Mari
Via della Circonvallazione 1,
Tel. 0759710400
Giulio Gialletti & C.
Via Tiberina Sud 304, Tel. 075972021
La Gioconda
Via G. Li Causi 8, Tel. 0759710080
Monotti Maioliche
Via Tiberina Sud 276, Tel. 075972002
Nazzareno Picchiotti & C.
Via dell'Artigianato 16, Tel. 075972271

FOLIGNO
WOOD RESTORATION
Alla Vecchia Maniera
Via Bettini 3, Tel. 0742320005

GUALDO TADINO
ARTISTIC CERAMICS
Ceramica Garofoli
Via Caduti Marcinelle, Tel. 0759108113
Ceramica Vecchia Gualdo
Via Matteotti 88, Tel. 0759140229

GUBBIO
ARTISTIC CERAMICS
Ceramiche Da Mastro Giorgio
Via Tifernate 10, Tel. 0759273616
Leo Grilli
Via Consoli 68, Tel. 0759275120
WOOD FURNITURE
Il Fratino
Via Fontevole 112, Tel. 0759271248
WROUGHT IRON WORKING
Artigianato Ferro Artistico
Via U. Baldassini 22, Tel. 0759273079

MONTEFALCO
FABRICS AND EMBROIDERY
Tessuti di Montefalco
Via Ringhiera Umbra 25, Tel. 0742378119

SPELLO
WROUGHT IRON WORKING
Artigianfer
Via Gigliara 13, Tel. 0742651387

L'Officina
Via A. Grandi 12, Tel. 0742301095

SPOLETO
JEWELRY
K.S. Creazioni in Oro
Via Martiri della Resistenza 119,
Tel. 0743221967
WOOD RESTORATION
Agostinelli Teofilo
San Paolo di Beroide 45/A,
Tel. 0743275208

TREVI
FABRICS AND EMBROIDERY
Bottega Artigianale "Casa de' Trinci"
Piazza Mazzini 8, Tel. 0742381270
WORKING DIFFERENT METALS
Fonderia Leghe Leggere Albi
Via Monte Ademelio 28, Tel. 074280508

UMBÈRTIDE
ARTISTIC CERAMICS
Ceramiche Rometti
Via Garibaldi 73, Tel. 0759413266
Le Crete di Pa.to'
Badia S. Cassiano, Tel. 0759302365

TERNI

ORVIETO
ARTISTIC CERAMICS
L.ar.ce.
Via Postierla 6, Tel. 0763393151
FURNITURE
Falegnameria Ars & Lignum
Via dei Fabbri 1, Tel. 0763316351

 TCI HIGHLIGHTS

UMBRIAN CLOTH
At Città di Castello in Piazza Costa
stands the 16th-century Palazzo
Bourbon Dal Monte, now seat of the
Tela Umbra weaving workshop,
created in 1909 by Baroness Alice
Franchetti to preserve knowledge
about old weaving techniques.
It contains the Collezione Tessile
di Tela Umbra, with traditional
spindles, spinning-wheels and looms,
and tools for making embroidery and
lace, as well as documents and early
photographs.

SHOPPING

MARKETS

Antique fairs, fairs of second-hand goods and arts and crafts fairs provide an alternative way of shopping or hunting for unusual items and souvenirs. People come to these delightful events, which, in many cases, blend into their settings like something out of a fairytale, to hunt for unusual or rare items in a sort of frantic treasure-hunt. Walking past the stalls you can find almost anything: old vinyl "33s", quaint farm tools, pieces of antique furniture and books whose pages have become yellowed with time. There is no shortage of precious objects and prints but also, for real enthusiasts, collections of stamps, postcards and coins.

PERUGIA

Fiera dei Morti
First week of November
An annual fair continuing
a hundred-year-old tradition.
Information: Tel. 0755736458,
www.comune.perugia.it

**Fiera dell'Antiquariato
e del Collezionismo**
Last week of every month
Held from April till October at the
Giardini Carducci and from November till
March at the Rocca Paolina, this is an
antique fair for real enthusiasts.
Many stalls exhibiting stamps and coins.
Information: Tel. 0755008731

Umbria Libri
End of November
Book fair featuring Italian and foreign
writers and intellectuals who
participate in meetings, debates
and conferences.
Information: Tel. 07553681,
www.umbrialibri.com

BASTIA UMBRA
**Mostra Mercato Nazionale
dell'Antiquariato**
End of April-Beginning of May
This fair attracts Italy's top antique
dealers and some foreign exhibitors,
and antiques collectors and enthusiasts
from all over Italy and abroad.
It has large sections devoted
to stamps and coins.
Information: Tel. 0758004005,
www.umbriafiere.it

CITTÀ DI CASTELLO
Fiera del rigattiere
Third weekend of every month
This old town center is occupied by
stalls offering all kinds of antique and
second-hand objects.
Information: Tel. 0758529225

Mostra del Mobile in Stile
End of April-Beginning of May
A chance to admire the quality and
tradition of Umbrian-style furniture
made by craftsmen from the upper
reaches of the Tiber, in walnut, cherry,
olive, chestnut and oak. One section of
the exhibition concentrates on antique
furniture made by local craftsmen.
Information: Tel. 0758554922

Mostra Nazionale del Cavallo
Mid-September
One of the most important Italian shows
in the sector, with horse-breeders from
all over Italy and abroad. Vast program
of events, from competitions for
selected breeds to all kinds of
equestrian events.The annual event is
held in the grounds of the town's old
tabacco factory.
Information: Tel. 0758554922
www.mostradelcavallo.com

TODI
Rassegna Antiquaria d'Italia
End of March-Beginning of April
Held at Palazzo del Vignola, for ten days
this fair is host to the most prestigious
names in the world of Italian antiques,
offering the public the chance to admire
some unique pieces, including furniture,
ceramics, jewelry, wrought iron, and
hand-made brass and copper.
Information: Tel. 07589561,
www.comune.todi.pg.it

TERNI

Anticherie
*Second weekend of every month, except
July and August*
The historic center is thronged with
stalls selling anything from shoes,
clothes, ornaments, farm tools and
books to antique jewelry.
Information: Tel. 0744549824

FASHION

Factory outlets are the new, modern way of shopping at discount prices. These "virtual villages" are designed with the aim of encouraging people to buy, places where shoppers can lose themselves in the maze of shops and enjoy the carefree atmosphere. In addition to boutiques selling Italy's top brands of clothes, shoes and accessories, you find all the services and facilities needed to make the customers' stay more pleasant: huge parking-lots, bars, places where you can get something to eat, ice-cream parlors with tables and chairs, as well as play areas designed specifically for young children.

PERUGIA

Luisa Spagnoli
Strada S. Lucia 35, Tel. 0754591-07540158
Casual and elegant ladies' wear. Also sells accessories like belts, bags and scarves. Excellent discounts compared to normal prices.

BASTIA UMBRA
Ellesse Unisport
Ospedalicchio, Via S. Cristoforo, Tel. 0758012765, www.unisport.it
Clothing for men, ladies and kids, casual and sportswear for skiing, tennis and the beach. Also sells accessories such as beach towels, bath-robes, beach sandals, swimwear, sports bags, gloves and hats. Footwear for leisure activities, trekking, the beach and tennis. Considerable savings compared to normal shop prices.

CANNARA
2C - Maglificio Artigiano
Via S. Angelo 5, Tel. 074272380
Artisan production and direct sale of tops, jumpers, skirts and trousers made of pure wool, wool/Merino and wool/cashmere blends. Factory prices.

CITTÀ DI CASTELLO
Camiceria Etrusca
Viale Romagna 73, Tel. 0758511328-0758511171
www.camiceriaetrusca.com
Artisan-made high-quality men's shirts and ladies' blouses. Accessories include ties, socks and boxer shorts. Fabrics vary depending on the season: cotton, brushed cotton, jeans and linen. Discounts on marked prices.

CORCIANO
Brunello Cucinelli
Solomeo, Piazza Carlo Alberto Dalla Chiesa 6, Tel. 075529481
www.brunellocucinelli.it
High-quality, artisan cashmere articles. Men's and ladies' wear. Accessories include scarves, hats and gloves. Generous discounts, especially on seconds.

Ellesse Unisport
Ellera, Via Fratelli Turati, Tel. 0755171523, www.unisport.it
Men's, ladies' and kids' casual and sports wear for skiing, tennis and the beach. Accessories available include beach towels, bath-robes, beach and pool sandals, sports bags, gloves and hats. Footwear for leisure activities, trekking, the beach and tennis.

Gunex
Solomeo, Via dell'Industria 5/2, Tel. 075529491, www.gunex.it
Ladies' wear sold under the Cucinelli group's Gunex label, specializing in skirts and trousers for smart occasions. Top-quality fabrics and artisan production. Only top-quality items at bargain prices.

Rivamonti
Solomeo, Via dell'Industria 5/1, Tel. 075697071, www.rivamonti.it
Within the Cucinelli group, the Rivamonti trade-mark represents the trendy fashion line for younger people. Specialized in knitwear crafted with top-quality yarn, with solutions for every kind of men's and ladies' wear. Generous discounts.

TERNI

Spaccio Conti
Via del Sersimone 2, Tel. 0744300088
Outer clothing, lingerie and household linen. Gifts and household objects such as picture- frames, cups, candles, glasses and trays. All items sold at discounted prices.

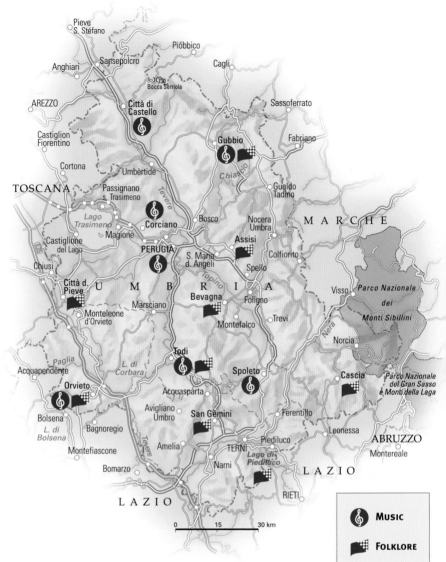

🎵	**MUSIC**
🏁	**FOLKLORE**

One reason why Umbria is so extraordinary is the sheer number and variety of events held throughout the year. All the traditional secular and religious festivals, the historical re-enactments, the jousting and the historic processions have been handed down through the centuries and are performed today in the just same way, with the same enthusiasm. For the local people, each event reinforces their roots and identity, while offering visitors a chance to learn about local folklore and even participate in the event first hand. In addition to these deep-rooted traditions, much energy is devoted to organizing contemporary cultural events attended by Italians and foreign visitors alike. There are also events focusing on the arts, like *Umbria Jazz* and the *Festival dei Due Mondi*, with music, ballet, theater, movies and exhibitions. Yet another facet of the important role played by this small region.

Highlights

■ Events of national and international importance like *Umbria Jazz* and the *Festival dei Due Mondi* in Spoleto.

■ The *Sagra Musicale Umbra* has been a success for more than 60 years, with first-class performances.

■ Every year in Assisi, in the first week of May, there is a competition to select *Madonna Primavera*, in a medieval and Renaissance setting .

■ Watch the *Corsa dei Ceri* in Gubbio: the wooden Ceri, which weigh 200kg, are 4m high.

Inside

MUSIC

In a region like Umbria, where many of the towns have preserved much of their medieval character, concerts are held in Roman amphitheaters and in the many squares, enclosed by buildings making them acoustically suitable, or in historic venues or charming old theaters. Music in this region has developed particularly in the last 50 or 60 years, thanks partly to the emergence of events of international importance, such as the *Festival dei Due Mondi* and *Umbria Jazz*. But the unusual thing about Umbria is that, in addition to the events organized in individual towns, there are also events like the *Sagra Musicale Umbra* involving many Umbrian towns, where not only historic theaters but also churches and other monuments provide delightful settings for musical events of all kinds.

PERUGIA

Festival Internazionale delle Figure Animate
End of August-beginning of September
Hosts companies from all over the world representing all kinds of Figure Theater.
For further information:
www.tieffeu.com

Perugia Classico
September
Held in the *Rocca Paolina* and the old town center, this important trade fair of hand-made musical instruments takes place against a background of concerts and conferences in the town's historic venues.
For further information:
www.perugiaclassico.it

Umbria Jazz
Mid-July
One of Europe's top jazz festivals, "the" jazz festival in Italy, involving the most famous names from the world jazz scene. Ten days of concerts from morning till night, many performed in the open air or in the theaters and on the stages of the towns of Umbria.
For further information:
www.umbriajazz.com

CITTÀ DI CASTELLO

Festival delle Nazioni
August
One of Italy's most important musical events. Each year a different country is invited to participate in the event, which offers the public the best of musical output against the charming backdrop of Città di Castello's natural scenery and historic buildings. The main focus is on music, but dance, theater, and visual arts also make an important contribution.
For further information:
www.festivaldellenazioni.com

CORCIANO

Corciano Festival
August
The festival involves the visual arts, music, theater and historical re-enactments, and has been enthusiastically received by the public and by cultural operators for the quality of the events and the charming setting. In Corciano castle, in the week of Ferragosto (August 15), there are re-enactments of scenes from medieval life with the *Processione del Lume* (Candle-lit Procession), the *Serenate dei Menestrelli* (Minstrels' Serenades) and the *Corteo del Gonfalone* (Procession of the Flags). There is also an unusual international competition for composers of band music.
For further information:
www.comune.corciano.pg.it

FOLIGNO

Segni Barocchi Festival
September
Exhibitions of paintings, concerts, theater performances and movies, dance, events in period costume and a traditional jousting competition. The attractions of this event, launched in 1981, all have a baroque focus, in keeping with the re-enactment of the 17th-century world of the *Giostra della Quintana*.
For further information:
www.comune.foligno.pg.it

GUBBIO

Gubbio Festival and Spettacoli Classici
July-August
These two separate events take place one after the other in the charming setting of Gubbio's well-preserved Roman theater. Concerts reflecting new musical ideas and trends are followed by traditional concerts of classical music.
For further information: www.gubbio.com

SPOLETO
Festival dei Due Mondi
First half of July

This unique and innovative festival gives voice to all forms of artistic expression, with the best in terms of producers, choreographers, conductors, staging and international soloists, in the enchanting setting of the ducal city of Spoleto.
For further information:
Tel. 800565600, www.spoletofestival.it

Settimana Internazionale della Danza
Beginning of April

In the marvelous setting of the cloister of S. Nicolò, this prestigious event focuses on an international dance competition for young talent specializing in classic, modern and contemporary dance and choreographic composition. The event culminates in a in a gala performance by the winners.
For further information:
www.settimanainternazionaledelladanza.it

Stagione del Teatro Lirico
Sperimentale A. Belli
August-September

This theater in Spoleto, founded in 1947, is associated with a competition for promising young opera singers who make their debut at the Spoleto opera season.
For further information:
Tel. 0743221645, www.tls-belli.it

TODI
Todi Arte Festival
End of July

A festival featuring drama and opera, dance, classical and ethnic music, the visual arts and literature, which promotes young talent from Italy and abroad.
For further information:
www.todiartefestival.it

TUORO SUL TRASIMENO
Missione Annibale
July-August

Theatrical event which recreates the warlike atmosphere of the Battle of Trasimeno in 217 B.C. in which Hannibal's Carthaginian army attacked and defeated the troops of the Roman consul Caius Flaminius. Spectators are encouraged to participate in the event and interact with the actors in a mobile production (moving from one scene to another by bus and on foot) with dramatic happenings at every turn. Spectators of all nationalities may

TCI HIGHLIGHTS

MUSIC IN THE SQUARES

Umbria Jazz is set in some of the most beautiful parts of Umbria. The idea behind the festival is to combine the music which began in the New World with the charming artistic and natural settings of Umbrian towns: medieval squares, churches, theaters, wine-cellars and gardens. It's one of Italy's oldest specialized festivals (the first was held in 1973) and has gained in popularity over the years, not only with the Italian audience, on account of its capacity to attract all the leading names in jazz (*in the photo, Lionel Hampton*) and, more particularly, because of the original idea of combining culture with tourism. Since it began, the festival has impressed musicologists and sociologists alike on account of the stimulating, spontaneous, dialectic relationship it creates between young people and music, casting off the narrow reputation of "specialist" music which jazz had previously enjoyed. Over the years, with the increasing attention that the festival has attracted, especially from the Italian and international Press, *Umbria Jazz* has become a diversified, multifarious series of events, lasting almost a month. The heart is *Umbria Jazz Estate*: the first ten days of July are devoted to concerts and other musical events held in the historic center of Perugia, a musical whirlwind of performances at all hours of the day and lasting well into the night. Before the event in Perugia, a smaller festival takes place in little towns around Lake Trasimeno, reflecting the same combination of music and water as New Orleans, where jazz began. During the week between Christmas and New Year, Umbria Jazz Winter is held at Orvieto, with a very different spirit from the summer festival. This is all about in-depth exploration of the innovative aspects of contemporary jazz, resulting in a more unusual, reserved, specialized event for true contemporary-jazz aficionados.

participate because the actors all speak several languages.
For further information: www.annibale.net

TERNI

Terni in Jazz
October, April and June
Set at various locations in the town, a series of jazz concerts, workshops, guides to new releases, and the chance to hear different sorts of music.
For further information:
Tel. 0744401346-0744801252,
www.terniinjazz.com

NARNI
Black Festival
August-September
For three evenings Narni's 14th-century square becomes the stage for gospel music, R&B, soul and jazz.
For further information:
www.comune.narni.tr.it

ORVIETO
Festival Internazionale Teatro di Strada
Beginning of September

 TCI HIGHLIGHTS

SAGRA MUSICALE UMBRA
A prestigious classical music festival with a long tradition (more than 60 have been held) organized in the Umbria's most important towns during the month of September.

For further information:
Tel. 0755722271
www.perugiamusicaclassica.com

For three days, the streets of the old town form the natural background for artistes from all over the world, who perform more than 50 shows a day for the public in the afternoons and evenings.
For further information:
www.comune.orvieto.tr.it

Umbria Jazz Winter
The week leading up to New Year
The winter edition of Perugia's Umbria Jazz festival organized in the most charming venues of this lovely Umbrian town.
For further information:
www.umbriajazz.com

 TCI HIGHLIGHTS

THE SPOLETO FESTIVAL
In an interview given back in August 1956, Maestro Gian Carlo Menotti, known the world over for his original and modern interpretation of opera, talked about a journey that he made in Italy in search of a dream: to find a town, a small town if possible, where he could organize an annual festival of chamber music, opera, theater and ballet. (*In the photo Carla Fracci during a peformance in Spoleto.*)

Having visited many towns and realized that many of the provincial theaters were falling into decay, he decided on Spoleto, a quiet little town with a cultural tradition, which was also the seat of an experimental opera company which had helped many promising young singers to embark on successful careers. The mayor had assured him that it was possible to organize a festival "where there will be no noise of passing traffic, no engine noise at all anywhere near the theater, there will be absolute silence". And he was right. On June 5, the Festival was launched with a production of Verdi's *Macbeth* directed by Luchino Visconti. It was a triumph. Since then, there have been more than 40 festivals. Every year it arouses interest and enthusiasm, attracting many thousands of spectators and critics from all over the world. The revolutionary idea of a festival including many different art forms, with artistes from different, distant cultures, creates new magic each year.

FOLKLORE

Despite being quite a small region, Umbria offers a great many folk events harking back to and reinforcing links with the medieval tradition, a charming way of reviving the costumes and customs of long ago, but, at the same time, still able to attract and delight, partly because we can still see so many testimonials dating from that period today. Pervaded by a strong sense of spirituality and religious fervor, many of the celebrations in this area are associated with mysticism and religious devotion. Many theatrical representations with sacred themes and festivals are associated with old farming and folk traditions, like the ones to mark the beginning of spring and the re-awakening of nature, and other festivals which refer to particular events. On these occasions, folk culture, often given scant consideration by the institutions, comes into its own. Through spectacular re-enactments in costume, folklore is recognized as representing the whole spectrum of a community, from the peasant and artisan classes to civic and religious authorities.

PERUGIA

ASSISI
Calendimaggio
First week in May
A tribute to spring in the form of a spectacular re-enactment of the centuries-old rivalry between '*Parte di sopra*' and '*Parte di sotto*' (the upper and lower parts of the town), whose residents challenge each other in contests of all kinds, including crossbow archery, singing and dancing, even the best-decorated district, with displays by tightrope-walkers, acrobats, flag-throwers and archers thrown in. The torch-lit streets with their taverns attempt to recreate the atmosphere between the Middle Ages and the Renaissance. The whole point of the festival is to choose "Madonna Primavera", the prettiest of the girls entered for the beauty contest by the two opposing factions.
For further information: Tel. 075812534, www.calendimaggio.com

The parade of the Calendimaggio festival.

Palio di San Rufino
Last Sunday in August
The festival is held in honor of its patron saint, St Rufinus, first bishop of Assisi. Locals dressed in Renaissance costume process through the town and there are flag-throwing displays prior to the Palio, the name given to an ancient crossbow contest between the three *terzieri* (districts) of the town: San Francesco, San Rufino and Dive Marie. The festival celebrates an edict of 1542 which divided Assisi into three parts with the aim of eliminating the fierce rivalry of the two opposing factions which had existed until then: "*Parte de Sopra*" and "*Parte de Sotto*".
For further information: Tel. 075812534, www.umbria2000.it

BEVAGNA
Mercato delle Gaite
June 16-25
The aim of this fascinating event is to re-create the daily life of Bevagna between 1250 and 1350. For 10 days, the town dives back into Middle Ages when it was divided into four parts, and the locals dress in medieval costume, vying with each other to create craft workshops, taverns and markets of typical local products.
For further information:
Tel. 0742361847,
www.ilmercatodellegaite.com

CASCIA
Festa di Santa Rita
May 21-22
The celebrations which Cascia dedicates to its patron saint include moments of meditation and prayer according to an ancient liturgy. The culmination of the festival is a torch-lit procession and a symbolic "fire of faith", when thousands of candles light up the windows in the town and the surrounding countryside.
For further information: Tel. 074371147, www.casciaonline.it

EVENTS

CASTIGLIONE DEL LAGO
Coloriamo i Cieli
End of April - beginning of May
For more than 20 years, the former military airport in the beautiful landscape by the shores of Lake Trasimeno has been the setting for a spectacular meeting of kite and hot-air ballooning enthusiasts.
For further information:
www.castiglionedellago.it

Rassegna Internazionale del Folklore
First half of August
This festival was conceived with the aim of encouraging people to learn about the traditions and cultures of different countries. In fact, many of the folk groups who participate in the festival come from other parts of the world (China, Bulgaria, Cyprus, Brazil, New Zealand, and so on) to give performances of traditional songs and dances, wearing the traditional costume of their culture. At weekends, the performances are held in the delightful setting of a theater mounted inside the medieval castle, whereas, on the other days of the week, the performers take turns to tour the neighboring towns where locals provide accommodation for the groups.
For further information: Tel. 075951125

CITTÀ DELLA PIEVE
Palio dei Terzieri
Mid-August
The festival sees members of the old *terzieri* (districts) of the town process through the streets in costumes inspired by the paintings of Perugino. The procession ends at the '*campo de li giochi*' where an archery contest is held. Archers fire arrows at rotating targets in the shape of a Chianino bull, evoking the bull-baiting contests that were held here in the 15th and 16th centuries.
For further information:
Tel. 05782919129-0578291291,
www.cittadellapieve.org

CORCIANO
Rievocazioni Storiche Medievali
August 13 - 15
The festival evokes some aspects of life in the Middle Ages which the people of Corciano reproduce down to the last detail. The first day begins with a serenade by minstrels. On the evening of the second day, the townsfolk

process in 15th-century costume, holding torches and lanterns, and the valets of the town carry a huge *cera* (candle) on their shoulders, which they offer to the church dedicated to the Assumption. The festival ends with another procession in 15th-century costume, this time with a display by flag-throwers. The festival is part of an event called "Agosto corcianese" which starts on the first Saturday in August and lasts for 16 consecutive days. It includes various cultural initiatives: art exhibitions, concerts and theatrical performances.
For further information: Tel. 0755188255
www.comune.corciano.pg.it

FOLIGNO
Giostra della Quintana
Mid-June and mid-September
Ever since 1946, when someone had the idea of reviving an old equestrian contest in period costume, based on a race held at Foligno during the carnival of 1613, the *Giostra della Quintana* has been performed as we see it today. This historic event—beautiful to watch because of the

The culminating moment of the Giostra della Quintana.

colorful costumes—involves the whole town and attracts hundreds of tourists.
For further information:
Tel. 0742354000-0742340653,
www.quintana.it

GUBBIO
Corsa dei Ceri
May 15
Possibly Umbria's most famous festival, involving the whole town and bringing back many of Gubbio's expat community, it also attracts large numbers of tourists. The festival consists of a long series of rituals which

take place on May 15, on the eve of the day of the town's patron saint, St Ubaldo. It is no coincidence that the three huge *ceri* (candles) carried on the shoulders of strongest men up to the church of S. Ubaldo situated on the hill above the town, have become the official symbol of the region. Tradition, religious devotion and the sheer enthusiasm of the local people blend, making this a very exciting event for participants and spectators alike.
For further information:
Tel. 0759220693, www.ceri.it

Torneo dei Quartieri
August 14
An archery contest using old Italian crossbows between the crossbow champions of the four districts of the town: San Martino, San Giuliano, San Pietro and Sant'Andrea. The contest is held in the evening by torchlight. There is a flag-throwing display and the contest is preceded and followed by a procession in Renaissance costume through the streets and squares of the town. The winner receives the *palio*, a piece of cloth hand-painted by local artists. At the end of the day, in the squares of the four districts there is music, and everyone has a chance to taste local gastronomic specialties.
For further information:
Tel. 0759220693,
www.gubbio-altochiascio.umbria2000.it

NOCERA UMBRA
Palio dei Quartieri
First Sunday in August
The festival begins on Wednesday, with processions, taverns offering local specialties and demonstrations of ancient skills. The contests between the districts of Borgo San Martino and Borgo Santa Croce are held the following Sunday. First an equestrian event where the riders try to pierce rings with spears. Next is a relay race and a race carrying a sedan chair, or *Dama infedele* (unfaithful lady). This is based on a dramatic event in 1421, when a lord of the Rocca di Nocera killed his wife's lover. Four athletes from each district carry a sedan chair on their shoulders containing a girl from their district. However, it is not the strength of the bearers' legs that decides the winner but the "betrayals" of the ladies. In fact,

in each district, the lady of the district in the lead must break open one of two jugs, and unless she finds the handkerchief with the colors of her own district inside, the district loses the points it has won.
For further information: Tel. 0742834011

NORCIA
Festa Patronale di San Benedetto
March 20-21
The torch-lit procession on the evening of March 20, which starts in one of the European capitals and is welcomed by ambassadors of various countries, is dedicated to St Benedict, patron saint of the town and of Europe. The following day, a historical re-enactment takes place between the six districts of the town. Dressed in medieval costume they challenge each other in a crossbow contest.
For further information: Tel. 0743828173, www.comune.norcia.pg.it

PASSIGNANO SUL TRASIMENO
Palio delle Barche
Last Sunday in July
This spectacular *palio* evokes an event during the civil war of Perugia, when the soldiers of the Oddi family, who were quarrelling with the Baglioni and the Della Corgna, were forced to flee the *castle of Passignano*. The approximately 160 competitors, 40 from each district, take part in an extremely tough relay race involving three feats of strength: rowing across the lake; running with the boat on their shoulders up and down the steep streets and staircases of the town center, and rowing back across the lake.
For further information: Tel. 075829801, www.passignanosultrasimeno.org

SPELLO
Infiorata
Corpus Domini
The ancient and delightful custom of strewing flower petals in front of sacred images as they process around the town lies behind the festival that takes places today (a much more elaborate festival than others in the region). Flower petals are used to create works of art which cover the streets of the town in a blaze of color.
For further information: Tel. 0742301009, www.comune.spello.pg.it

EVENTS

TODI

Gran Premio Italiano Mongolfieristico
July

Hot-air balloons from all over Europe and even the United States decorate the sky above Todi. Flights take place twice a day. A delightful and unusual way to spend a day.
For further information:
Tel. 0758945416-0758942526, www.todi.umbria2000.it

TREVI

Appuntamenti d'Autunno
October (begins on the first Saturday)

The Palio dei Terzieri, preceded by a colorful procession of locals in period costume, is the focus of a series of events held in this hillside town in early autumn. It evokes events which took place here in 1214 and consists in an exciting race between representatives of the various districts who push heavy carts through the streets of the town. There is an exhibition on the third Sunday to promote the locally-grown black Trevi celery, and, on the fourth Sunday, demonstrations of medieval craft skills bring the event to an end.
For further information:
Tel. 0742781150, www.protrevi.com

TERNI

Cantamaggio
End of April - beginning of May

For over a month, various exhibitions and other events revolve around the processions of allegorical floats, held on the evenings of April 30 and May 1. The floats are produced by the districts of Terni and other nearby towns to celebrate the arrival of spring.
For further information:
Tel. 0744431044, www.cantamaggio.it

AMELIA

Rievocazione degli Statuti Amerini e Palio dei Colombi
End of July - mid-August

To evoke the municipal statutes of 1346, the five districts of the town challenge each other to a traditional equestrian contest with duels between the riders. Riding in opposite directions at a gallop, they must cross the circular, 90-m

---

 TCI HIGHLIGHTS

THE CERI OF ST UBALDO

The aim of the race is not to arrive first, because the order of the procession is always the same: first comes the *cero* of St Ubaldo, followed by that of St George, and the *cero* of St Anthony is always last. The aim, at the end of the run up to the church of St Ubaldo, situated at 827m, which takes between 9 and 11 minutes, is for the team of the *cero* of St Ubaldo to succeed in closing the church doors, shutting out the other two teams, who must try to get at least part of the *ceri* through the doorway. This ritual is repeated in exactly the same way every year on May 15, the eve of the festival of Gubbio's

patron saint. The *ceri*, which are the symbol of Umbria, are three wooden structures each weighing about 200kg and 4m high, consisting of two superimposed hollow prisms held together by a central shaft. Each *cero* is then fixed upright onto a platform which is carried on the shoulders of the bearers. Being chosen for the race requires not only technical skill and precise training but is very important to all the citizens of Gubbio, who are proud to take part in this tribute to their local saint. In fact, statues of St Ubaldo, patron saint of stonemasons and sculptors, St George (craftsmen and pedlars) and St Anthony Abbot (farmers and students) are mounted on top of the *ceri*.
The rituals surrounding the event, the procession and the race not only exciting but highly spectacular.

ground as fast as possible, and strike a small target with their spears. Each rider has a man with a crossbow who, after every gallop, must fire an arrow towards a target connected to a dovecote, and must hit the center to release a dove.
For further information: www.amelia.it

LAGO DI PIEDILUCO
Festa delle Acque
End of June - beginning of July
The festival on the shores of this lake in the province of Terni dates back to an ancient tradition of celebrating the summer solstice. The many initiatives include nocturnal processions of illuminated boats, fireworks displays, but also theater performances and concerts of classical music.
For further information:
Tel. 0744423047, www.umbria2000.it

NARNI
Corsa all'Anello
End of April - second Sunday in May
A competition between riders of the various districts of the town, in the traditional way, with all the trimmings of bunting, processions, shows and concerts with a medieval flavor.
For further information:
Tel. 0744726233, www.corsallanello.it

ORVIETO
Corpus Domini
Corpus Domini
The festival evokes the Miracle of Bolsena in 1264, when a Bohemian priest who was saying mass above the tomb of St Cristina saw drops of blood falling from the consecrated wafer. A procession in period costume involving more than 400 local people carries the precious relic (a bloodstained piece of linen) around the town.
For further information:
Tel. 0763341772, www.comune.orvieto.tr.it
Festa della Palombella
Pentecost
This festival dates from the 15th century, when the noble family of the Monaldeschi began the custom of flying a dove on a metal wire stretched between a shrine on the front of the Duomo and a tabernacle on the steps leading up to the church. The flight of the dove, always timed for the moment when the bells strike midday, sets off a firework display. The success of

the flight of the dove augurs good luck for the coming year. On the eve of this event, there is another event, the Palio dell'Oca, a historic re-enactment of a dispute between riders of the factions of the town.
For further information:
Tel. 0763341772, www.orvietoturismo.it
Palio dell'Oca
Weekend after Pentecost
The festival begins on the Friday evening when the two teams are presented, names are drawn to decide who is to take part in the competitions and dinners are held in each of the two competing districts. On the Saturday afternoon, the horses and riders are blessed, and there is a procession of residents of the districts, archers, crossbowmen, musicians, flag-throwers and other Orvieto citizens. The Palio dell'Oca race takes place at night. The participants must gallop towards a sort of puppet and throw a ring over it. Then comes the award ceremony when two prizes are presented: the Palio di Contrada to the winning district and the Paliotto, awarded to the best rider. The Sunday is devoted to other events, shows and medieval happenings.
For further information:
Tel. 0763341772, www.comune.orvieto.tr.it

SAN GEMINI
Giostra dell'Arme
Last Sunday in September – mid-October
In honor of the patron saint, St Gemine (October 9), for two weeks, the districts of Rocca and Piazza organize a series of events in a spirit of healthy competition: processions of locals dressed in 15th-century costume, re-enactments of historical events and various other events take place in this town, colorfully decorated for the occasion. Highlights include the procession in costume to the cathedral to make offerings to the patron saint and, the following Sunday, the equestrian contest or Giostra dell'Arme, a tournament in which the riders of the teams have to gallop towards their goal, throw a spear and hit a target in the form of a coat-of-arms. Throughout the festival, taverns offer dishes of local gastronomic specialties.
For further information:
www.comune.sangemini.tr.it

EVENTS

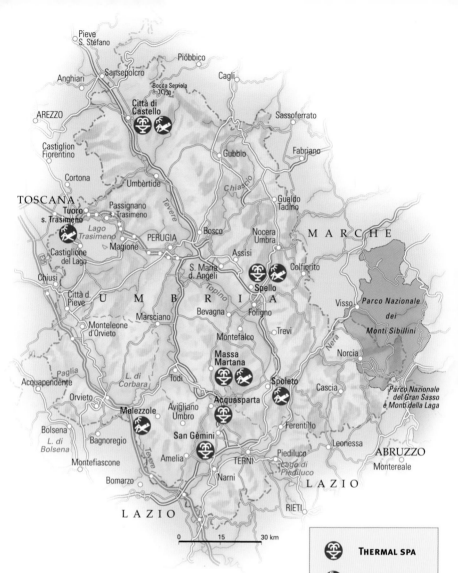

Symbol	
	THERMAL SPA
	HEALTH CENTER

This region might be far from the sea, but it is a realm of water. Water is everywhere in Umbria, even when it is not visible at first sight. The numerous springs were even used in Roman times. This water, though, is not merely a source of pride for historical reasons, but also because this land places great value on nature and protecting the environment. The groundwater is particularly rich in minerals that are beneficial to one's health and have been used for thousands of years in various cures as well as being bottled as drinking water. These pages contain a genuine "water trail" that explores both past

Wellness

and present as it makes it way through the lovely valleys that have inspired painters and poets, the picturesque medieval hamlets and the vestiges of ancient towns. This land seems almost to be the answer to man's need to find, in nature, an element of balance and wellness.

Highlights

- Città di Castello, the fame of the therapeutic properties of this water dates back to the 1st century AD.
- The Parco della Fonte Sangemini has numerous pines and oaks as well as free roaming fallow deer.
- Some of the springs at Spello, with sulfurous water, were used as early as the Middle Ages.
- Mud baths are one of the most important and oldest thermal cures at Massa Marittima.

Inside

ACQUASPARTA

Parco Terme Amerino

Via S. Francesco 1, Tel. 0744943622,
www.amerino.com
Open June to October
The Amerino springs in the province of
Terni were used in Roman times,
although their use in the modern age
dates from the early 20th century.
They are sometimes called St Francis'
springs as the water is said to have been

blessed by the saint. The water is quite
pure and so is mainly bottled for drinking
and used in cures centered on drinking
water. The actually site of the spring
is in a park next to the modern
production plant. The properties of this
water have been studied since the
18th century and, from then, they have
been used by both locals, foreigners
and various celebrities.

CITTÀ DI CASTELLO

Terme di Fontecchio

Loc. Fontecchio 4, Tel. 0758520614,
www.termedifontecchio.it
Open all year – disabled facilities

**The neoclassical building that houses the Terme
di Fontecchio.**

These thermal baths near Perugia first
came to fame in the time of the lawyer,
philosopher and author Pliny
the Younger when, at the end of the
1st century AD, he went there with his
third-wife wife, Calpurnia. This story
was confirmed during excavations in
1879, when a statue of this young
woman pouring water from a jar was

found. Today, the Terme di Fontecchio
is a highly respected facility and the
alkaline water is rich in bicarbonate
and sulfur. The baths are located
about 3km from Città di Castello in a
lovely neoclassical building (1868) that
was constructed on the ruins of an
earlier construction (perhaps from the
Roman era and destroyed by the
earthquake in 1789). In addition to the
traditional thermal treatments
department, there are sections dealing
with heart and lung problems, a
section for orthopedic rehabilitation,
one for sport and work medicine and
the Calpurnia beauty center. The
surrounding park also has a hotel with
a restaurant, pool, tennis courts,
fitness trail, mini golf and a
playground. There is also another
spring, the Cappuccini one (this water
has more calcium and magnesium),
that is 500m away. There, the old,
adjacent convent is used as a historical
residence. There is a beauty center
that offers various deals for week-long
and weekend treatments.

MASSA MARTANA

Terme di San Faustino

Loc. Terme di San Faustino,
Tel. 0758856421, www.sanfaustino.it
Open all year – disabled facilities
The Terme di San Faustino complex
lies 5km south of the panoramic,
lush-green town of Massa Martana
(in the province of Perugia), at Villa
San Faustino, on the left side of the
Naia stream. The S. Faustino spring

Lush greenery surrounds Massa Martana.

gets its name from a nearby Benedictine abbey that was founded in the 12th-century. The water from the spring tends to be cold, with a percentage of clay and bicarbonate. It also has amounts of lithium and fluorine, giving it diuretic properties. As a matter of fact, this water has been studied and researched by various institutions and scientists for over a century, meaning its therapeutic properties are now well-known. The water is sometimes used in locomotive rehabilitative treatments as well as a part of other cures (mineral and mud baths being the most common). Recent studies have also shown the high degree of bioavailability of the calcium in this water. The actual complex is modern and includes a hotel, restaurant – serving Umbrian food and catering for specific diets -, a thermal

Mud-therapy is one of the most important and oldest spa treatments.

cures section, pool, garden, gym, reading room and an internet access point. All of these aspects are designed to help reduce stress and allow one to find some balance between modern life and the traditional "living slowly" that was once such an integral part of this area.

MELEZZOLE

Health Center Marc Mésségué
Via Torre Errighi 7,
Tel. 0744951666,
www.marcmessegue.it
See calendar for opening times
This center is at Torre Errighi in an old, fortified country house located in the verdant countryside of Umbria near Todi and the thousand-year old hamlet

toxins from the body and restoring physical health. The Health Center Marc Mésségué was conceived as a place for herbal medicine and beauty and other types of treatment aimed at improving physical and mental health in natural surrounds. The center has a covered pool, spa bath, sun terrace, Turkish bath and water exercise route

that allows you to enjoy a good workout without stressing the body. All of these facilities are designed so that the center can offer its clients complete physical therapy. Indeed, treatment is only carried out once certain tests/examinations have been carried out by a doctor. These personalized treatments include diet, exercise in the gym, stretching, beauty treatments and massages,

The old manor house in now home to the Marc Mésségué center.

of Melezzole. Set in a large private garden, the facility has a bar, reading room, gym, tennis court, private parking and a garage (4 parking spaces). The cuisine served follows the diet designed for you during a medical examination and is aimed at removing

thus ensuring complete physical regeneration. In essence, this center combines herbal medicine, beauty treatments and more traditional medicine with physical therapy to help people rid themselves of bad habits and find harmony once more.

W
E
L
L
N
E
S
S

Parco delle Fonti

Via Tiberina 1, Tel. 0744630130,
www.prosangemini.com
Open April to October
San Gemini, in the province of Terni, is known for its mineral water that comes from aquifers deep in the Martani Mountains. Sangemini mineral water – as it is known – has various curative properties and has often been studied by scientists. Indeed, the first chemical analysis was done way back in the 19th century, in 1837 to be precise. The Parco della Fonte Sangemini is located in a magnificent natural setting with pines, age-old oaks and fallow deer roaming freely. It is only 2.5km from the old town center. The actual spa center has a medical section for cures based on drinking the Sangemini and Fabia water (a low mineral water with bicarbonate and lime) as well as a bar and various other recreational options, such as mini golf, tennis, bowls and a fitness trail.

The historic inscription at the San Gemini spring.

Terme Francescane Village

Via delle Acque, Tel. 0742301186,
www.termefrancescane.com
Open all year – disabled facilities
The road from Spello (in the province of Perugia) to Cannara runs near the Ose stream, which was subjected to land reclamation efforts and other measures to ensure the safety of the surrounding land in the 15th century. Here, a little before the 16th-century Chiesa Tonda (or church of S. Maria della Rotonda), the local springs are used by the Terme Francescane Village spa complex. The alkaline water, with traces of sulfur, bicarbonate and clay, was used as early as the Middle Ages for curative purposes. The actual complex has a hotel with various treatments rooms, a medical center - the specialty here is curing ear, nose and throat problems – a covered pool with a water fitness route and against-current swimming, and suites with spa baths, showers and thermal hydromassage. The garden area (an impressive 50,000m²) has pools with hydromassage jets, waterfalls, fountains, a private lake where guests can try their hand at fishing and, finally, on an island in the center, a restaurant.

The Terme Francescane Village is set in a large park in Spello.

SPOLETO

Convento di Agghielli
Loc. Pompagnano, Tel. 0743225010,
www.agghielli.it
Open all year
Scenically located only a few
kilometers from Spoleto, this is a farm
holiday complex of about 100 hectares.
The building was once a villa owned by
the Dukedom of Spoleto and later
became a convent for the Poor Clares.
The complex has subsequently been
refurbished in an environmentally
friendly manner while making sure
guests can enjoy an elegant and
welcoming setting. The
11 suites and 5 double
rooms have numerous
modern facilities and
services as well as being
furnished with natural
materials and specially
protected from
electromagnetic waves.
The center offers a range
of massages, including
shiatsu, ayurvedic,
orthopedic and
reflexology. The setting is
also crucial and is even
the basis for some of the
treatments, such as the

guided walks in the woodlands to
sharpen sensory perception. The
cuisine is based on traditional Umbrian
food, with various recipes traceable
back to the Romans and Etruscans. The
products used are organic, with
appropriate certification. The aim is to
allow guests to find their natural
harmony using holistic means and
treatments for the body and mind. All
of these aspects, along with the chance
to follow a personalized program to
ensure you eat properly and cleanse
your body, ensure you get a complete
mind and body treatment.

The old convent at Agghielli lies in the undulating Umbrian countryside.

TUORO SUL TRASIMENO

Antico Casale di Monte Gualandro
Via Montecchio 1, Tel. 0758230295,
www.anticocasale.it
Open all year – disabled facilities
Once a customs house for the Grand
Duchy of Tuscany and later an estate
owned by the Counts Ranieri di
Corbello, the old Monte Gualandro
country house has recently been
refurbished, paying careful attention
to the building's history. The floors
are brickwork or stone, the beams are
visible in the frescoed rooms and the
canopy beds are made of wrought iron.
These features, along with the
fireplaces, give this place a truly
distinctive feel. The building has 14
apartments (interconnected) that are
each divided into various rooms: a
main bedroom, a room with two beds,

a living room with a kitchenette and
bathroom. The outside pool,
overlooking Lake Trasimeno and
the Chiana valley, is surrounded by
age-old olive groves. The center
focuses on beauty and body
treatments. It has a heated indoor pool
with against-current swimming and
mini waterfalls for head massages, a
sauna, a Turkish bath, a Scottish
shower and a spa bath for six people.
The small fitness area has modern
equipment and can be used by guests
to help build muscle strength. A small
room is used for color and aroma
therapy, which help the mind to relax.
This is also quite a good setting for
excursions, with Cortona, Perugia,
Arezzo, Assisi, Orvieto and Siena all
being less than 100km away.

WELLNESS

THE A-Z OF WHAT YOU NEED TO KNOW

GETTING TO

By plane to Umbria

PERUGIA – Aeroporto Internazionale dell'Umbria (Sant'Egidio)
Information about flights and services Tel. 075592141, www.airport.umbria.it
TO AND FROM AEROPORTO INTERNAZIONALE DELL'UMBRIA
The Aeroporto Internazionale dell'Umbria is located 12 km east of Perugia, and there are two daily return flights to Milan's Malpensa Airport.
To reach the airport from Perugia, take the SS 3bis road and the E45 highway, following signs for Assisi, and exit at the Sant'Egidio junction.
There is a shuttle bus service between the airport and the center of Perugia, where it stops at the train station in Piazza Italia; it meets Alitalia flights. The journey takes about 30 minutes.
Alternatively you can reach the city center by taxi (the taxi rank is just outside the Arrivals Hall) (RADIOTAXI Tel. 0755004888) or hire a car.
You can also get to Umbria from Rome's Fiumicino Airport, where coach services operate daily to Perugia and Assisi (it takes about 3.5 hours to reach Perugia by coach).

By train

The most frequent train services to Perugia are from Rome. There is one Intercity train to Perugia a day from Milan (the IC Tacito) which stops at Perugia, Assisi, Foligno, Spoleto and Terni. The regional train network runs a fairly comprehensive local service.
In fact there are regular train services to Assisi, Foligno, Gualdo Tadino, Orvieto, Spoleto and Terni.
For timetables and fares: **TRENITALIA**, Tel. 892021, www.trenitalia.com

By car

The main highway is the A1 (Milano-Napoli). Coming from the north, take the Valdichiana or Chiusi/Chianciano Terme exit. Coming from the south, take the Orte, Attigliano, Orvieto or Fabro exit.

For moving about within the region, the key road is the E45, which runs north-south linking Città di Castello, Perugia, Terni and Todi, with various roads leading off it to other destinations: at Perugia, the SS 75 road leads to Assisi, Spello and Foligno; north of Perugia, the SS 298 road leads to Gubbio; for Orvieto turn onto the SS 448 at Todi; for Lake Trasimeno take the SS 75bis road.
Motorway information center: freephone 800269269; www.autostrade.it

By bus

There is an excellent bus network. The main local operator is SULGA, which runs services between the main towns (Perugia, Deruta, Todi, Gubbio etc.). It also operates services from Assisi and Perugia to Florence, Rome and Naples, and between Perugia and Milan.
For timetables and fares:
SULGA, Tel. 800099661 (freephone); www.sulga.it

TRANSPORT

Public Transport

PERUGIA – APM
Tel. 800512141 (freephone); 075506781
www.apmperugia.it
TERNI – ATC
Tel. 0744492711
www.atcterni.it
FOLIGNO – SSIT
Tel. 0743212208
www.spoletina.com
There is a shuttle bus service linking the main car parks with the town center.
ORVIETO – ATC
Tel. 0744492711
www.atcterni.it
SPOLETO – SSIT
Tel. 0743212208
www.spoletina.com

Bus and bike

You may take your bike with you on the bus services operated by APM between Perugia and Gubbio, Gualdo Tadino, Assisi, Todi, Castiglione del Lago, between Gubbio and Gualdo Tadino, and between Gualdo Tadino and Assisi. This is an efficient, cheap way of exploring Umbria which maximizes the enjoyment of exploring the more scenic parts of the region by bike and minimizes the amount of tiresome long-distance cycling on main roads. For a small extra charge, bikes can be stowed in the hold.

Car rental in Umbria

AVIS – www.avisautonoleggio.it
PERUGIA: Aeroporto Sant'Egidio,
Tel. 0756929796 -
Train Station,
Piazza V. Veneto,
Tel. 0755000395
TERNI: Via XX Settembre 80 D/E, Tel. 0744287170
CITTÀ DI CASTELLO: Via Pier della Francesca 20,
Tel. 0758558534
FOLIGNO: Train Station Piazzale Unità d'Italia,
Tel. 0742340919

SPOLETO: Industrial Estate, San Chiodo 164,
Tel. 074346272
EUROPCAR – www.europcar.it
PERUGIA: Aeroporto Sant'Egidio,
Tel. 0755731704 -
Via R. D'Andreotto 7 (Perugia town center),
Tel. 0755731704
TERNI: Strada Maratta Bassa km 2.8, Tel. 0744306615
HERTZ – www.hertz.it
PERUGIA: Aeroporto Sant'Egidio,
Tel. 0755928590 –
Train Station,
Piazza V. Veneto,
Tel. 0755002439
TERNI: Via Curio Dentato 42,
Tel. 0744403902
CITTÀ DI CASTELLO: Industrial Estate, Cerbara,
Via E. Kant 29/G,
Tel. 0758511766
ORVIETO: Train Station,
Via 7 Martiri 32/F,
Tel. 0763301303
SPOLETO: Via Cerquiglia 144,
Tel. 074347195

Practical info

CLIMATE

Since Umbria has no coastline, it has a somewhat attenuated form of the Mediterranean climate, with fairly damp winters and hot summers. However, the fact that typical Mediterranean vegetation, such as the olive, grows here is proof that the climate is fairly mild.
The area around Lake Trasimeno has its own mild, temperate micro-climate throughout the year, while the more mountainous areas have cool summers and cold winters, with a fair amount of snow.
The highest rainfall is in fall and winter, whereas the summer tends to be dry, especially from June to September. Late spring is the ideal time to visit Umbria, when it is pleasantly warm but not too hot. Not only is the vegetation at its greenest, but the temperature is such that you can visit the tourist sights without the oppressive heat of the summer months. The fall, especially September, is also a pleasant time of year to visit Umbria.

INFORMATION

Official tourism website site of Regione Umbria:
www.umbria2000.it
Website of the Provincia di Perugia:
www.provincia.perugia.it
Website of the Provincia di Terni: www.provincia.terni.it

Boats on Lake Trasimeno

There is a boat service which stops at the main towns on Lake Trasimeno. The main jetty is at Passignano sul Trasimeno (other scheduled stops include Castiglione del Lago, Tuoro Navaccia and San Feliciano), and there is also a boat service to the islands of Isola Maggiore and Isola Polvese.
APM, Tel. 800512141 (freephone); 075506781
www.apmperugia.it

Umbria by Motorbike

The diverse nature of the landscape and the fact that there are many scenic drives mean that Umbria is an ideal place for bikers. Some of the most popular routes, in the north of the region, in the upper Tiber valley, include the passes of Bocca Trabaria, where there is a famous uphill section of hairpin bends (known as the *sette voltate* or seven bends), and Bocca Serriola.

Another classic motorbike route runs south-east of the Valnerina, from Norcia to Forca Canapine, crossing the picturesque town of Castelluccio and the Pian Grande: a huge plateau (we especially recommend this route in the summer when the flowers are spectacular), dominated by the highest peak of the Sibillini Mountains, Mt Vettore.

Access for the disabled in Umbria

The nature of the Umbrian landscape combined with the medieval layout of the largest towns (many on hills with steep streets) mean that they are not ideal for people with physical disabilities. However, useful and detailed information about Perugia and Assisi is available on the following websites about Perugia
(www.comune.perugia.it/ disabilita/index.asp) and Assisi
www.assisiaccessibile.it

Inside

Tourist information
Hotels and restaurants
At night
Museums and Monuments

EMERGENCY NUMBERS

112	Military Police (Carabinieri)
113	State Police (Polizia)
115	Fire Department
117	Financial Police
118	Medical Emergencies
1515	Fire-watch
1518	Road Information
803116	Road Assistance

ASSISI

Hotels

Country House 3 Esse ★★
Via di Valecchie 41,
Tel. 075816363
www.countryhousetreesse.com
15 rooms.
Parking, air conditioning, swimming pool
Credit cards: American Express, Visa, Mastercard
Set in a lovely, peaceful park, with a panoramic terrace and swimming pool, this converted rustic building is a charming, relaxing place to stay.

Dei Priori ★★★ ♿ ★
Corso Mazzini 15,
Tel. 075812237
www.assisi-hotel.com
34 rooms.
Restaurant, parking, air conditioning
Credit cards: American Express, Diners Club, Visa, Mastercard, Bancomat
This elegant noble palazzo right in the middle of Assisi has bright, comfortable rooms and a sweet and savory breakfast buffet.

Fontebella ★★★ ♿
Via Fontebella 25, Tel. 075812883
www.fontebella.com
Open April-December
40 rooms.
Restaurant, parking, air conditioning
Credit cards: American Express, Diners Club, Visa, Mastercard, Bancomat
A 17th-century palazzo only 300m away from the Basilica S. Francesco, with spacious, comfortable rooms.

Il Maniero ★★
Via Biagiano 3, Tel. 075816379
www.ilmaniero.com
17 rooms.
Restaurant, parking, swimming pool
Credit cards: American Express, Visa, Mastercard, Bancomat
Set on the edge of the town in the medieval castle of Biagiano; the dullness of the rooms is compensated by the splendid views of the surrounding hills.

Il Castello ★★★ ♿
Viale Marconi 1/B, Tel. 075812384
www.hotelcastelloassisi.it
Open March – mid-November
46 rooms. Restaurant, air conditioning
Credit Cards: Visa, Mastercard
Situated in the historic center, this recently renovated building has been a hotel since the early 1900's; sweet and savory breakfast buffet, large restaurant serving typical Umbrian cuisine.

San Francesco ★★★
Via S. Francesco 48,
Tel. 075812281
www.hotelsanfrancescoassisi.it
44 rooms.
Restaurant, air conditioning
Credit cards: American Express, Diners Club, Visa, Mastercard, Bancomat, JCB
Behind the 15th-century facade of this palazzo is a modern, lively hotel which has been run by the same family for over 40 years.

San Giacomo ★★ ♿
Via S. Giacomo 6, Tel. 075816778
www.hotelsangiacomoassisi.it
25 rooms.
Restaurant, parking
Credit cards: Visa, Mastercard, Bancomat
In the historic center, friendly comfortable hotel with classic lines inside and out. Excellent cuisine with an open fire for grills.

San Pietro ★★★ ♿
Piazza S. Pietro 5,
Tel. 075812452
www.hotel-sanpietro.it
37 rooms.
Restaurant, parking, air conditioning
Credit cards: American Express, Visa, Mastercard
Medieval stone building (part of the facade is a listed monument), completely renovated inside with AC, family-run.

Subasio ★★★★
Via Frate Elia 2,
Tel. 075812206
www.hotelsubasio.com
61 rooms.
Restaurant, parking, air conditioning
Credit cards: American Express, Diners Club, Visa, Mastercard, Bancomat
Next to the Basilica S. Francesco, with unbeatable views, a historic building with a high degree of comfort.

Rural lodgings

Il Noceto Umbro ♿
Loc. Petrignano,
Via Campagna 43,
Tel. 075800838
www.ilnocetoumbro.com
Restaurant, swimming pool, bicycle hire
Credit cards: American Express, Visa, Mastercard, Bancomat
Near Assisi, set in the quiet Umbrian countryside; rooms each has own entrance, furnished in the arte povera style. Real home-cooking.

La Rocchicciola delle Upupe ★
Via Eremo delle Carceri 15,
Tel. 075837790
www.larocchiccioladelleupupe.it
Mountain-bike
A typical 15th-century house set in the Parco del Subasio, only 300m from the center of Assisi. Apartments furnished simply but with good taste; yoga courses available.

Le Colombe ♿ ★
Loc. Rocca Sant'Angelo 42/43,
Tel. 0758098101
www.lecolombe.com
Restaurant, swimming pool
Credit cards: Visa, Mastercard
In a panoramic position, the original building has been renovated to create a very welcoming ambience.

Malvarina ★
Via Pieve di S. Apollinare 32,
Tel. 0758064280
www.malvarina.it
Restaurant, swimming pool
Credit cards: Diners Club, Visa, Mastercard, Bancomat
Four stone buildings with rustic and antique furnishings, set in the countryside. Friendly ambience with attention to detail.

Podere la Fornace ♿ ★
Loc. Tordibetto di Assisi
Via Ombrosa 3,
Tel. 0758019537
www.lafornace.com
Swimming pool, mountain-bike
Credit cards: Visa, Mastercard
Two stone peach-colored farm buildings with first-class fittings and a homely atmosphere.

Restaurants

Buca di San Francesco 🍴🍴 ♿
Via E. Brizi 1,
Tel. 075812204
bucasanfrancesco@libero.it
Closed Mondays
Credit cards: American Express, Diners Club, Visa, Mastercard
Medieval ambience, with rustic decor and run by the same family for 30 years. Real Umbrian cuisine.

Enoteca San Pietro 🍴
Via Borgo San Pietro 18/B,
Tel. 075813303
www.enotecasanpietro.com
Closed Tuesdays
Credit cards: Diners Club, Visa, Mastercard, Bancomat
Former café in the town center, ideal for quick meal or a romantic dinner by candle-light.

Il Duomo †
Via Porta Perlici 11, Tel. 075816326
www.assisiduomo.com
Closed Wednesdays
Credit cards: American Express, Diners Club, Visa, Mastercard
Characteristic venue in medieval style, with car park nearby. Pizza, grilled meat, Umbrian specialties, also vegetarian dishes.

La Fortezza †
Vicolo della Fortezza 2/B,
Tel. 075812418
www.lafortezzahotel.com
Open evenings (Saturdays and Sundays also midday)
Closed Thurdays
Credit cards: American Express, Visa, Mastercard
This restaurant in the heart of Assisi, occupies a 19th-century building with two charming small dining-rooms; serves regional cuisine.

San Francesco †† ★
Via S. Francesco 52,
Tel. 075812329
www.ristorantesanfrancesco.com
Closed Wednesdays
Credit cards: American Express, Diners Club, Visa, Mastercard, Bancomat
A warm welcome awaits you in this taverna-wine-bar that serves both classical and local dishes.

Museums

Museo del Foro Romano e Collezione Archeologica
Via Portica,
Tel. 075813053
www.sistemamuseo.it
Open: March-May, September-October: 10-13, 14.30-18.
June-August: 10-13, 14.30-19.
November-February: 10-13, 14-17.
Closed 1 January, 25 December

Museo della Basilica di San Francesco - Tesoro e Collezione Perkins
Piazza S. Francesco 2,
Tel. 075819001
www.sanfrancescoassisi.org
Open: April-October: Mondays-Saturdays 9.30-17.
In other periods visiting by request

Museo della Porziuncola
Loc. Santa Maria degli Angeli, Piazza Porziuncola 1,
Tel. 0758051430
www.porziuncola.org
Open: Mondays-Sundays 9-12.30, 15-18.30. Closed: variable

Museo della Cattedrale e Cripta di San Rufino ★
Piazza S. Rufino 3,
Tel. 075812712
www.assisimuseocattedrale.com
Open: 16 March-31 July, 1 September-15 October:
Mondays-Sundays 10-13, 15-18.
August, holidays and bank holidays: 10-18. 16 October-15 March: Mondays-Sundays 10-13, 14.30-17.30. Christmas holidays: Mondays-Sundays 10-17.30.
Closed Wednesdays, 1 January, 25 December

Museo di San Pietro ★
Piazza S. Pietro 1,
Tel. 0758155204-3398812301
www.museiecclesiastici.it
Open: June-October: Mondays-Sundays 10-19. November-May: Mondays-Sundays 10-13, 15-19

Pinacoteca Comunale
Via S. Francesco 10,
Tel. 075812033
www.sistemamuseo.it
Open: March-May, September-October: 10-13, 14.30-18.
June-August: 10-13, 14.30-19.
November-February: 10-13, 14-17.
Closed 1 January, 25 December

BEVAGNA

> ☑ **Ufficio Informazioni**
> **Comune di Bevagna**
> **Tel. 0742368111**

Hotels

Il Chiostro di Bevagna ★ ⅊ ★
Corso Matteotti 107,
Tel. 0742361987
www.ilchiostrodibevagna.com
14 rooms.
Restaurant, parking
Credit cards: Diners Club, Visa, Mastercard, Bancomat
A former 14th-century monastery furnished in the arte povera style with a frescoed hall. Sweet and savory options at breakfast and home-made bread.

Locanda Piazza Onofri
Via Piazza Onofri,
Tel. 0742361920
www.enotecaonofri.it
13 rooms.
Restaurant, air conditioning
Credit cards: American Express, Diners Club, Visa, Mastercard
A charming inn consisting of two medieval buildings with Gothic windows, exposed beams and rustic furnishings; apartments of various sizes with kitchenette.

L'Orto degli Angeli
Via Dante Alighieri 1,
Tel. 0742360130
www.ortoangeli.it
14 rooms.
Restaurant, air conditioning
Credit cards: American Express, Diners Club, Visa, Mastercard, Bancomat
Two elegant, romantic noble residences with plenty of atmosphere, connected by a hanging garden. Lovely rooms each furnished differently.

Palazzo Brunamonti ★★★ ⅊ ★
Corso Matteotti 79,
Tel. 0742361932
www.brunamonti.com
16 rooms.
Credit cards: American Express, Diners Club, Visa, Mastercard, Bancomat
In the town center, elegant noble 18th-century palazzo: beautiful brick ceilings with cross-vaulting and period furnishings. Warm welcome.

Rural lodgings

Borgovivo ⅊
Loc. Torre del Colle,
Tel. 0742362001
www.borgovivo.it
Open from April to mid-January
Restaurant, swimming pool, mountain-bike
Credit cards: American Express, Diners Club, Visa, Mastercard, Bancomat
A cleverly converted 19th-century farmhouse, set in an old village 5 minutes from Bevagna.

Casa Cantone ⅊
Vocabolo Cantone,
Tel. 074236187
www.casacantone.it
Restaurant, swimming pool, bicycles
Credit cards: American Express, Diners Club, Visa, Mastercard, Bancomat
Country house with rooms and apartments with late-19th century furniture.

Restaurants

El Rancho †
Via Flaminia 55, Tel. 0742360105
www.elrancho.it
Closed Mondays
Credit cards: American Express, Visa, Mastercard, Bancomat
Charming country restaurant with a long family tradition and excellent value for money. Typical Umbrian cuisine with grilled meat.

Enoteca Piazza Onofri ††
Piazza Onofri 2,
Tel. 0742361926
www.enotecaonofri.it
Open evenings only (Saturdays, Sundays and holidays also midday)
Closed Wednesdays
Credit cards: Visa, Mastercard, Bancomat
Set in a medieval olive-mill, informal ambience. Traditional dishes, cured meats and excellent cheeses.

Ottavius ††
Via del Gonfalone 4,
Tel. 0742360555

Credit cards: American Express, Diners Club, Visa, Mastercard, Bancomat

This family-run place has a rustic atmosphere and serves typical Umbrian cuisine.

Museums

Complesso Termale e Mosaico Romano
Via di Porta Guelfa,
Tel. 0742360031
sociali@comune.bevagna.pg.it
Open: April-May, September: Mondays-Sundays 10.30-13, 14.30-18. June-July: Mondays-Sundays 10.30-13, 15.30-19. August: Mondays-Sundays 10.30-13, 15-19.30. October-March: Tuesdays, Sundays 10.30-13, 14.30-17. In other periods visits by request

Museo Civico di Bevagna
Corso Matteotti 70,
Tel. 0742360031
www.sistemamuseo.it
Open: April-May, September: Mondays-Sundays 10.30-13, 14.30-18. June-July: Mondays-Sundays 10.30-13, 15.30-19. August: Mondays-Sundays 10.30-13, 15-19.30. October-March: Tuesdays, Sundays 10.30-13, 14.30-17. Visits by request also

CASCIA

i IAT Cascia
Piazza Garibaldi 1,
Tel. 074371147
info@iat.cascia.pg.it

Hotels

Cursula *** &
Viale Cavour 3, Tel. 074376206
www.hotelcursula.com
40 rooms.
Restaurant, parking, air conditioning
Credit cards: American Express, Diners Club, Visa, Mastercard, Bancomat, JCB
Family ambience, modern furnishings in the reception rooms and new bathrooms.

Monte Meraviglia *** &
Via Roma 15, Tel. 074376142
www.montemeraviglia.com
138 rooms. Restaurant, parking, air conditioning, swimming pool, sauna, tennis court, gym
Credit cards: Visa, Mastercard, Bancomat
Modern hotel with comfortable rooms; buffet breakfast with home-made cakes.

Rural lodgings

Casale Sant'Antonio
Loc. Casale Sant'Antonio,
Tel. 074376819
www.casalesantantonio.it

In Valnerina, a converted farmhouse, ideal for people who love the mountains.

Museums

Museo Civico di Palazzo Santi
Via G. Palombi, Tel. 0743751010
www.sistemamuseo.it
Open: April: Saturdays and holidays 10.30-13.00, 16.00-18.00. May-June: Fridays, Saturdays and Sundays 10.30-13.00, 16.00-18.30. July and September: Tuesdays-Sundays 10.30-13.00, 16.00-18.30. August: Mondays- Sundays 10.30-13.00, 16.00-19.00. October-March: Saturdays and holidays 10.30-13.00, 15.00-17.00

CASTIGLIONE DEL LAGO

i IAT Castiglione del Lago
Piazza Mazzini 10,
Tel. 0759652484
info@iat.castiglione-del-lago.pg.it

Hotels

Fazzuoli **
Piazza Marconi 11, Tel. 075951119
27 rooms.
Parking
Comfortable and well-finished; bedrooms with modern decor.

La Torre ***
Via Vittorio Emanuele 50,
Tel. 075951666
www.trasinet.com/latorre
8 rooms.
Air conditioning
Credit cards: American Express, Diners Club, Visa, Mastercard, Bancomat
Early 20th-century building, a warm welcome and family ambience; large bedrooms with modern decor.

Miralago ***
Piazza Mazzini 6,
Tel. 075951157
www.hotelmiralago.com
19 rooms.
Restaurant, air conditioning
Credit cards: American Express, Diners Club, Visa
This late 19th-century building has been converted and has comfortable bedrooms.

Rural lodgings

Casal de' Cucchi &
Loc. Petrignano del Lago
Vocabolo I Cucchi,
Tel. 0759528116
www.agriturismofanini.it
Restaurant, swimming pool, mountain-bike hire
Well-known winery with rooms and apartments in converted farm buildings.

Romitorio
Loc. Pozzuolo,
Tel. 075959517
www.romitorio.com
Swimming pool, tennis court, mountain-bike
Set in the hills, accommodation in typical stone and brick buildings.

Villa Osvaldo
Loc. Salticchio 7,
Tel. 0759527241
villaosvaldo@virgilio.it
Restaurant, swimming pool, mountain-bike hire
A 17th-century farmhouse in the country with independent apartments, furnished in rustic style.

Restaurants

Acquario ⫴
Via Vittorio Emanuele 69,
Tel. 0759652432
www.castiglionedellago.it/acquario
Closed Wednesdays
(in winter also Tuesdays)
Credit cards: Visa, Mastercard
In the old town center, pleasant atmosphere, serves typical local meat and fish dishes.

Cantina ⫴ ★
Via Vittorio Emanuele 93,
Tel. 0759652463
www.castiglionedellago.it/cantina
Closed Mondays except summer
Credit cards: American Express, Diners Club, Visa, Mastercard, Bancomat
This restaurant with lovely vaulted brick ceilings serves fish from the lake, grilled meat and pizza.

Vinolento ⫶
Via Vittorio Emanuele 112,
Tel. 0759525262
www.vinolento.it
Closed Mondays
Credit cards: Visa, Mastercard, Bancomat
Osteria and wine-bar with 19th-century frescoes on the ceiling and an open fire; home-made pasta and desserts; excellent selection of cured meats and cheese.

CITTÀ DELLA PIEVE

i Ufficio informazioni
Comune di Città della Pieve, Tel. 0758291111

Hotels

Relais dei Magi
Loc. Le Selve Nuove 45,
Tel. 0578298133
www.relaismagi.it
13 rooms.
Restaurant, air conditioning, swimming pool, sauna
Credit cards: American Express, Diners Club, Visa, Mastercard

A refined country-house furnished with antiques; fitness and wellness facilities.

Vannucci *** &
Via I. Vanni 1,
Tel. 0578298063
www.hotel-vannucci.com
30 rooms.
Restaurant, parking, air conditioning, sauna, gym
Credit cards: American Express, Diners Club, Visa
Villa Mirafiori is a carefully-restored Art-Nouveau building; elegant, sophisticated ambience; rooms have been tastefully furnished, some have balconies.

Rural lodgings

Madonna delle Grazie ★
Vocabolo Madonna delle Grazie 6,
Tel. 0578299822
www.madonnadellegrazie.it
Restaurant, swimming pool, mountain-bike hire
Credit cards: American Express, Diners Club, Visa, Mastercard
Carefully-restored stone and brick farmhouse, run by a young family; rooms and apartments furnished in rustic style.

Miralaghi ★
Loc. Monte Pausillo,
Via Bianche,
Tel. 3483701085
www.miralaghi.com
Swimming pool, mountain-bike hire
Farm offering hospitality in comfortable apartments in two converted farm buildings and a villa; two swimming pools.

Restaurants

Il Pinzimonio ⅋
Loc. San Litardo 27,
Tel. 0578298105
www.ristoranteilpinzimonio.it
Closed Tuesdays
Credit cards: American Express, Diners Club, Visa, Mastercard, Bancomat
Smart venue, a few steps away from the lake. Exellent pizza, game dishes and specialties with mushrooms and truffles.

Museums

Raccolta d'Arte diocesana della Cattedrale
Piazza Gramsci 4,
Tel. 0759652738
www.cittadellapieve.org/page10.html
Temporarily closed for restoration

CITTÀ DI CASTELLO

> ⓘ **IAT Città di Castello**
> *Piazza Matteotti,*
> *Tel. 0758554922*
> *info@icittà-di-castello.pg.it*

Hotels

Delle Terme *** &
Loc. Terme di Fontecchio 4,
Tel. 0758520614
www.termedifontecchio.it
105 rooms.
Restaurant, parking, swimming pool, sauna, tennis court, gym
Credit cards: Visa, Mastercard, Bancomat
This charming, comfortable hotel set in a large park offers visitors the chance to benefit from thermal treatments, recharge their batteries, relax and keep fit.

Garden **** ★
Via A. Bologni, Tel. 0758550587
www.hotelgarden.com
56 rooms.
Restaurant, parking, air conditioning, swimming pool, sauna
Credit cards: American Express, Diners Club, Visa, Mastercard
Located 1 km from the town center, peaceful, sophisticated ambience, with views over the Umbrian hills and the town. Comfortable rooms and restaurant serving Mediterranean and Umbrian cuisine with some new ideas.

Le Mura *** &
Via Borgo Farinario 24,
Tel. 0758521070
www.hotellemura.it
35 rooms.
Restaurant, parking, air conditioning
Credit cards: American Express, Diners Club, Visa, Mastercard, Bancomat
Situated next to the walls of the old town; bedrooms have all mod cons.

Tiferno **** ★
Piazza R. Sanzio 13,
Tel. 0758550331
www.hoteltiferno.it
47 rooms.
Restaurant, parking, air conditioning
Credit cards: American Express, Diners Club, Visa, Mastercard, Bancomat
In the heart of the old town, a 17th-century noble palazzo with modern, functional bedrooms.

Rural lodgings

La Terrazza sul Macchietto &
Loc. Morra,
Via S. Crescenziano 1,
Tel. 0758574102
www.laterrazzasulmacchietto.com
Swimming pool, bicycle hire
Credit cards: Visa, Bancomat
A 19th-century farmhouse and a 17th-century villa with open fires and antique furniture.

Villa Lugnano &
Loc. Lugnano,
vocabolo La Villa,
Tel. 0758649000
www.villalugnano.com
Restaurant, swimming pool, bicycles
Credit cards: Diners Club, Visa, Mastercard, Bancomat
Typical Umbrian farmhouse converted into a charming farm holiday establishment. Accommodation in five delightful apartments.

Restaurants

Amici Miei ⅋⅋
Via del Monte 2,
Tel. 0758559904
Closed Wednesdays (in winter also Thursday midday)
Credit cards: Visa, Mastercard, Bancomat
Two dining-rooms with period furnishings in the wine-cellars of a 16th-century palazzo; fish and meat options on the menu.

Bersaglio ⅋⅋ &
Via Vittorio Emanuele Orlando 14,
Tel. 0758555534
bersaglio@technet.it
Closed Wednesdays
Credit cards: Mastercard, Bancomat
An unpretentious, friendly restaurant, with a delightful terrace for the summer and cuisine based on local raw ingredients.

Il Postale di Marco e Barbara ⅋⅋⅋
Via Raffaele de Cesare 8,
Tel. 0758521356
www.ristoranteilpostale.it
Closed Mondays and Saturday midday (October-May also Sunday evenings)
Credit cards: American Express, Diners Club, Visa, Mastercard, Bancomat
Interesting, spacious airy venue with a difference: the bright young chef in the kitchen has some innovative ideas.

Museums

Fondazione Palazzo Albizzini - Collezione Burri ★
Via Albizzini 1,
Tel. 0758554649-0758559848
www.fondazioneburri.org
Open: Tuesdays-Saturdays 9-12.30, 14.30-18; holidays 10.30-12.30, 15-18. Closed Mondays weekday, 1 January, 25 December

Fondazione Palazzo Albizzini - former Seccatoi del Tabacco ★
Via Pierucci, Tel. 0758559848
www.fondazioneburri.org
Open: April–mid-November: Tuesdays-Saturdays 9-12.30, 14.30-18; holidays 10.30-12.30, 15-18. Mid-November—March:

Saturdays 9-12.30, 14.30-18;
holidays 10.30-12.30, 15-18.
Bookings on request for groups.
Closed Mondays weekday,
1 January, 25 December

Museo del Duomo ★
Piazza Gabriotti 3/A,
Tel. 0758554705
www.museoduomocdc.it
Open: summer, Tuesdays-Sundays
9.30-13.00. August: Mondays-
Sundays 9.30-13.00, 14.30-19.00.
Winter: Tuesdays-Sundays
10.00-13.00, 14.30-18.30.
Closed 1 January, 25 December

Pinacoteca Comunale
Via della Cannoniera 22/A,
Tel. 0758520656
www.cdcnet.net/pinacoteca
Open: April-September: Tuesdays-
Sundays 10-13, 14.30-18.30.
October-March: Tuesdays-Sundays
10-13, 15-18

DERUTA

☐ **Pro Loco**
Piazza dei Consoli 4,
Tel. 0759711559

Museums

**Museo Regionale
della Ceramica ★**
Largo San Francesco,
Tel. 0759711000
www.museoceramicaderuta.it
Open: April-June: Mondays-
Sundays 10.30-13, 15-18.
July-September: Mondays-Sundays
10-13, 15.30-19. October-March:
Mondays, Wednesdays, Sundays
10.30-13, 14.30-17.

FOLIGNO

☐ **IAT Città di Foligno**
Corso Cavour 126,
Tel. 0742354459
info@iat.foligno.pg.it

Hotels

Italia * ⅟**
Piazza Matteotti 12,
Tel. 0742350412
www.hotelitaliafoligno.com
39 rooms.
Restaurant, air conditioning
Credit cards: American Express,
Diners Club, Visa, Mastercard,
Bancomat
Designer furnishings in this two-
storey palazzo with absolutely all
mod cons.

Le Mura * ⅟**
Via Bolletta 29, (corner
Via Mentana), Tel. 0742357344
www.lemura.net
36 rooms.
Restaurant, parking, air
conditioning

Credit cards: American Express,
Diners Club, Visa, Mastercard,
Bancomat
Situated inside the section of
medieval walls near the Topino
Stream; a harmonious, friendly
place; restaurant serves Umbrian
specialties.

Poledrini *
Viale Mezzetti 3, Tel. 0742341041
www.folignohotel.com
42 rooms.
Restaurant, parking, air
conditioning
Credit cards: American Express,
Diners Club, Visa, Mastercard,
Bancomat
This modern hotel with a classic
ambience has excellent facilities
and services; warm welcome.

Villa Roncalli *
Viale Roma 25, Tel. 0742391091
10 rooms.
Restaurant, parking, air
conditioning, swimming pool
Credit cards: American Express,
Visa, Mastercard
On the edge of the town, a
cleverly converted 17th-century
villa with a lovely garden;
bedrooms have high level of
comfort and modern furnishings.

Restaurants

Il Bacco Felice ⅟ ⅟
Via Garibaldi 73/75,
Tel. 3356622659
www.ilbaccofelice.it
Closed Mondays
Credit cards: American Express,
Diners Club, Visa, Mastercard,
Bancomat
This 16th-century palazzo in the
town center is a characteristic
venue with a jolly atmosphere;
Umbrian and classic Italian cuisine
with pulses, truffles and snails.

**Locanda del Cavaliere
Che Non C'è ⅟⅟**
Via dei Molini 16, Tel. 0742353623
Credit cards: Visa, Mastercard
Rustic yet sophisticated with local
cuisine reproducing the flavors of
long ago.

Sparafucile ⅟ ⅟
Piazzetta Duomo 30,
Tel. 0742342602
Open evenings
Credit cards: Visa, Mastercard,
Bancomat
Typical osteria in the center of
town, with a family atmosphere,
good home-cooking and
traditional dishes.

Museums

**Museo della Città - Museo
Archeologico e Pinacoteca ★**
Palazzo Trinci, Piazza della
Repubblica, Tel. 0742357697
www.comune.foligno.pg.it

Open: Tuesdays-Sundays and
holidays 10-19. Closed Mondays
weekday, 1 January, 25 December

**Museo della Città - Museo
dell'Istituzione comunale**
Palazzo Trinci,
Piazza della Repubblica
Tel. 0742357989-0742357697
www.comune.foligno.pg.it/cultura/
musei.htm
Open: Tuesdays-Sundays and
holidays 10-19. Closed Monday
weekday, 1 January, 25 December

**Museo della Città - Museo
Multimediale dei Tornei delle
Giostre e dei Giochi**
Palazzo Trinci,
Piazza della Repubblica,
Tel. 0742357989-0742357697
www.comune.foligno.pg.it/cultura/
musei.htm
Open: Tuesdays-Sundays and
holidays 10-19. Closed Monday
weekday, 1 January, 25 December

Museo diocesano
Largo Carducci, Tel. 0742350473
curiavescovile@diocesi-
foligno.191.it
www.diocesidifoligno.it
Visits by request

GUALDO TADINO

☐ **Ufficio Informazioni**
Comune di Gualdo Tadino
Tel. 075915021

Rural lodgings

Bonomi Fabrizia ★
Loc. San Pellegrino,
a Monte Camera, Tel. 075918145
www.montecamera.it
Bicycles
A delightful place up in the hills,
surrounded by oak forests, olive-
groves and arable land.

Museums

Museo Civico Rocca Flea
Via della Rocca, Tel. 075916078
www.sistemamuseo.it
Open: April-May: Thursdays-
Sundays 10.30-13, 15-18. June-
September: Tuesdays-Sundays
10.30-13, 15.30-19. October-March:
Saturdays, Sundays and holidays
10.30-13, 14.30-17.
Closed 1 January, 25 December

GUBBIO

☐ **IAT Città di Gubbio**
Via Repubblica 15,
Tel. 0759220693
info@iat.gubbio.pg.it

Hotels

Gattapone * ⅟**
Via Ansidei 6, Tel. 0759272489
www.mencarelligroup.com
18 rooms.

Air conditioning

Credit cards: American Express, Diners Club, Visa, Mastercard, Bancomat

Central small hotel of great charm, tastefully furnished. Warm, family atmosphere, bedrooms well-appointed and private garden.

Grotta dell'Angelo **
Via Gioia 47, Tel. 0759271747
www.grottadellangelo.it
18 rooms.
Restaurant
Credit cards: American Express, Diners Club, Visa, Bancomat

Right in the center of town, a small hotel with comfortable rooms. The wine-cellar in a cave dates from the 13th century.

Oderisi-Balestrieri **
Via Mazzatinti 2-12,
Tel. 0759220662
www.rosatihotels.com
40 rooms.
Credit cards: American Express, Diners Club, Visa, Mastercard, Bancomat

The hotel has rooms in two separate buildings; some rooms overlook the rooftops of the old town center while others have wrought-iron beds.

Park Hotel
ai Cappuccini **** ⅃ ★
Via Tifernate, Tel. 0759234
www.parkhotelaicappuccini.it
95 rooms.
Restaurant, parking, air conditioning, swimming pool, sauna, tennis court, gym
Credit cards: American Express, Diners Club, Visa, Bancomat

Situated in a converted 17th-century monastery, this hotel has great atmosphere, a high degree of comfort and modern facilities: a beauty center, heated swimming pool and rooms furnished in rustic or modern style.

Rural Lodgings

Marano
Loc. Colonnata, Tel. 0759302126
www.maranoholidays.com
Swimming pool, bicycle and mountain-bike hire

This establishment of 100 hectares is part of an animal sanctuary. A warm welcome and the apartments are spacious and comfortable.

Oasi Verde Mengara
Loc. Mengara 1,
Tel. 0759227004
www.oasiverdemengara.it
Restaurant, swimming pool, mountain-bike
Credit cards: Diners Club, Visa, Mastercard, Bancomat
Situated on the hillside, a

converted 17th-century stone farmhouse and barn; large rooms with rustic furnishings.

Sant'Erasmo ⅃
Loc. Padule
Vocabolo S. Erasmo 37,
Tel. 0759271017
www.agrisanterasmo.it
Bicycles
Credit cards: Visa, Mastercard, Bancomat

In the countryside, 5km from Gubbio, a large farmhouse offering five spacious apartments with modern facilities and comforts.

Restaurants

La Fornace di
Mastro Giorgio ⅋ ★
Via Mastro Giorgio 2,
Tel. 0759221836
www.rosatihotels.com
Closed Tuesdays and Wednesday midday
Credit cards: American Express, Diners Club, Visa, Mastercard, Bancomat

In the town center, this 14th-century ambience serves traditional cuisine.

Piatto d'Oro ⅋
Loc. Branca
Via Ponte Rosso 205,
Tel. 0759256238
Closed Fridays
Credit cards: Visa, Mastercard, Bancomat

Large, popular restaurant out of the town center, serving genuine local cuisine: excellent value.

Taverna del Lupo ⅋⅋⅋ ⅃ ★
Via Ansidei 6,
Tel. 0759274368
www.mencarelligroup.com
Closed Mondays (except bank holidays, holidays, August and September)
Credit cards: American Express, Diners Club, Visa, Mastercard, Bancomat

Sophisticated restaurant associated with the Gattapone Hotel; serves local cuisine based on local products (truffles and mushrooms) and home-made pasta.

At night

Bar Bosone "Don Navarro"
Piazza Bosone 2,
Closed Mondays

A small, jolly cake-shop, popular with young people, serving ice-cream, cakes and savory snacks.

The Village
Piazza dei Quaranta Martiri 29
Closed Tuesdays

This bar has a pleasant atmosphere, ideal for a beer or a quick snack.

Museums

Museo Civico e Pinacoteca
Comunale ★
Piazza Grande 1,
Tel. 0759274298
www.comune.gubbio.pg.it/
musei/palconsoli2.htm
Open: April-September: Mondays-Sundays 10-13, 15-18. October-March: Mondays-Sundays 10-13, 14-17. Closed 1 January, 13-15 May, 25 December

Museo Diocesano ★
Via Federico da Montefeltro 1,
Tel. 0759220904
www.museogubbio.it
Open: summer, Mondays-Sundays 10-19. Winter: Mondays-Sundays 10-18. Closed 15 May and next two Sundays

Museo di Palazzo Ducale
Via Federico da Montefeltro,
Tel. 0759275872
www.provincia.perugia.it
Open: Tuesdays-Sundays 8.30-19.30. Closed 1 January, 25 December

MAGIONE

> ℹ **Ufficio Informazioni**
> Comune di Magione
> Tel. 075847701

Museums

Museo della Pesca
del Lago Trasimeno
Località San Feliciano,
Lungolago della Pace
e del Lavoro 20,
Tel. 0758479261
www.museodellapesca.it
Open: February-March-October: Thursdays-Sundays 10.30-12.30, 14.30-17.30. April-June and September: Tuesdays-Sundays 10-12.30, 15-18. July-August: 10.30-13, 16-19. November-January: Saturdays and Sundays 10.30-13, 14.30-17

MONTEFALCO

> ℹ **Ufficio Informazioni**
> Comune di Montefalco,
> Tel. 0742378673

Hotels

Villa Pambuffetti **** ⅃ ★
Viale della Vittoria 20,
Tel. 0742379417
www.villapambuffetti.com
15 rooms.
Restaurant, parking, air conditioning, swimming pool
Credit cards: American Express, Diners Club, Visa, Mastercard
Very comfortable rooms in a 19th-century villa furnished in the same style.

Rural lodgings

Camiano Piccolo ★
Via Camiano Piccolo 5,
Tel. 0742379492
www.camianopiccolo.com
Restaurant, swimming pool, bicycles
Credit cards: American Express, Diners Club, Visa, Mastercard
A complex of converted farm buildings surrounded by olive groves, with well-lit, tastefully furnished rustic-style rooms and apartments.

Restaurants

Coccorone ₸₸
Via N. Fabbri 7,
Tel. 0742379535
www.coccorone.com
Closed Wednesdays (except summer)
Credit cards: Diners Club, Visa, Bancomat
Time-tested family-run restaurant with a charming ambience, excellent service and traditional cuisine.

Museums

Museo Civico di San Francesco ★
Via Ringhiera Umbra 6,
Tel. 0742379598
montefalco@sistemamuseo.it
www.montefalco.it/sfranc.htm
Open: March-May, September-October: Mondays-Sundays 10.30-13, 14-18. June-July: Mondays-Sundays 10.30-13, 15-19. August: Mondays-Sundays 10.30-13, 15-19.30. November-February: Tuesdays-Sundays 10.30-13, 14.30-17

NARNI

> **ℹ️ Associazione Turistica Pro-Narni**
> *Piazza dei Priori 3,*
> *Tel. 0744715362*

Hotels

Dei Priori ★★★ ★
Vicolo del Comune 4,
Tel. 0744726843
www.loggiadeipriori.it
19 rooms.
Restaurant
Credit cards: American Express, Diners Club, Visa, Mastercard, Bancomat
A 15th-century palazzo, beautifully converted with successful juxtaposition of historic features and modern furnishings.

Terra Umbra ★★★★ ⚕ ★
Loc. Narni Scalo
Strada Maratta 61,
Tel. 0744750304
www.terraumbra.it
29 rooms.

Restaurant, parking, air conditioning, swimming pool, sauna, gym
Credit cards: American Express, Diners Club, Visa, Mastercard
Delightful modern hotel with well-lit, well-appointed rooms.

Rural lodgings

Colle Abramo delle Vigne
Loc. Vigne,
Strada di Colle Abramo 34,
Tel. 0744796428
www.colleabramo.com
Swimming pool, mountain-bike
Accommodation in rooms and apartments, furnished in traditional Umbrian style.

Restaurants

Cavallino ₸
Via Flaminia Romana 220,
Tel. 0744761020
Closed Tuesdays
Credit cards: American Express, Diners Club, Visa, Mastercard, Bancomat
This delightful trattoria has been run by the same family for more than 30 years; traditional cuisine.

Il Pincio ₸
Via XX Settembre 115/117,
Tel. 0744722241
www.ristoranteilpincio.it
Closed Wednesdays October to mid-April
Credit cards: American Express, Diners Club, Visa, Mastercard, Bancomat
An 18th-century palazzo, with an unusual dining-room in a natural cave. Umbrian cuisine, friendly service.

Museums

Museo della Città
Palazzo Eroli, Via A. Saffi,
Tel. 0744717117-0744747269
www.museoeroli.it
Open: April-June, September: Tuesdays-Sundays 10.30-13, 15.30-18. July-August: Tuesdays-Sundays 10.30-13, 16.30-19.30. October-March: Fridays-Sundays, holidays and bank holidays 10.30-13, 15-17.30. Closed 1 January (mornings), 25 December

NOCERA UMBRA

> **ℹ️ Ufficio Informazioni**
> *Comune di Nocera Umbra,*
> *Tel. 0742834011*

Rural lodgings

Antico Monastero di S. Biagio
Loc. Lanciano 42,
Tel. 0742813589
www.sanbiagio.info
Restaurant, mountain-bike
This former 15th-century

monastery has recently been restored to its former splendor; large, sophisticated, and elegantly furnished rooms.

La Lupa
Loc. Colpertana,
Tel. 0742813539
www.agriturismo.com/alupa
Restaurant, swimming pool, mountain-bike
Credit cards: Bancomat
Fine stone building on top of a hill with unusual, rustic-style furnishings.

Restaurants

La Costa ₸ ⚕
Loc. Costa, Tel. 0742810042
gaspmass@interfree.it
Closed Monday midday
Credit cards: Visa, Mastercard, Bancomat
Unpretentious, clean farm-holiday complex, serving traditional cuisine.

Museums

Museo civico di San Francesco
Piazza Caprera,
Tel. 0742818640
www.sistemamuseo.it
Open: April-September: Tuesdays-Sundays 10.30-13, 16.30-19 (August: also Mondays). October-March: Saturdays and Sundays 10.30-13, 15-17.30

NORCIA

> **ℹ️ Ufficio Informazioni**
> *Comune di Norcia*
> *Tel. 0743828173*

Hotels

Best Western
Hotel Salicone ★★★ ⚕ ★
Strada Montedoro,
Tel. 0743828081
www.bestwestern.it/salicone_pg
71 rooms.
Parking, air conditioning, swimming pool, sauna, tennis court, gym
Credit cards: American Express, Diners Club, Visa, Mastercard, Bancomat
Just outside the walls, about 300m from town center; spacious very well-appointed rooms.

Grotta Azzurra ★★★ ⚕ ★
Via Alfieri 12, Tel. 0743816513
www.bianconi.com
46 rooms.
Restaurant, air conditioning, swimming pool, sauna, tennis court, gym
Credit cards: American Express, Diners Club, Visa, Mastercard, Bancomat
This traditional hotel set in an old palazzo also has some suites.

| ⋮⋮⋮ ⋮⋮⋮ ⋮⋮⋮ ⋯⋯⋯ ⋯⋯ ⋆ Hotels | ₸₸₸₸₸ ₸₸₸₸ ₸₸₸ ₸₸ ₸ Restaurants | ⚕ Disabled | ★ Special TCI Rates |

Hermitage ***
Località Savelli, Via Abruzzese 4,
Tel. 0743829177
www.norciavacanze.com

24 rooms.

Restaurant, parking, swimming
pool, tennis courts

Credit cards: Diners Club, Visa,
Mastercard, Bancomat

Built in the late 1970's, the
furnishings in the bedrooms and
the general facilities have been
renovated; heated swimming pool
with hydro-massage, good
restaurant.

Rural lodgings

**Casale nel Parco
dei Monti Sibillini**
Loc. Fontevena,
Tel. 0743816481
www.casalenelparco.com

13 rooms.

Restaurant, parking,
swimming pool

Credit cards: Visa, Mastercard

Old, traditionally furnished
farmhouse with occasional
modern touches.

Il Casale degli Amici
Vocabolo Cappuccini 157,
Tel. 0743816811
www.ilcasaledegliamici.it

10 rooms.

Restaurant, parking

Credit cards: American Express,
Diners Club, Visa, Mastercard,
Bancomat

Stone and wood are the salient
features of this 16th-century
farmhouse.

Restaurants

Beccofino ♔ ★
Piazza S. Benedetto 12,
Tel. 0743816086
beccofino.enoteca@tiscalinet.it

Closed Wednesdays
(except summer)

Credit cards: American Express,
Diners Club, Visa, Mastercard,
Bancomat

Characteristic venue serving
traditional and innovative cuisine.

Taverna de' Massari ♔
Via Roma 13, Tel. 0743816218
www.tavernademassari.com

Closed Tuesdays in winter

Credit cards: American Express,
Diners Club, Visa, Mastercard

In a 14th-century palazzo, serving
regional cuisine, including
specialties from the Valnerina
based on mushrooms and truffles.

Trattoria dal Francese ♔
Via Riguardati 16,
Tel. 0743816290

Closed Fridays
(except July-September)

Credit cards: American Express,
Visa, Mastercard, Bancomat

Near the Duomo, a family-run
trattoria with rustic decor; cuisine
based on truffles, game and
grilled meat.

Museums

**Museo della Castellina - Civico e
Diocesano - Collezione Massenzi**
Piazza S. Benedetto 1,
Tel. 0743817030
www.artenorcia.net

Open: May, October: Tuesdays-
Sundays 10-13, 16-18.
June-September: 10-13, 16-19.30
(August: also 22-24 in variable
days). November-April: Tuesdays-
Sundays 10-13, 15-17

ORVIETO

⑂ IAT Città di Orvieto
Piazza Duomo 24,
Tel. 0763341772
info@iat.orvieto.tr.it

Hotels

La Badia **** ♿
Loc. La Badia 8, Tel. 0763301959
www.labadiahotel.it

28 rooms.

Restaurant, parking, air
conditioning, swimming pool,
tennis court

Credit cards: American Express,
Visa, Mastercard, Bancomat

A clever conversion of a
12th-century abbey; vaulted
ceilings and antique-style
furnishings resulting in a
sophisticated, elegant ambience.

Palazzo Piccolomini **** ♿ ★
Piazza Ranieri 36,
Tel. 0763341743
www.hotelpiccolomini.it

32 rooms.

Parking, air conditioning

Credit cards: American Express,
Diners Club, Visa, Mastercard,
Bancomat

In the 14th century, this palazzo
was the home of the noble
Piccolomini family; now a hotel,
its rooms are pleasant and well-
appointed, with terracotta tiled
floors and antique-style furniture.

Picchio * ** ♿ ★
Via G. Salvatori 17,
Tel. 0763301144
hotelpicchio@tin.it

27 rooms.

Credit cards: American Express,
Diners Club, Visa, Mastercard,
Bancomat

A typical family-run hotel with
charmingly simple rooms. Parking.

Valentino * ** ♿
Via Angelo da Orvieto 32,
Tel. 0763342464
www.valentinohotel.com

19 rooms.

Air conditioning

Credit cards: American Express,
Diners Club, Visa, Mastercard,
Bancomat

Right next to the Duomo, a
tastefully converted three-storey
16th-century palazzo.

Rural lodgings

Borgo San Faustino
Loc. Morrano di Orvieto,
Via San Faustino 11,
Tel. 0763215745
www.agriturismoborgosanfaustino.it

Restaurant, swimming pool

Credit cards: Diners Club, Visa,
Mastercard, Bancomat

A few kilometers from Orvieto, a
farm using organic farming
methods with accommodation in
comfortable converted farm
buildings, tastefully and
thoughtfully furnished.

Fattoria di Titignano
Loc. Prodo, Via Centro 7,
Tel. 0763308000
www.titignano.com

Restaurant, swimming pool,
mountain-bike

In the medieval part of town,
bedrooms have modern
bathrooms and rustic decor.

La Rocca Orvieto
Loc. Rocca Ripesena 62,
Tel. 0763344210
www.laroccaorvieto.com

Restaurant, swimming pool,
mountain-bike

Credit cards: American Express,
Diners Club, Visa, Mastercard,
Bancomat

A carefully converted complex, in
a quiet setting in the hills.

Restaurants

L'Asino d'Oro ♔ ♿
Vicolo del Popolo 9,
Tel. 0763344406
luciosforza@hotmail.com

Open mid-March–mid-October and
mid-December–mid-January

Closed Mondays

Credit cards: Diners Club, Visa,
Mastercard, Bancomat

In a narrow alley in the medieval
center, this early 20th-century
trattoria serves traditional
peasant fare.

Le Grotte del Funaro ♔ ★
Via Ripa Serancia 41,
Tel. 0763343276
www.grottedelfunaro.it

Closed Mondays (except August)

Credit cards: American Express,
Diners Club, Visa, Mastercard

Central venue in a characteristic
tufa cave; cuisine based on
truffles, mushrooms, grilled meat
and game. Also a pizzeria and
piano bar.

Osteria dell'Angelo ♔ ♿
Piazza XXIX Marzo 8/A,
Tel. 0763341805

iginepri@iginepri.it
Closed Sunday evenings,
Mondays and Tuesday midday
Credit cards: American Express,
Diners Club, Visa, Mastercard,
Bancomat
Modern designer ambience, and
cuisine based exclusively on
genuine Italian ingredients.

Trattoria la Grotta ¶ & ★
Via Luca Signorelli 5,
Tel. 0763341348
Closed Tuesdays
Credit cards: American Express,
Diners Club, Visa, Mastercard,
Bancomat
A converted stables with frescoes,
in the historic center, with home
cooking.

At night

Internet@caffè Montanucci
Corso Cavour 23
Closed Wednesdays
Good salads, snacks and
chocolate specialties.

Museums

Museo Archeologico «Claudio Faina» ★
Palazzo Faina,
Piazza del Duomo 29,
Tel. 0763341216-0763341511
www.museofaina.com
Open: April-September: Mondays-
Sundays 9.30-18. October-March:
Mondays-Sundays 10-17.
November-February: Wednesdays-
Mondays 10-17. Closed 1 January,
25-26 December

Museo Archeologico Nazionale Palazzo papale
Piazza del Duomo,
Tel. 0763341039
www.archeopg.arti.beniculturali.it
Open: Mondays-Sundays
8.30-19.30. Closed 1 January,
1 May, 25 December

Museo d'Arte Moderna «Emilio Greco» ★
Palazzo Soliano, Piazza Duomo,
Tel. 0763344605
www.sistemamuseo.it
Open: January-February, October-
December: Fridays-Sundays
10.30-16.30. March: Fridays-
Sundays 10.30-17. April-July:
Tuesdays-Sundays 10.30-13, 15.30-
17. August: Tuesdays-Sundays
11-17. September: Tuesdays-
Sundays 10.30-13, 14.30-17

Museo dell'Opera del Duomo
Piazza del Duomo 23,
Tel. 0763343592
www.opsm.it
Open: March: Tuesdays-Sundays
9.30-13, 15-18. April-September:
Mondays-Sundays 9.30-19.
October: Tuesdays-Sundays 9.30-
13, 15-18. November-February:
Tuesdays-Sundays 9.30-13, 15-17

PANICALE

> ### ⓘ Ufficio Informazioni Turistiche
> Piazza Umberto I
> Tel. 075837319
> info@panicaleturismo.it

Hotels

Le Grotte di Boldrino ★★★
Via V. Ceppari 30, Tel. 075837161
www.grottediboldrino.com
10 rooms.
Credit cards: Diners Club, Visa,
Bancomat
On the edge of town, rooms
furnished with 19th-century
furniture; famous restaurant.

Villa di Monte Solare ★
Loc. Colle San Paolo,
Via Montali 7, Tel. 075832376
www.villamontesolare.it
28 rooms.
Restaurant, parking, air
conditioning, swimming pool,
sauna, tennis court
Credit cards: American Express,
Diners Club, Visa, Mastercard
Late 18th-century country
residence with lovely garden;
bedrooms and reception rooms
have open fireplaces, terracotta-
tiled floors and antique furniture.

Rural lodgings

La Fonte ★
Loc. Migliaiolo, Via Vannucci 15,
Tel. 075837469
www.agriturismolafonte.it
Swimming pool
Credit cards: American Express,
Diners Club, Visa
Large farm offering
accommodation in the main
farmhouse and in converted farm
buildings.

Restaurants

Lillotatini ¶¶
Piazza Umberto I, Tel. 075837771
Closed Mondays
Credit cards: American Express,
Diners Club, Visa, Mastercard
This small, delightful venue
occupies some of the rooms of an
old castle. Cuisine based on top-
quality raw ingredients.

Museums

Museo dei Paramenti Sacri
Chiesa Madonna della Sbarra,
Via Roma,
Tel. 075837319-0758373531
www.panicaleturismo.it
Visits by request

Museo del Tulle «Anita Belleschi Grifoni»
Piazza Regina Margherita 5/A,
Tel. 075837319-0758373531
www.panicaleturismo.it
Visits by request

PERUGIA

> ### ⓘ IAT Città di Perugia
> Piazza Novembre 3
> Tel. 0755736458
> info@iat.perugia.it
> www.iat.perugia.it

Hotels

Brufani Palace ★★★★★L & ★
Piazza Italia 12, Tel. 0755732541
www.brufanipalace.com
94 rooms.
Restaurant, air conditioning,
swimming pool, sauna, gym
Credit cards: American Express,
Diners Club, Visa, Mastercard
This place has been a hotel
offering tradition and hospitality
for more than 100 years. It has
magnificently decorated reception
rooms and large stone fireplaces,
elegant rooms and suites, all
furnished with antiques; a fitness
center and a splendid swimming
pool.

Castello dell'Oscano & ★
Loc. Oscano-Cenerente
Strada della Forcella 37,
Tel. 075584371
www.oscano.com
20 rooms.
Restaurant, parking, swimming
pool, sauna, gym
Credit cards: American Express,
Diners Club, Visa, Mastercard
Peaceful setting in an ancient
park, refined accommodation in a
neo-Gothic castle with elegant
rooms, each one different, antique
furniture, parquet floors and open
fireplaces.

Fortuna ★★★ & ★
Via Bonazzi 19,
Tel. 0755722845
www.umbriahotels.com
51 rooms.
Air conditioning
Credit cards: American Express,
Diners Club, Visa, Mastercard
13th-century palazzo with frescoes
in the reception rooms and some
of the bedrooms.

Ideal ★★
Via Tuderte 1/G, Tel. 07530869
www.hotel-ideal.it
20 rooms.
Parking.
Credit cards: American Express,
Visa, Mastercard
This small family-run
establishment in a rural setting
offers bed sits for week-long stays
and rooms with a kitchenette.

Rosalba ★★
Piazza del Circo 7,
Tel. 0755728285
www.hotelrosalba.com
11 rooms.
Air conditioning

In the historic center, a simple, pleasant 18th-century villa; rooms thoughtfully furnished in the arte povera style.

Sangallo Palace Hotel **** ♿ ★
Via Masi 9, Tel. 0755730202
www.sangallo.it

100 rooms.

Restaurant, parking, air conditioning, swimming pool, sauna, gym

Credit cards: American Express, Diners Club, Visa, Mastercard, Bancomat, JCB

Large, comfortable, beautifully furnished rooms; indoor pool with hydromassage and fitness center.

Sirius ***
Via Padre Guardiano 9,
Tel. 075690921
www.siriush.com

15 rooms.

Restaurant, parking, air conditioning

Credit cards: American Express, Diners Club, Visa, Mastercard, Bancomat

Close to the historic center, this modern hotel with a garden has well-appointed rooms.

Rural lodgings

Il Covone ★
Loc. Ponte Pattoli
Strada Fratticiola 2,
Tel. 075694140
www.covone.com

Restaurant, mountain-bike

Credit cards: Diners Club, Visa, Mastercard

In the Tiber valley, a lovely medieval villa with frescoes, valuable paintings and a delightful patio.

Il Romitorio di Monte Tezio ♿
Loc. Cenerente,
Strada Colognola-Migiana di Monte Tezio 1,
Tel. 075690859
www.montetezio.com

Restaurant, bicycles

Credit cards: American Express, Visa, Mastercard

In the 13th-century hermitage of S. Maria di Monte Tezio, this hotel has modern comforts in a charming ancient setting.

Restaurants

Caffè di Perugia ❙❙ ♿
Via Mazzini 10-14,
Tel. 0755731863
www.caffediperugia.it
Closed Tuesdays

Credit cards: American Express, Visa, Mastercard

The restaurant has 13th-century vaulted brick ceilings and offers several options: it serves meat and fish, and is also a grill-pizzeria and wine-bar.

Enoteca Giò ❙❙ ♿ ★
Via R. D'Andreotto 19,
Tel. 0755731100
www.hotelgio.it
Closed Sunday evenings and Monday midday

Credit cards: American Express, Diners Club, Visa, Mastercard, Bancomat

Simple, spotless ambience, excellent value, genuine local cuisine.

Fortebraccio ❙❙ ♿
Via Palermo 88, Tel. 07534643
www.umbriahotels.com
Closed Mondays

Credit cards: American Express, Diners Club, Visa, Mastercard, Bancomat

Delightful ambience serving cuisine based on typical local raw ingredients; excellent selection of wines, olive oil and vinegar.

Il Falchetto ❙❙
Via Bartolo 20, Tel. 0755731775
www.ilfalchetto.it
Closed Mondays

Credit cards: American Express, Diners Club, Visa, Mastercard, Bancomat

Both dining-rooms have ancient stone and brick walls, genuine traditional Umbrian cuisine.

Locanda degli Artisti ❙ ★
Via Campo Battaglia 10,
Tel. 0755735851
www.perugiaonline.com/
locandadegliartisti
Closed Tuesdays

Credit cards: American Express, Diners Club, Visa, Mastercard, Bancomat

Set in a beautifully-kept medieval palazzo, with rustic decor and regional cuisine. Excellent pizza.

Osteria Fiorucci ❙
Via Fabbretti 27,
Tel. 0755735273
Closed Sundays

Credit cards: Diners Club, Visa, Mastercard

Jolly family-run trattoria, serving straightforward home-cooking at a reasonable price.

At night

The Merlin Pub
Via del Forno 19
Closed Sundays

Venue mainly frequented by students. Happy hour from 5pm to midnight (except Saturdays).

Birreria Bratislava
Via Fiorenzuola 12
Closed Mondays

The clientele here ranges from the very young to people in their 40s, a venue specializing in jazz and rock. Vaulted ceilings and various makes of beer.

Caffè Morlacchi
Piazza Morlacchi 8
Closed Sundays

Opposite the university, a trendy café in a charming venue with vaulted ceilings and soft lighting. DJ on some evenings.

Downtown
Via Bulagaio 5
Closed Tuesdays

Open until the early hours of the morning, this pub is popular with students, and also serves kebabs.

Cinastik
Via dei Priori 39
Closed Sundays

The owners call this venue a "literary refuge", since they organize poetry and other readings here; a charming place to sip Umbrian wines.

Milano
Corso Garibaldi 2
Closed Sundays

Lounge bar which, depending on the time of day, is a self-service, cake-shop or bar. Trendy ambience, good cocktails but also wines, beer, tea and snacks.

Museums

Galleria Nazionale dell'Umbria
Corso Vannucci 19,
Tel. 0755741400-0755721009
www.gallerianazionaleumbria.it
Open: Tuesdays-Sundays 8.30-18.30. Closed Mondays except holidays, 1 January, 25 December

Ipogeo dei Volumni - Antiquarium
Loc. Ponte San Giovanni,
Via Assisana 53,
Tel. 075393329-075397969
www.archeopg.arti.beniculturali.it/
canale.asp?id=456
Open: July-August: Mondays-Sundays 9-12.30, 16.30-19. September-June: Mondays-Sundays 9-13, 15.30-18.30. Visits by request. Closed 1 January, 1 May, 25 December

Museo Archeologico Nazionale dell'Umbria
Piazza Giordano Bruno 10,
Tel. 0755727141
www.archeopg.arti.beniculturali.it
Open: Mondays 10-19.30; Tuesdays-Sundays 8.30-19.30. Closed 1 January, 25 December

Museo capitolare di San Lorenzo
Piazza IV Novembre,
Tel. 0755724853
museo@diocesi.perugia.it
Open: Tuesdays-Sundays 10-13, 14.30-17.30

Museo Storico della Perugina -
Stabilimento Nestlè Italiana S.p.a.
Loc. San Sisto
Via Pievaiola 207/C,
Tel. 0755276796
www.perugina.it
Open: Mondays-Fridays 9-13, 14-
17.30. Factory: visits by request

SPELLO

Hotels

Del Teatro ★★★
Via Giulia 24,
Tel. 0742301140
www.hoteldelteatro.it
11 rooms.
Credit cards: American Express,
Diners Club, Visa, Mastercard,
Bancomat
This small, converted 18th-century
palazzo has a quiet ambience and
a high degree of comfort.

La Bastiglia ★★★★
Via Salnitraria 15,
Tel. 0742651277
www.labastiglia.com
33 rooms.
Restaurant, parking, air
conditioning, swimming pool
Credit cards: American Express,
Diners Club, Visa, Mastercard,
Bancomat
This old mill has been enlarged
and converted into a delightful
hotel with a friendly atmosphere
and tasteful furnishings. Excellent
sophisticated restaurant.

Palazzo Bocci ★★★★ ♿ ★
Via Cavour 17,
Tel. 0742301021
www.palazzobocci.com
23 rooms.
Parking, air conditioning
Credit cards: American Express,
Diners Club, Visa, Mastercard,
Bancomat
A hotel with lots of atmosphere
and all the latest facilities. The
rooms have high ceilings,
terracotta floors and classic-style
furnishings.

Rural lodgings

Le Due Torri ♿ ★
Loc. Limiti di Spello
Via Torre Quadrano 1,
Tel. 0742651249
www.agriturismoleduetorri.com
Restaurant, swimming pool,
bicycles
Credit cards: American Express,
Diners Club, Visa
Accommodation in two converted
farm buildings of white and pink
stone; tastefully furnished.

Restaurants

Il Molino ❡❡
Piazza Matteotti 6/7,
Tel. 0742651305
ristoranteilmolino@libero.it
Closed Tuesdays
Credit cards: American Express,
Diners Club, Visa, Mastercard,
Bancomat
A converted 14th-century oil mill,
an elegant venue serving regional
cuisine with an innovative touch.

At night

Bar Giardino
Via Garibaldi
Closed Thurdays
Open until midnight in summer
(in winter up to 10pm), this venue
with tables outside serves ice-
cream, snacks and also a variety
of pasta dishes.

Museums

Pinacoteca civica
Piazza Matteotti 10,
Tel. 0742301497-0742300039
www.sistemamuseo.it
Open: April-September: Tuesdays-
Sundays 10.30-13, 15-18.30.
October-March: Tuesdays-Sundays
10.30-12.30, 15.30-17.30

Villa Fidelia -
Collezione Straka-Coppa
Via Centrale Umbra 70,
Tel. 0742651726-0742652547
www.comune.spello.pg.it/musei/m
enustrakacoppa.htm
Open: April-October: Tuesdays-
Sundays 10.30-19. November-
March: Tuesdays-Sundays 10.30-18

SPOLETO

Hotels

Aurora ★★★ ♿
Via Apollinare 3,
Tel. 0743220315
www.hotelauroraspoleto.it
23 rooms.
Restaurant, parking, air
conditioning
Credit cards: American Express,
Diners Club, Visa, Mastercard,
Bancomat
This converted medieval convent
with renovated bedrooms lies in a
beautiful position. Well-run by
local family.

Charleston ★★★
Piazza Collicola 10,
Tel. 0743220052
www.hotelcharleston.it
18 rooms.
Parking, sauna
Credit cards: American Express,

Diners Club, Visa, Mastercard,
Bancomat
This 17th-century building has a
peaceful atmosphere and bright
rooms with exposed wooden
beams.

Clitunno ★★★ ♿ ★
Piazza Sordini 6,
Tel. 0743223340
www.nih.it/hotelclitunno
45 rooms.
Restaurant, air conditioning sauna
In a late-19th century palazzo with
exposed wooden beams,
terracotta floors and period
furniture.

Dei Duchi ★★★★ ♿ ★
Viale Matteotti 4,
Tel. 074344541
www.hoteldeiduchi.com
49 rooms.
Restaurant, parking, air
conditioning
Credit cards: American Express,
Diners Club, Visa, Mastercard,
Bancomat
Central, with a garden, this is the
place to stay for the "Festival dei
Due Mondi".

San Carlo Borromeo ★★ ♿ ★
Via S. Carlo 13, Tel. 0743225320
www.geocities.com/sancarlo
borromeo
38 rooms.
Restaurant, parking
Credit cards: American Express,
Diners Club, Visa, Mastercard,
Bancomat
A restored convent with simple,
tastefully furnished rooms and
modern furniture. Very good
value.

San Luca ★★★★ ♿ ★
Via interna delle Mura 21,
Tel. 0743223399
www.hotelsanluca.com
35 rooms.
Air conditioning
Credit cards: American Express,
Diners Club, Visa, Bancomat
Sophisticated hotel furnished with
antiques, very well-run by the
family who own it. No restaurant.

Rural lodgings

Convento di Agghielli ♿ ★
Loc. Pompagnano,
Tel. 0743225010
www.agghielli.it
Restaurant, swimming pool,
mountain-bike hire
Credit cards: Diners Club, Visa,
Mastercard
A few kilometers from Spoleto, a
whole monastic complex has been
converted into a farm holiday
establishment according to bio-
architectural principles, yet it
retains its ancient charm.
Spacious, elegant rooms and a
first-class wellness center.

Umbria

Il Castello di Poreta
Loc. Poreta, Tel. 0743275810
www.ilcastellodiporeta.it
Restaurant
Credit cards: American Express,
Diners Club, Visa, Mastercard,
Bancomat
This 14th-century castle offers
simply but tastefully furnished
rooms and a lounge-cum-library.

Le Logge di Silvignano
Località Silvignano 14,
Tel. 0743274098
www.leloggedisilvignano.it
Open March-November
Restaurant, swimming pool
Credit cards: Visa, Mastercard
In a good strategic position, this
medieval residence has a superb
15th-century arched loggia.
Recently renovated and converted
into rooms with tasteful
furnishings in warm colors.

L'Ulivo ★
Loc. Bazzano Inferiore,
Tel. 074349031
www.agrulivo.com
Swimming pool, bicycles
A tastefully converted house in
the country with a large garden.

Restaurants

Il Tempio del Gusto ￭￭￭
Via Arco di Druso 11,
Tel. 074347121
www.iltempiodelgusto.com
Closed Thurdays
Credit cards: American Express,
Diners Club, Visa, Mastercard,
Bancomat
A small, pleasant modern venue,
where the expert chef prepares
dishes with beautifully balanced
flavors.

Palazzaccio ￭
Loc. San Giacomo
S.S. 3 - km 134, Tel. 0743520168
Closed Mondays
Credit cards: American Express,
Visa, Mastercard, Bancomat
This converted farm has rustic yet
elegant decor and serves classic
Umbrian cuisine.

Pentagramma ￭￭
Via T. Martani 4,
(Piazza della Libertà),
Tel. 0743223141
www.ristorantepentagramma.com
Closed Sunday evenings and
Mondays
Credit cards: Diners Club, Visa,
Mastercard, Bancomat
A popular meeting-place for
artists performing at the Festival;
serves traditional cuisine based
on soups, fresh pasta and grilled
meat.

Tartufo ￭￭￭ ★
Piazza Garibaldi 24,
Tel. 074340236
www.ristoranteiltartufo.it

Closed Sunday evenings and
Mondays
This place has been a restaurant
since 1927; it serves classic
cuisine and places particular
emphasis on local specialties.

Taverna dei Duchi ￭
Via Saffi 1, Tel. 074340323
duchi@libero.it
Closed Friday evenings
Credit cards: American Express,
Diners Club, Visa, Mastercard,
Bancomat
This restaurant serves pizza,
traditional cuisine and has a good
selection of wines; the rooms
have 18th-century vaulted stone
ceilings or exposed wooden
beams.

Trattoria del Festival ￭ ♿ ★
Via Brignone 8, Tel. 0743220993
www.trattoriadelfestival.com
Closed Thurdays
Credit cards: American Express,
Diners Club, Visa, Mastercard,
Bancomat
A typical venue with fireplace in a
16th-century palazzo. Expert
cuisine, including local specialties.

At night

Tric Trac Wine Bar
Piazza del Duomo
Closed Wednesdays
This is a popular, quite trendy bar
with tables outside, a good place
to sip a glass of wine, open until
2am.

Pub Silver
Via Cavallotti 1
A small pub with a good
atmosphere, the perfect place
to listen to music while sipping a
cocktail. Stays open until 2am
(from Thursdays to Saturdays
until 3am).

Excalibur
Via M. Quadrio 5
Closed Thurdays and July
A small but very pleasant pub,
in a quiet little square. Snacks
and set menu every day, as well
as beer.

Museums

Galleria Civica
di Arte Moderna - GCAM
Palazzo Collico, Piazza Collicola,
Tel. 074346434
www.spoletopermusei.it
Open: 16 March-15 October:
Wednesdays-Mondays 10.30-13,
15-19. 16 October-14 March:
Wednesdays-Mondays 10.30-13,
14.30-17. Closed Tuesdays,
1 January, 25 December

Museo Archeologico
Nazionale di Spoleto
Via S. Agata 18/A,
Tel. 0743223277-0743225531
www.archeopg.arti.beniculturali.it

Open: Mondays-Sundays
8.30-19.30. Closed 1 January,,
1 May, 25 December

Museo del Teatro
Via Filitteria 1,
Tel. 0743223419
Temporarily closed for restoration.
Opening first months 2008

Museo Diocesano di Spoleto-
Norcia e Basilica di Santa
Eufemia ★
Palazzo Arcivescovile,
Via A. Saffi 13, Tel. 0743231022
www.museiecclesiastici.it
Open: April-September: Mondays-
Fridays 10.30-13, 15.30-19;
Saturdays and holidays 10-18.
October-March: Mondays-Fridays
10.30-13, 14.30-17; Saturdays and
holidays 10-18. Closed Tuesdays

Pinacoteca Comunale
Palazzo Spada, Piazza Sordini,
Tel. 074345940
spoleto@sistemamuseo.it
www.spoletopermusei.it
Open: 16 March-14 October:
Wednesdays-Mondays 16-19. 15
October-15 March: Wednesdays-
Mondays 14.30-17. Closed
Tuesdays, 1 January, 25 December

TERNI

☒ **IAT Città di Terni**
Viale C. Battisti 7
Tel. 0744423047
info@iat.terni.it

Hotels

Best Western
Garden Hotel ★★★★ ♿
Viale Bramante 4/6,
Tel. 0744300041
www.gardenhotelterni.it
94 rooms.
Restaurant, parking, air
conditioning, swimming pool,
sauna, gym
Credit cards: American Express,
Diners Club, Visa, Mastercard,
Bancomat
This modern hotel with its terrace
fits beautifully into its rural
setting. The interior is well-
arranged and comfortable, plenty
of accommodation; all rooms
have a small terrace and the
"Il Melograno" restaurant serves
traditional cuisine.

ClassHotel Terni ★★★ ♿ ★
Via C.A. Dalla Chiesa 24,
Tel. 0744306024
www.classhotel.com
67 rooms.
Restaurant, parking, air
conditioning
Credit cards: American Express,
Diners Club, Visa, Mastercard,
Bancomat
New hotel with comfortable rooms
and modern wooden furnishings.

PRACTICAL INFO

185

Locanda del Colle d'Oro *** &

Strada di Palmetta 31,
Tel. 0744432379
www.colledelloro.it

11 rooms.

Restaurant, parking,
swimming pool

Credit cards: American Express,
Diners Club, Visa, Mastercard

An old country residence in the
woods with well-appointed rooms
and rustic-style furnishings.

Valentino ****

Via Plinio il Giovane 3/5,
Tel. 0744402550
www.hotelvalentinoterni.com

60 rooms.

Restaurant, parking,
air conditioning

Credit cards: American Express,
Diners Club, Visa, Mastercard,
Bancomat

Centrally located; good facilities
and rooms with all mod cons.

Restaurants

La Fontanella ¶¶ &

Via Plinio il Giovane 3/5,
Tel. 0744402550
www.hotelvalentinoterni.com

Closed Sundays

Credit cards: American Express,
Diners Club, Visa, Mastercard,
Bancomat

A modern ambience with a spit in
the restaurant, specializing in
grilled meat and home-made
desserts.

La Mora ¶

Strada S. Martino 44,
Tel. 0744421256
lamoratr@libero.it

Closed Tuesdays (except holidays)

Credit cards: American Express,
Diners Club, Visa, Mastercard,
Bancomat

This cosy little restaurant with
family run serves good local
cuisine

Villa Graziani ¶¶ &

Località Papigno, Villa Valle 11,
Tel. 074467138

Closed Sunday evenings and
Mondays

Credit cards: American Express,
Diners Club, Visa, Mastercard,
Bancomat

This restaurant in an old villa has
been expertly run by the same
family for a long time. Meals
served on terrace with views in
summer.

Museums

Museo Diocesano e Capitolare

Via XI Febbraio 4,
Tel. 0744546561
www.museieiecclesiastici.it/museisin
goli.asp?museoId=23

Open: Thursdays-Fridays 10-13,
14.30-17.30; Saturdays 10-13

Pinacoteca Comunale
«Orneore Metelli»

Via del Teatro Romano 13,
Tel. 074459421
www.comune.terni.it/arte_cultura_
pinacoteca.asp

Open: Tuesdays-Sundays 10-13,
16-19

TODI

> **i IAT Città di Todi**
> Piazza Umberto I 6,
> Tel. 0758943395
> info@iat.Todi.pg.it

Hotels

Bramante **** &

Via Orvietana 48,
Tel. 0758948381
www.hotelbramante.it

57 rooms.

Restaurant, parking, air
conditioning, swimming pool,
tennis courts, gym

Credit cards: American Express,
Diners Club, Visa

This 14th-century monastery has
been renovated and provided with
modern facilities; lunch is served
on the large terrace and the pool
has views over the valley.

Fonte Cesia **** &

Via L. Leony 3,
Tel. 0758943737
www.fontecesia.it

35 rooms.

Restaurant, parking, air
conditioning

18th-century palazzo with plenty of
atmosphere where the
architectural features are
enhanced by furnishings of the
same period.

Relais Todini &

Loc. Collevalenza,
Vocabolo Cervara,
Tel. 075887521
www.relaistodini.com

12 rooms.

Restaurant, parking, air
conditioning, swimming pool,
sauna, tennis court, gym

Credit cards: American Express,
Diners Club, Visa, Mastercard,
Bancomat

A prestigious period residence in
a 14th-century mansion. A friendly,
slightly old-fashioned atmosphere,
with stone walls, terracotta floors
and antique paintings and
furniture.

Villa Luisa *** &

Via A. Cortesi 147,
Tel. 0758948571
www.villaluisa.it

40 rooms.

Restaurant, parking, air
conditioning, swimming pool

Credit cards: American Express,
Diners Club, Visa

This hotel is set in a large garden;
beautifully furnished with good
facilities, recently renovated
bedrooms, swimming pool and
relaxation areas.

Rural lodgings

Casale delle Lucrezie &

Loc. Palazzaccio,
Contrada Due Santi,
Tel. 0758987488
www.casaledellelucrezie.com

13 rooms.

Restaurant, parking, swimming
pool

Credit cards: Visa, Mastercard,
Bancomat

This former convent of the
Lucrezia nuns dating from the
13th century offers spacious, well-
appointed bedrooms and
charming apartments, all
furnished in rustic style, with all
mod cons.

Castello di Porchiano

Loc. Porchiano,
Tel. 0758853127
maxbern@tin.it

A medieval village of recently
restored stone buildings divided
into elegant apartments, with
wonderful views.

Tenuta di Canonica

Loc. Canonica 75,
Tel. 0758947545
www.tenutadicanonica.com

Open: March-November

Restaurant, swimming pool

Credit cards: Visa, Bancomat

A charming, early-20th-century
stone house with an old lookout
tower.

At night

Gran Caffè Todi

Piazza del Popolo 47,

Situated opposite the Duomo.
Here you can admire the splendid
view while you sip coffee or enjoy
an ice-cream.

Restaurants

Cavour ¶

Corso Cavour 21/23,
Tel. 0758943730

Credit cards: American Express,
Diners Club, Visa, Mastercard,
Bancomat

This spacious, busy restaurant has
a garden with magnificent views;
regional cuisine and good pizza.

La Mulinella ¶ &

Loc. Pontenaia 29,
Fraz. Vasciano,
Tel. 0758944779

Closed Wednesdays

Credit cards: American Express,
Diners Club, Visa, Mastercard,
Bancomat

Rustic friendly trattoria, with
space for tables outside in
summer.

Umbria ¶ ★
Via S. Bonaventura 13,
Tel. 0758942737
Closed Tuesdays
Credit cards: American Express,
Diners Club, Visa, Bancomat
Typical venue, serving traditional
cuisine; run by the same family
since 1953.

Museums

Museo - Pinacoteca ★
Piazza del Popolo,
Tel. 0758944148
www.sistemamuseo.it
Open: April-October: Tuesdays-
Sundays 10-13.30, 15-18.
November-March: Tuesdays-
Sundays 10.30-13, 14.30-17.
Closed Mondays weekday, 1
January (mornings), 25 December

TREVI

ⓘ Ufficio Turismo -
Pro Loco
Tel. 0742781150

Hotels

Antica Dimora alla Rocca ★★★★ ♿
Piazza della Rocca,
Tel. 074238541
www.hotelallarocca.it
Open April-December
44 rooms.
Restaurant, parking, air
conditioning
Credit cards: American Express,
Diners Club, Visa, Mastercard,
Bancomat
Noble mid 17th-century palazzo;
bedrooms and suites with
exposed wooden beams,
reception rooms furnished in
19th-century style.

Della Torre ★★★ ♿
S.S. Flaminia al km 147,
Tel. 07423971
www.folignohotel.com
135 rooms.
Restaurant, parking, air
conditioning, swimming pool,
sauna, tennis court, gym
Credit cards: American Express,
Diners Club, Visa, Mastercard,
Bancomat
Surrounded by a large garden,
with very comfortable rooms
and suites.

Trevi Hotel ★★★ ♿ ★
Via Fantosati 2, Tel. 0742780922
www.trevihotel.net
11 rooms.
Restaurant, parking, sauna
Credit cards: American Express,
Visa, Bancomat
Set in a Renaissance palazzo, with
rooms and suites furnished in the
typical Umbrian style; wellness
center with aromatherapy.

Rural lodgings

I Mandorli ♿
Loc. Bovara,
Fondaccio 6,
Tel. 074278669
www.agriturismoimandorli.com
Restaurant, swimming pool,
bicycle hire
The farm buildings of this old
village have been converted into
houses with gardens linked by
stone paths.

Villa Silvana ♿ ★
Loc. Parrano,
Via Fonte Pigge 6,
Tel. 074278821
www.villasilvana.it
Restaurant, swimming pool,
mountain-bike
Credit cards: American Express,
Diners Club, Visa, Mastercard,
Bancomat
Situated in an olive-grove below
the walls of a medieval village,
accommodation in three houses
and wooden buildings (bio-
structures rather like chalets).

Restaurants

L'Ulivo ¶ ♿
Loc. Matigge,
Via Monte Bianco 23,
Tel. 074278969
Closed Mondays and Tuesdays
Credit cards: American Express,
Diners Club, Visa, Mastercard,
Bancomat
Pleasant rustic ambience, with
menus offering tastes of local
specialties.

Taverna del Pescatore ¶ ♿
Loc. Pigge, Via Chiesa Tonda 50,
Tel. 0742780920
www.latavernadelpescatore.com
Closed Mondays and Sunday
evenings
Credit cards: Visa, Mastercard
On the banks of the Clitunno
River, this venue with a rustic
ambience serves inventive cuisine.

Museums

**Complesso Museale di San
Francesco**
Largo Don Bosco 14,
Tel. 0742381628
www.sistemamuseo.it
Open: April, May and September:
Tuesdays-Sundays 10.30-13, 14.30-
18. June-July: Tuesdays-Sundays
10.30-13, 15.30-19. August:
Mondays-Sundays 10.30-13, 15-
19.30. October-March: Fridays,
Saturdays and Sundays 10.30-13,
14.30-17. Closed 1 January and
25 December

UMBÈRTIDE

ⓘ IAT Città di Umbèrtide
Tel. 0759417099

Hotels

Moderno ★★
S.S. Tiberina 3 bis,
Tel. 0759413759
hotelmoderno@hotmail.com
21 rooms.
Parking, air conditioning
Credit cards: Visa, Mastercard,
Bancomat
This three-storey house offers a
high degree of comfort, well-
appointed rooms and a restaurant
serving Umbrian cuisine.

Rural lodgings

Casale degli Olmi ♿
Via Romeggio 566,
Tel. 800903618
www.casaledegliolmi.com
Swimming pool, mountain-bike
Credit cards: American Express,
Diners Club, Visa, Mastercard,
Bancomat
This typical Umbrian farmhouse
with lovely views has comfortable,
tastefully furnished independent
apartments. Kids' playground,
computer, games room, library
and large garden.

I Casali di Caicocci ♿
S.P. 142,
Tel. 0759410305
www.caicocci.it
Restaurant, swimming pool, tennis
court, mountain-bike hire
Credit cards: American Express,
Visa, Mastercard
Near Lake Trasimeno, various
farmhouses have been converted
into spacious, charming
apartments furnished in the arte
povera style, with the best
comforts.

La Chiusa ♿ ★
Loc. Niccone,
S.S. 416 al km 2,3,
Tel. 0759410848
www.nih.it/relaislachiusa
Swimming pool, mountain-bike
19th-century farm in the country,
with two suites and three mini-
apartments, all beautifully
furnished, and a good restaurant.

Museums

**Centro per l'Arte Contemporanea
La Rocca**
Piazza Fortebraccio,
Tel. 0759413691
www.comune.umbertide.it
Open: April-November: Tuesdays-
Sundays 9.00-13.00, 16.00-19.00.
In other days visits by request

Museo di Santa Croce
Piazza S. Francesco,
Tel. 0759420147
www.sistemamuseo.it
Open: June-September:
Fridays-Sundays 10.30-13.00,
16.00-18.30. October-May: Fridays-
Sundays and holidays 10.30-13.00,
15.00-17.30

METRIC CONVERTIONS

DISTANCE

Kilometres/Miles

km to mi	mi to km
1 = 0.62	1 = 1.6
2 = 1.2	2 = 3.2
3 = 1.9	3 = 4.8
4 = 2.5	4 = 6.4
5 = 3.1	5 = 8.1
6 = 3.7	6 = 9.7
7 = 4.3	7 = 11.3
8 = 5.0	8 = 12.9

Meters/Feet

m to ft	ft to m
1 = 3.3	1 = 0.30
2 = 6.6	2 = 0.61
3 = 9.8	3 = 0.91
4 = 13.1	4 = 1.2
5 = 16.4	5 = 1.5
6 = 19.7	6 = 1.8
7 = 23.0	7 = 2.1
8 = 26.2	8 = 2.4

WEIGHT

Kilograms/Pounds

kg to lb	lb to kg
1 = 2.2	1 = 0.45
2 = 4.4	2 = 0.91
3 = 6.6	3 = 1.4
4 = 8.8	4 = 1.8
5 = 11.0	5 = 2.3
6 = 13.2	6 = 2.7
7 = 15.4	7 = 3.2
8 = 17.6	8 = 3.6

Grams/Ounces

g to oz	oz to g
1 = 0.04	1 = 28
2 = 0.07	2 = 57
3 = 0.11	3 = 85
4 = 0.14	4 = 114
5 = 0.18	5 = 142
6 = 0.21	6 = 170
7 = 0.25	7 = 199
8 = 0.28	8 = 227

TEMPERATURE

Fahrenheit/Celsius

F	C
0	-17.8
5	-15.0
10	-12.2
15	-9.4
20	-6.7
25	-3.9
30	-1.1
32	0
35	1.7
40	4.4
45	7.2
50	10.0
55	12.8
60	15.5
65	18.3
70	21.1
75	23.9
80	26.7
85	29.4
90	32.2
95	35.0
100	37.8

LIQUID VOLUME

Liters/U.S. Gallons

l to gal	gal to l
1 = 0.26	1 = 3.8
2 = 0.53	2 = 7.6
3 = 0.79	3 = 11.4
4 = 1.1	4 = 15.1

Liters/U.S. Gallons

l to gal	gal to l
5 = 1.3	5 = 18.9
6 = 1.6	6 = 22.7
7 = 1.8	7 = 26.5
8 = 2.1	8 = 30.3

INDEX OF NAMES

GENERAL INDEX

**la rocca
orvieto
country house
and
restaurant**

ZUP ASSOCIATI - PG

RESTORED RESPECTING THE SURROUNDING ENVIRONMENT, EQUIPPED WITH CARE AND DIRECTLY RUN FROM THE OWNERS, AGRITURISMO LA ROCCA ORVIETO IS A VERY SPECIAL LOCATION: BETWEEN SECULAR OAKS, VINEYARDS AND OLIVE-GROVES, OFFERS COMFORT AND HIGH LEVEL SERVICES IN A SUGGESTIVE AND QUIET HILL CONTEXT.

ROOMS, APARTMENTS, WIDE SWIMMING POOL, JACUZZI WHIRLPOOL, PANORAMIC GYMNASIUM, WELLNESS CENTRE WITH HOT TUB AND STEAM BATH, TERRACE RESTAURANT, RECEPTION HALL BY THE POOL. LA ROCCA'S RESTAURANT PROPOSE TYPICAL MEALS OF UMBRIA REGION, THE ROASTED MEATS AND FISH ON REQUEST. ALSO AVAILABLE HOME MADE PRODUCTS: EXTRA VIRGIN OLIVE OIL AND WINES CANTINA ALTAROCCA.

LA ROCCA ORVIETO
LOC. ROCCA RIPESENA, 62
ORVIETO (TR) ITALY
TEL. +39 0763 344 210
FAX +39 0763 395 155
www.laroccaorvieto.com
info@laroccaorvieto.com

Antico casale di Montegualandro

Country House and Wellness Centre
Via Montecchio, 1 - 06069 Tuoro sul Trasimeno (PG)
Tel. +39 075 8230295 - +39 075 8230289 - www.anticocasale.it - info@anticocasale.it

This noble residence is surrounded by a 100,000 m2 century-old olive grove, with a beautiful view over Lake Trasimeno. In the park, the large outdoor swimming pool with lakeside view is equipped with an extensive sundeck. The careful restoration, inspired by eco-friendly building criteria, has preserved the antique materials - terracotta, stone and exposed wooden beams – as well as the fireplaces, and some precious antique frescoes.

In the country house there are 15 suites made up of a double bedroom, living room with kitchenette, double sofa-bed, and bathroom. Refined and elegant, these rooms have four-poster beds, embroidered textiles, Persian rugs, a safe, satellite TV, telephone and internet connections, and ceiling fans. Some of the suites have a small garden or a terrace. The hose also hosts a convention centre for meetings and incentives.

There is a charming restaurant for candlelight dinners and a large gazebo with a lakeside view for the summer.

Inside the residence there is a modern and complete Wellness Centre: Beauty Farm, Day Spa, indoor heated swimming pool, cervical waterfalls, sauna, Turkish bath, six-seater Jacuzzi whirlpool, relaxation room, chromotherapy, aromatherapy and gym.

Beauty treatments, relaxing massages, ayurvedic massages, essential oil massages, Swedish massages, and low pressure tanning salon.

Holiday Farms
Casale delle Lucrezie

A beautiful holiday between history and nature...
Todi, in Umbria, the green heart of Italy!

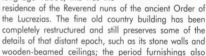

The structure rises up amidst the green vegetation of the hills which surround Todi; in the long ago 1200's, this was the residence of the Reverend nuns of the ancient Order of the Lucrezias. The fine old country building has been completely restructured and still preserves some of the details of that distant epoch, such as its stone walls and wooden-beamed ceilings; the period furnishings also contribute to giving the rooms a warm and relaxing atmosphere. The country house is set in the backdrop of a landscape composed of a mosaic of olive groves, ploughed fields, vineyards and woodlands with the ancient town of Todi in the distance. Our guests have at their disposal comfortable rooms and pleasant independent apartments with private bathrooms, independently controlled heating, TV and a large swimming pool from which they may enjoy a magnificent panorama. The Italian style breakfast, with cakes, home-made jams and typical local products is served in spacious rooms and, upon request, lunch and evening dinner may also be organised. Our establishment is also strategically placed geographically for reaching the most beautiful and culturally important cities and towns of Umbria such as Perugia, Assisi, Spoleto, Orvieto and Todi which may be reached in a short time by car. **Selected for "Premio Stanze Italiane 2007" - Best Italian Hotels' Prize.**

Fraz. Due Santi - Loc. Palazzaccio - Todi (PG)
Tel. (+39) 075 8987488-8989271 - Cel. 335/326269 - Fax 075 8987488
www.casaledellelucrezie.com - info@casaledellelucrezie.com